IB STUD ES

Business and Management

FOR THE IB DIPLOMA

Standard and Higher Level

Lloyd Gutteridge

OXFORD

UNIVERSITY PRESS

UNIVERSITY PRESS

Great Clarendon Street, Oxford OX2 6DP

Oxford University Press is a department of the University of Oxford.
It furthers the University's objective of excellence in research, scholarship,
and education by publishing worldwide in

Oxford   New York

Auckland   Cape Town   Dar es Salaam   Hong Kong   Karachi
Kuala Lumpur   Madrid   Melbourne   Mexico City   Nairobi
New Delhi   Shanghai   Taipei   Toronto

With offices in

Argentina   Austria   Brazil   Chile   Czech Republic   France   Greece
Guatemala   Hungary   Italy   Japan   South Korea   Poland   Portugal
Singapore   Switzerland   Thailand   Turkey   Ukraine   Vietnam

Oxford is a registered trade mark of Oxford University Press
in the UK and in certain other countries

British Library Cataloguing in Publication Data

Data available

ISBN 9780199135318

10 9 8 7 6 5 4 3 2 1

Printed in Great Britain by Bell and Bain Ltd., Glasgow

Paper used in the production of this book is a natural, recyclable product made
from wood grown in sustainable forests. The manufacturing process conforms to
the environmental regulations of the country of origin.

Mixed Sources
Product group from well-managed
forests and other controlled sources
www.fsc.org   Cert no. TT-COC-002769
© 1996 Forest Stewardship Council

FSC

Introduction

Thank you for purchasing this study guide.

The number of textbooks and resources dedicated to the IB Business and Management course was until recently very small. Since 2007, a number of textbooks have been written. Of course, outside the domain of IB business and management study, there exists a multitude of resources both written and on the Internet concerning business decision-making, marketing, leadership, operations management, finance and of course the external environment.

In such a small volume, the author cannot hope to compete with the detail and depth accorded to the modern-day textbook. This guide has been written by a current senior examiner of the IB Business and Management course to sit alongside the standard business textbook. It is hoped that it will provide a concise and engaging resource which will help students and teachers to navigate a course through a syllabus which on first viewing can be intimidating.

The rationale of this guide is to provide clarity and concise analysis to complement study of this subject in class. Although it contains some previous examination questions with suggested answers, and 'Examiner's hints' to help students improve their performance, this guide has not been written as a 'crammer' for last-minute revision.

Some important features of the Study Guide

The guide has been written to cover as fully as possible the requirements of the new Business and Management syllabus which was examined in May 2009 for the first time. Previous questions from examination papers from 2003 to 2008 are included. Questions for Higher level students only are marked HL as appropriate.

Chapters and units follow the syllabus closely and use is made of learning outcomes taken directly from the IB *Business and Management Guide*, with clear guidance in 'Notes for teachers' as to the required depth and detail of key topics.

At the beginning of each chapter, the material covered is designed for both Higher level and Standard level students. Higher level extension material is clearly marked HL in each topic area.

The examples given reflect the author's passion for movies and music and are intended to help engage the reader. They are as up to date as possible and include material from 2009.

The current uncertainties in the world economy and weakening economic environment play a role in some of the contexts used. After reading the guide, the reader may feel disheartened by the dilemmas facing business decision-making. It is not the intention of the guide to be too downbeat but to reflect the difficult times ahead for all stakeholders involved in business decision-making as we move through this challenging period.

At various points of the guide there are cognitive exercises (marked with a 'cogs' icon) where students are asked to think for themselves or to develop a discussion idea. In other instances students are invited to undertake their own research or consider an idea in greater depth (marked with a 'magnifying' icon).

Teachers may find some of these ideas useful to explain or analyse topics such as leadership or motivation, in keeping with the IB learner profile which is now considered the appropriate way to deliver teaching materials and to develop students' abilities.

In order to preserve clarity and brevity, students will be directed to their textbook if more depth or further individual study of a topic is warranted.

Acknowledgments

I am grateful to the IBO for granting permission for the use of past examination questions.

Unit 1.2 contains extracts from www.woopidoo.com.

Units 1.8 contains extracts from www.mindtools.com.

Units 4.1 and 4.3 contain data from www.macrumors.com.

The diagram on page 40 of the shamrock organization is redrawn from Gillespie (2001). The diagrams on page 49 are redrawn from Dearden and Foster (1994). The diagrams on page 52 are adapted from Google Images. The diagram on page 58 is redrawn from Handy (1995).

My thanks also go to Oxford University Press and Fern Watson for giving me the opportunity to write this guide and supporting me through the writing process. I would like to thank Gloria McDowell of the IBO for her review of the manuscript and for her many valuable suggestions. Heather Addison has also provided invaluable guidance in the editing stage.

Many colleagues both past and present have had a direct and indirect influence on my teaching and preparation of this material. Thank you to John, Patrick, Ian, Steve, Mark, Phil, Mahendra, Nick, Manoj, James and Graeme for your professional friendships and guidance in the UK, Singapore and New Zealand over the last 20 years. You are all in this book somewhere and I leave it for you to decide which parts you have influenced. All errors however remain my own.

My thanks also to the IB Business and Management 'A Team' of Richard Taylor, Susan James, Paul Clark, Andy Beharrell, Robert Pierce, Loykie Lomine and Roni Hameiri for their encouragement and enthusiasm for this project.

My final thanks must go to my wife Elaine for her constant encouragement and for giving me the time and space to complete the manuscript, and to my two boys Sam and Joel – one of whom I am sure will enjoy seeing his name in print and hopefully the other one will one day soon.

A donation from the royalties earned through the sale of this guide will go to the Motuora Special Needs Charitable Trust, Auckland, New Zealand.

Lloyd Gutteridge
May 2009

Contents

1.1 Nature of business activity

WHAT IS A BUSINESS?

Given the enormous impact of the Internet and the subsequent growth of new e-commerce start-ups, defining a business can prove quite difficult. A traditional definition would look something like:

> *A business is an entity which tries to combine human, physical and financial resources into processing goods or services to respond to and satisfy customer needs.*

However, with the growing ubiquity of the World Wide Web there are a number of examples (Google, Second Life) which, apart from their head office, do not exist in the physical sense.

It is also possible with a laptop and a secure Internet connection to create an online business with no additional human resources and at very little or no cost.

We must also remember that despite the impact of large multinational and global brands, the majority of businesses in both the developed and developing world are classed as small.

The traditional idea that a business must contain a production/operations division with marketing, finance and human resources departments is being challenged. The rise of outsourcing and off-shoring has led to a number of large companies now having their production facilities located well away from the country of origin.

A fundamental point which is often missed by students is that the creation of any business relies heavily on the ability of the entrepreneur to calculate and manage risk. We must not forget that the creation of a business involves considerable opportunity costs when combining human and financial resources. Students may wish to research successful entrepreneurs and investigate their attitudes to risk taking.

ROLE OF DIFFERENT BUSINESS DEPARTMENTS AND THEIR CONTRIBUTION TO OVERALL BUSINESS ACTIVITY

Whatever the size of organization, we typically see four main departments:

*   Production or operations management
*   Marketing
*   Finance
*   Human resource management

These areas are interrelated.

Consider:

*   A new T-shirt manufacturing company has a very successful domestic product but no finance to promote or distribute this into an overseas market.
*   The marketing department of a fast-food company become very excited about the possibility of a zero saturated-fat French fry but the production department do not have the knowledge or financial resources to do this.
*   A shortage of skilled labour forces a technology company to relocate its main production facility.

All of these issues highlight the dilemma facing all firms, that they must integrate all departments in order to satisfy consumer wants and needs.

The nature of business activity

We generally classify business activity into three areas:

*   Primary or the extraction of natural resources
*   Secondary to include construction and manufacturing processes
*   Tertiary to include providers of services and technology industries

In the developed world the share of both the primary and secondary activity towards an economy's total output has been decreasing (see below). The tertiary sector's contribution has naturally risen. For developing countries, the trend from OECD data reveals that manufacturing remains the most important sector, especially in China and India. These changes in the economic structure of the economy have significant implications for business decision-making.

ANALYSING THE IMPACT ON BUSINESS ACTIVITY OF CHANGES IN ECONOMIC STRUCTURE **HL**

For most of the developed world, economies have experienced a process called *de-industrialization*. A full discussion of this is beyond the scope of this guide. However, as we shall see in unit 1.9 on globalization, this combination of de-industrialization and globalization has had profound effects on human resource planning, production and marketing. It has also impacted on organizational structure, decision-making, stakeholder activity and objectives.

1.2 Types of organization (1)

PRIVATE AND PUBLIC SECTOR

The recent dramatic events of the credit crisis and the deteriorating global economic situation have been accompanied by significant government 'bail-outs' or rescue packages. On 3 April 2009, the Heads of State of the leading 20 economies in the world announced a trillion US dollar stimulus package. A number of large private banks and companies such as General Motors have received government assistance and have effectively become public sector companies. The term 're-nationalization' has begun to appear in the business pages.

This would have been unthinkable during the 1980s and 1990s when the private sector was being heralded as innovative, efficient and flexible. The public sector on the other hand was viewed as bureaucratic, complacent and most certainly wasteful. Students are encouraged to undertake research in their own countries to determine whether there has been a paradigm shift in thinking on the virtues of the two different sectors.

DISTINGUISHING BETWEEN ORGANIZATIONS IN THE PRIVATE AND PUBLIC SECTOR

If we were to identify the differences between the two sectors, as the IB asked students to do in the May 2008 exam, a typical student answer would contain a sentence very similar to the following:

> The private sector focuses on profit maximization and the public sector tries to provide a service to consumers.

While this has some truth for many countries, increasingly many public sector corporations – which we define as being principally controlled, financed and operated by the government – are:

- Expected to provide greater levels of customer satisfaction and demonstrate private sector type behaviour such as rising levels of efficiency, innovation and flexibility

- Expected to be more accountable for public funding and return, in some industries, a surplus back to the government. Public sector schools in the UK are ranked in 'league tables' according to student performance.

Many students assume that the public sector's only function is to provide goods or services to consumers at reasonable cost which private sector companies are either unwilling or unable to provide. Interested students may wish to look at the 'free-rider' problem in economics and investigate merit and public goods to clearly see this distinction between the two sectors on a theoretical basis.

1.2 Types of organization (2)

REASONS FOR SETTING UP A BUSINESS

> *My first 6 years of business were hopeless. There were lots of times when I sat and said, "Why am I doing this? I will never make it. It is just not going to happen. I should go out and get a real job."*
>
> George Lucas, creator of *Star Wars*
>
> Lucas's case is interesting, not because he has been so successful, but because every major film studio but one turned down his original *Star Wars* project. His risk-taking and ambition to get his 'vision' of the future onto the big screen despite numerous setbacks in production should be an inspiration to all film-makers.

We can summarize some of the key reasons why any individual would want to set up their own business. They include:

- to become artistically and financially independent (a strong driver for George Lucas)
- to pursue a passion or transform a hobby into a financially viable business
- to exercise a degree of control over one's future, especially if one has been made redundant by a larger corporation as an employee
- having identified a market opportunity where customer needs have not been satisfied with a desire to do so profitably (a market gap?)
- the ease with which it is possible to set up a new business.

The last point may seem slightly odd. However, a key factor in the decision-making process about starting up a new business may be the bureaucratic hurdles one has to go through in order to register a new start-up.

Consider the table below.

Country	No. of procedures to register each firm	Days for each procedure
New Zealand	2	12
United States	5	5
Singapore	7	8
United Kingdom	6	18
Kazakhstan	9	25
Nigeria	10	44
China	12	41
Paraguay	17	74
Indonesia	12	151

Adapted from The Economist *Business Miscellany*, 2004

It may not be surprising for the reader to discover that New Zealand has one of the highest per capita start-up rates for new businesses.

ANALYSING THE PROBLEMS THAT A BUSINESS START-UP MAY FACE

We can identify a number of problems. These factors will be influenced by the type of economy the business resides in and the state of the external environment. Both of these facts are of course outside the control of the individual firm.

However, we can identify the following reasons:

1. Lack of initial finance
2. May have knowledge and enthusiasm for the product or service but may lack the ability to prepare and monitor financial accounts, organize suitable promotional activities or delegate responsibilities
3. Incorrect pricing in the short run leading to lower or higher than forecasted sales
4. The need for clear, accurate and unbiased market research is overwhelming but new start-ups may not be able to afford independent objective market research provided by specialist agencies
5. The role of venture capital and technology start-ups. With just a computer and an Internet connection, a business can be created. Even start-ups such as these will need some operational or working capital. During the dot.com boom of the late 1990s, venture capital poured into Internet start-ups at an unsustainably fast pace. This capital demanded a quick return or it would be removed and 'invested in the next big thing'. This external pressure, without allowing time for the business to build a customer base in an increasingly competitive market, led to many start-ups failing.

We must remember that the issues facing all new start-ups depend on whether the business operates in the developed or developing world. Some of the issues will be identical but some will be completely different depending on the economy concerned. Check to make sure that you have the correct context for your answer.

DVD resource

There is an excellent documentary on the DVD boxed set of the first Star Wars Trilogy entitled *Empire of Dreams*. George Lucas is candid about the making of the *Star Wars* films, his struggles with the major studios, his determination to keep managerial control, the production and marketing nightmares and so on. It is a long documentary but provides an excellent overview of one man's determination to pursue his vision.

1.2 Types of organization (3)

DISTINGUISHING BETWEEN DIFFERENT TYPES OF BUSINESS ORGANIZATION AND IDENTIFYING THEIR MAIN FEATURES

A table may be useful at this point. Please refer to a textbook for a full discussion of the features, especially the detail behind a partnership agreement.

Type of business	Ownership and transparency	Finance	Examples	Control/decision-making
Sole trader	One owner Limited need for published accounts except those for tax purposes	Past savings, Government grants and loan schemes Retained profits after trading begins	Service-based firms such as home help Car and computer repairs	Usually one overall person in control
Partnership	Up to 20 depending on the country of operation Limited need for published accountability	Savings Loans Capital from new partners Retained profits	Lawyers, doctor practices	According to the terms of the agreement Sleeping partners have limited liability
Private limited company	Depends on the country of operation. Some restrictions Have to send financial statements to Registrar of Companies in some countries	Contributing capital from partners New partners could be introduced as per partnership agreement	Family-run business with desire to avoid unlimited liability Lego Illy Ferrari	According to agreement signed Authority usually handed down through family connections
Publicly traded company	Unlimited if shares advertised on local or global exchanges Period reporting with absolute transparency	Wide access to funds if shares are sold on various exchanges Success depends on the sentiment of the financial markets	Larger corporations with successful transparent financial histories Sony Wal-Mart	Shareholders will vote at AGM to decide on board of directors and dividend to be paid or retained
Public sector	Depends on the nature of government ownership. Some public-private enterprise combinations possible	Funded principally from the public purse through collective taxation	Health, Education Sewage Transport Individual country variations	Public sector is regarded as bureaucratic and structured by a tall hierarchy. This may be an old-fashioned view
Non-governmental (NGO)	Volunteer organizations/charities Some NGOs are run in partnership with government	Donations and funds from some government sources. A lot depends on the size and objectives of the NGO	Charities, Oxfam, World Vision	According to the terms of individual agreement. There is no one agreed accepted method to organize an NGO

Evaluating the most appropriate form of ownership for a firm

This is a difficult question to answer briefly. We can highlight a few key points.

- The objectives of the firm in terms of growth, profit, vision and mission
- The degree to which the owner wishes to retain control
- The degree to which the business wishes to be transparent about its financial position (there is nothing sinister in this proposition!)
- The extent to which the firm wishes to compete in international or global markets
- The speed and degree of flexibility in decision-making required by the owners

1.2 Types of organization (4)

In a future unit on organizational structure, we shall argue the proposition that the most appropriate structure for an organization is one which allows a firm to achieve its objectives. Students are encouraged to discuss a similar view that the most appropriate form of ownership for an organization is one which also helps it to achieve its objectives (to be covered in unit 1.3).

NON-GOVERNMENTAL ORGANIZATIONS

Although increasingly associated with charities and other not-for-profit organizations, over the last 10 years, the number of NGOs with some significant governmental input has been rising. The student will need to check carefully if researching an NGO, how the organization is financed, structured, its mission and vision. There is a very wide spectrum of debate as to what actually constitutes an NGO, and their effectiveness.

The impact of NGOs has become significant. For example:

- Global participation through social networking sites and the Internet has dramatically sharpened the influence of NGOs.

- There are estimated to be 40,000 NGOs working in an International context, with many more working on a national basis.

- In individual countries such as India and Russia, the number of active NGOs has reached over 2 million.

RELATIONSHIP BETWEEN PRIVATE AND PUBLIC SECTORS   HL

This part of the syllabus would normally have remained fairly inconspicuous had it not been for the events of 2008/9.

As already mentioned, the private sector would clearly have regarded the public sector model as outdated especially during the 1980s and 1990s when wholesale privatization was a key government objective for a number of developed countries.

However, with the financial rescue packages now being launched by a number of governments, it would be reasonable to suggest that there will be a much closer examination of the relationship between the two sectors and certainly a re-assessment of the virtues of the private sector model being based on maximizing profit and shareholder value exclusively.

Given the diverse range of public/private sector enterprise initiatives around the world, the reader is left to research their own country's position. Needless to say, this has become a contentious issue among stakeholders and we may need to wait until the financial storm clouds of 2009 have cleared before we can make any reasoned judgments.

1.3 Organizational objectives (1)

The course encourages the appreciation of ethical concerns and issues of social responsibility in the global business environment.

Source: IB *Business and Management Guide* (2007), 'Nature of the Subject', p.3.

It is recommended that Standard level students read through the Higher level material in this unit.

INTRODUCTION

By attracting growing interest from the media, non-governmental organizations and pressure groups, the objectives of organizations have come under renewed scrutiny. In response, organizations have encouraged feedback from their other stakeholders either directly via their websites or indirectly through the numerous social networking online communities. There has hopefully been a greater degree of transparency than ever before and this is reflected by the number of organizations that place ethical and social responsibilities at the top of their 'objectives agenda'.

In this unit we examine:

- Traditional objectives to help differentiate between strategic and tactical objectives
- The increasing use of mission and vision statements
- The growing importance of ethical and socially responsible objectives with an evaluation as to how effective they can be

Traditional objectives

Despite the growing awareness and importance of the last point above, all firms will still consider the following objectives as important. They have been termed traditional as they form the natural starting point for all organizations whether large or small.

These objectives will depend on the 'age' of the firm and also the prevailing external environment:

- Survival/breakeven
- Cost minimization
- Growth (market share)
- Profit maximization
- Profit satisficing

The importance of the profit motive

In economic terms, profit is considered as the **reward** for risk taking. If the entrepreneur has decided to combine human and non-human resources and land to create a business, then profit is seen as the incentive. Without the profit motive, risk taking would not be rewarded and very few new businesses would be created.

Profit satisficing

From observation it has been noticed that, as some private limited companies reach a certain size and level of profitability, the owners may decide to satisfice, i.e. agree not to focus on profit maximization but to try to satisfy other objectives such as debt repayment or innovation through increased research and development.

Strategic and tactical objectives

It may be useful to classify the above objectives according to whether they can be perceived as strategic or tactical.

- A **strategic** objective is usually defined as a longer-term aim of the business, defined perhaps by the vision of the owner as represented in the vision statement.
- A **tactical** or **operational** objective is more short term in nature and is usually defined as an aim or mechanism designed to help achieve the strategic objective and support the overall vision.

As a business begins trading:

- A tactical objective may be survival of the first year of trading in order to preserve and guarantee that a vision has a chance of being realized.
- Second, a tactical move to reduce costs and waste may allow a future goal of profit maximization or growth to take place.
- Generally, tactical objectives are designed to be subordinate to but also try to affect the overall strategic direction.

MISSION AND VISION STATEMENTS

There is some confusion about the difference between mission and vision statements.

A **mission statement** is a way of defining briefly and succinctly the reason for the business's existence. Some examples may help to clarify this point.

- Nokia: Connecting people has always been, and continues to be, our reason for business.
- Tesco: Our core purpose is to create value for our customers to earn their lifetime loyalty.
- Google's mission is to organize the world's information and make it universally accessible and useful.

A **vision statement** defines where the company sees itself moving to in the future.

- Some writers have called this a **strategic declaration** although some are purposely vague because it is clearly impossible to predict, given the external environment, where the company will be in 5 years' time, let alone 50 years.

For this reason some companies only construct mission statements to avoid being accused of making too bold and extravagant claims.

(continued)

1.3 Organizational objectives (2)

MISSION AND VISION STATEMENTS *(continued)*

Some examples of vision statements (**source:** *Business Miscellany* 2004) are:

- Heinz: Our vision, quite simply, is to be the world's premier food company, offering nutritious, superior tasting foods to people everywhere.

- Ford: Our vision is to become the world's leading company for automotive products and services.

We can briefly analyse the roles for companies creating and utilizing mission and vision statements.

- It can help clarify in the minds of stakeholders the purpose of the businesses. This may have important considerations for customers, investors and suppliers, both present and potential.

- A vision can reassure shareholders that the business is forward-looking and willing to create and pursue new opportunities. A vision could be perceived as unobtainable in the short term, but stakeholders may feel that the company is striving to do the best that it can within its market.

- But the mission and vision must be credible and realistic in the minds of the stakeholders too and this is one chief criticism laid at the door of those companies who set them, that they can be too vague or too imprecise.

As a discussion point let us consider the mission statement of Philip Morris International, the producers of Marlboro cigarettes, the most popular brand of cigarette in the world.

> *Our goal is to be the most responsible, effective and respected developer, manufacturer and marketer of consumer products, especially products intended for adults. Our core business is manufacturing and marketing the best quality tobacco to adults who use them.*

To what extent is this an appropriate mission statement?

ETHICAL OBJECTIVES

An ethical objective is a deliberate attempt on the part of the company to take a position which is viewed as morally correct and appropriate in the eyes of stakeholders.

We can examine an ethical position by asking a number of key questions.

- Should a multinational firm operate in a country that imposes harsh working conditions on its citizens and encourages the use of child labour?

- Should a pharmaceutical company that plans to produce an important vaccine in an area with a high prevalence of malaria charge high prices to those consumers who may be most affected and most in need?

- Should tobacco or alcohol producers be allowed to sponsor sporting events where young children may be in the crowd?

Students should be able to come up with their own examples from their own experiences.

Evaluation

Why should a company pursue ethical objectives?

- Considerable stakeholder pressure to 'do the right thing' in business after a number of high-profile and damaging corporate scandals (Enron, WorldCom).

- Linked to this point is the need for the company to differentiate itself from the competition by building a credible ethical stance (e.g. Fair Trade Movement and the plight of coffee growers in the developing world). This could be the basis for a new mission and vision to develop a new strategic direction.

Why should a company think carefully about adopting an ethical position?

- If we consider opportunity costs, then an ethical position may conflict with the profit motive. Shareholders may not be happy to forgo future profits if the business is not allowed to compete in some markets or geographical regions.

- If the ethical stance is leaning towards environmental concerns, the firm may have to spend vast sums of capital in the short term implementing environmental assurances on production processes. This will raise costs and impact on profitability.

- The ethical stance will need to be credible and effective in the eyes of the market in order for the firm to build a competitive position. This again will take time and capital.

- Finally, in a deteriorating economic environment, an ethical stance may mean redundancy for some line workers if contracts are not won or projects refused on ethical grounds. This could be an unpopular move in the wider community.

EXAMINER'S HINT

With ethical objectives receiving greater attention in the course guide, the student can expect many case studies and questions to have a strong ethical and social responsibility focus.

1.3 Organizational objectives (3)

CORPORATE SOCIAL RESPONSIBILITY (CSR)

The topics of business ethics and social responsibility are closely linked. In his excellent review of CSR, Walling (2007) argues that in the US the two topics are seen as one, while in the UK and Europe, CSR is more idealistically associated with businesses wanting to leave the world a better place.

It may surprise the reader to note that the adoption of CSR is not accepted by all. Milton Friedman famously remarked that:

Businesses have no social responsibility other than to increase profits and refrain from deception and fraud. When businesses seek to maximise profits they always do what is good for society.

And *The Economist* said:

Firms should not do the work of governments.

In this unit, we will not have the space for a full investigation. The reader is asked to consider some of the ideas presented and perhaps again undertake some independent research on what constitutes CSR and its impact on stakeholders.

DEFINITION OF SOCIALLY RESPONSIBLE OBJECTIVE

Russell-Walling (2007) argues that there is no single definition of CSR. The World Business Council defines sustainable development as:

The continuing commitment by business to behave ethically and contribute to economic development while improving the quality of life of the workforce and their families as well as of the local community at large.

The Global Reporting Initiative which provides a framework for companies to report on their CSR commitment has 32 different performance indicators ranging from customer privacy and anti-competitive behaviour to the use of child labour.

Environmental audits

A number of governments have also set up guidelines for firms that wish to carry out environmental audits, given the growing concerns of climate change and threats to sustainability. An environmental audit can form part of an organization's commitment to a socially responsible objective.

The Australian government, for example, has developed a series of guidelines for firms to follow if they wish to benchmark their environmental credentials against accepted government protocols.

They include:

- how a firm can readily change its influence on the environment
- how a firm can prioritize actions to reduce impact
- how a firm can demonstrate accountability to government, customers and shareholders.

This last point is important as clearly the value of an environmental impact or a decision to implement a CSR policy must have credibility and accountability in the minds of the stakeholders. Russell-Walling provides some interesting statistical work on this point in an international context (table in HL box on the next page).

1.3 Organizational objectives (4)

CSR AND CHANGES IN FIRMS' BEHAVIOUR

Consider the following table produced by Russell-Walling (2007).

A survey ranking the most ethically perceived brands

Rank	UK	US	France	Germany	Spain
1	Co-op	Coca-Cola	Danone	Adidas	Nestle
2	Body Shop	Kraft	Adidas/Nike	Nike/Puma	Body Shop
3	Marks & Spencer	Proctor & Gamble			Coca-Cola
4	Traidcraft	Johnson & Johnson Kellogg's Nike Sony	Nestle	BMW	Danone
5	Café Direct		Renault	Demeter gepa	Corte Ingles

Benefits of adopting a CSR approach: two examples

- Nike has adapted well to a UK-led campaign that accused it of employing child labour with very low wages and poor conditions in developing countries. It has responded proactively with a clear CSR strategy including the appointment of a director of sustainable development. However, perceptions take a long time to change and it is revealing that Nike does not appear in the UK rankings in the table above.

- Stung by criticism after the release of the film *Super Size Me*, McDonald's has responded positively by taking certain sweet fizzy drinks off the menu and introducing low-fat and low-sugar options, including fruit, for its 'Happy Meals' targeted at children.

Drawbacks of pursuing a socially responsible approach

Russell-Walling notes some of the difficulties:

- There are statistics that purport to show the beneficial impact of CSR on a company's profits but they are not yet overwhelmingly convincing.

- Second, the costs of compliance with environmental audits or preparing CSR strategies may take up valuable time and resources, adding to the reporting and administrative burden of new start-ups especially. This could force them to increase prices to the consumer.

CHANGES IN STEEPLE AND ETHICAL INVESTMENT: IMPACT ON CSR

Clearly, as we will see in unit 1.5, there have been a number of changes in the external environment which could explain why CSR has become an important part of some companies' philosophies over the last 20 years. Through the increased use of technology of the World Wide Web, we could point to the growing awareness and importance of social, environmental and ethical factors. It will be interesting to see whether, given the recent deterioration in the world economy, the tightening of credit opportunities and the rise in unemployment, a CSR approach can survive.

You could now attempt question 1, page 35.

A NEW MODEL OF ETHICAL INVESTMENT: MICRO-FINANCE

In addition there has been a small but growing body of evidence that ethical investment can in fact outperform other types of investment.

In 2006, the Grameen Bank founder, Muhammad Yunus, was awarded the Nobel Peace Prize for his outstanding work in developing a lending facility (which has been subsequently transferred to the Internet) to allow investment funds from the developed world (principally the US) to be accessed by firms in the developing world, in particular, in Africa. The capital is in the first instance used to develop socially responsible projects such as health, education and social infrastructure and has been very successful. Although the amounts invested can be quite small, US investors have been delighted with the returns they have received. The Grameen model is clear evidence that the ethical investment model can be sustainable.

The Kenyan Equity Bank, the Acumen Fund and Kiva.org are other examples and students are encouraged to research these to enhance their understanding of ethical investment.

1.4 Stakeholders (1)

THE ROLE OF STAKEHOLDERS

Definition: a stakeholder can be a person, group, or system that affects or can be affected by an organization's action.

Internal stakeholders include but are not limited to:

- Employees
- Shareholders
- Managers

External stakeholders include:

- Suppliers
- Customers
- Special interest or pressure groups to include NGOs
- Competitors
- Local and national government

All of the above could have a potential interest in a company's performance for a variety of reasons, as the table illustrates.

Stakeholder	Examples of interest towards company
Owners/Shareholders	Profit, vision, liquidity, efficiency
Government	Taxation (direct/indirect), compliance with legislation such as health and safety
Senior management	Financial performance, customer perception, profit and sales targets
Non-managerial staff	Pay, conditions, job security
Customers	Value, service, quality, ethical considerations
Creditors	Liquidity, gearing
Local community	Social responsibility, jobs, environment

Clearly, it would be very difficult for any company to be able to satisfy all these interests at the same time.

The following example will illustrate how conflicts of interest can arise.

STAKEHOLDER CONFLICT

Fisher & Paykel (F & P) today announced plans to move more of its manufacturing of quality whiteware such as fridges and cookers overseas. Local suppliers to F & P and employees were very concerned. The CEO announced however that the move was essential for the company to remain competitive in global markets as many of F & P's competitors have moved to Thailand and Mexico already with much lower labour costs. Shareholders and the financial markets seem delighted with the news with shares rising 34c on the day to $2.54.

Source: *New Zealand Herald*, 2007

A number of conflicts can be identified:

- Fisher & Paykel customers will welcome the lower prices but may have quality concerns about production moving overseas.
- Current and potential shareholders will be anticipating higher profits and returns due to efficiency gains leading to the higher share price.
- Local suppliers and workers will be concerned about job losses. The local and national government may be concerned about the impact on local communities.
- Senior management may be excited about the possibility of managing a larger multinational company with increased power and prestige. Lower-level workers may fear change.

The ability to analyse possible areas of stakeholder conflict is an important theme for the Business and Management course.

You may now attempt to answer questions 2, 3 and 4 on page 35.

1.4 Stakeholders (2)

EVALUATING POSSIBLE WAYS TO OVERCOME STAKEHOLDER CONFLICT

Many students would be able to suggest ways to overcome possible conflict but the key here is **to evaluate** methods and suggest why they may or may not work. Finally, an overall judgment for an evaluation question would be required.

Consider the following excerpt from an examiner answer with reference to the Fisher & Paykel case study, with sections broken up to highlight analysis, evaluation and judgment.

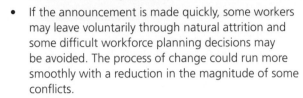

Evaluate solutions to the potential stakeholder conflicts outlined in the Fisher & Paykel case study.

Possible solutions

- Fisher & Paykel may have to carry out a carefully managed public relations exercise to reassure workers that job losses will be kept to a minimum and/or offer retraining schemes to those directly affected.

- Customers will need to be reassured that there will be no reduction in quality of the finished products.

- The company will have to present this new strategy as a way of protecting current jobs and future shareholder value.

Analysis and evaluation in context

- To implement the above ideas will take time and resources and there may be short-term goodwill losses to the firm such as customer resentment and dissatisfaction from the local community.

- Decisions will also need to be made as to how to communicate the details to the various stakeholders.

- Should Fisher & Paykel use formal methods or rely on informal groups? Use of the latter is risky as the messages to the wider community may become distorted via the 'grapevine'.

- If the announcement is made quickly, some workers may leave voluntarily through natural attrition and some difficult workforce planning decisions may be avoided. The process of change could run more smoothly with a reduction in the magnitude of some conflicts.

Judgment

- Ultimately, to a publicly traded company such as Fisher & Paykel the shareholders represent the key stakeholder. Senior management have to be aware of their responsibilities in a highly competitive financial global market.

- If shareholders are not satisfied with Fisher & Paykel's new strategy, they could sell their shares, driving down the value of the company, with important implications for gearing and future financing.

- This could lead to further unpopular action having to be taken. The company would wish to avoid any further poor publicity.

NOTE FOR TEACHERS

This answer contains some material which we have not yet fully covered in this guide but it is given to show how an evaluation answer involving analysis in context and judgment could be written. It is not a model answer and we could have identified a number of other conflicts. However, we will use this approach in future examples to highlight to the student the importance of being able to construct and present a reasoned and balanced argument.

1.5 The external environment; SLEPT analysis (1)

In the external environment (EE), we look at a whole range of external factors outside the individual control of the firm which can impact considerably, both positively and negatively, on decision-making. As well as the economic framework which operates in a country, we must consider political, social, technological, legal and environmental factors.

PESTLE analysis is simply an enlarged version of the more traditional PEST analysis. Some textbooks refer to an enlarged PEST as PEST-G where G represents green or environmental factors.

Consider the example below.

THE INDIAN FILM INDUSTRY

The Indian Hindi language movie industry – popularly known as Bollywood – is stepping up its fight against film piracy both at home and overseas.

Infringement of copyright laws is rampant in India. A recent study estimated that India's entertainment industry loses $4bn and 800,000 jobs because of piracy. The figures are higher if we include those Western countries such as the USA and the UK which are home to large Indian populations where Bollywood films provide an important link to their homeland.

With ever increasing technology making the copying of movies easier coupled with the availability of home theatre systems and an impending economic recession reducing discretionary spending on items such as visits to the cinema, the trend in buying pirated DVDs of new films is likely to continue unless Government legislation, penalties and the legal process are tightened up.

For the Indian film industry the following SLEPT analysis could be carried out:

- Social (S) — Societal needs of expatriates to watch Indian movies
- Legal (L) — Legal framework needs to support the film-makers
- Economic (E) — Economic downturn reducing spending on leisure
- Political (P) — Government trying to enforce a legal framework
- Technological (T) — The increasing ability to copy and distribute movies

It is interesting to note that not all the external factors are represented as threats. Firms or industries can look at opportunities such as supportive government assistance or favourable legal rulings which can justify a certain course of action being taken.

The key point to remember is that these factors are outside the control of the firms but they must be incorporated into their decision-making framework and be considered in developing any strategic move (a point which will become more apparent when we look at business decision-making tools and strategy in later units in the guide).

EVALUATING THE IMPACT ON A FIRM'S OBJECTIVES AND STRATEGY OF A CHANGE IN ANY OF THE SLEPT FACTORS

Having carried out a SLEPT analysis, the next step of the process would be for senior management to try and obtain additional research to work out the magnitude of these external factors and perhaps take some appropriate action and consider a new course of action.

Some large firms employ political, social and economic analysts for this purpose or may subcontract to specialist technological services in order to be aware of the latest external developments.

As an example, we could look at the online retailer Amazon's decision in January 2008 to offer its American customers the opportunity to download songs in response to a number of changes in the external environment.

- **Economic** Sales of compact discs had fallen with a US recession forecast. Fierce competition from the market leader in legal downloads – Apple iTunes.
- **Social** The increasing confidence of consumers to order and pay for songs over the Internet.
- **Legal** In order to build a library of songs, Amazon forms a strategic alliance with Warner Brothers to facilitate sales.
- **Technological** Increased use of broadband and the increasing threat of rival, free, peer-to-peer sites such as Limewire.
- **Political** Perceived weak government action in prosecuting 'music pirates'.

(continued)

1.5 The external environment; SLEPT analysis (2)

EVALUATING THE IMPACT ON A FIRM'S OBJECTIVES AND STRATEGY OF A CHANGE IN ANY OF THE SLEPT FACTORS (continued)

Evaluation of the impact

- Amazon's decision, given the difficult trading conditions since January 2008, would appear to have been successful. A number of electronic retailers in the US and UK have since gone into administration (Circuit City and Zavvi, November 2008) and sales of legally downloaded songs have increased. Confidence in online retailing has also grown dramatically.

- The only drawback to this decision is that Amazon may have 'cannibalized' some of its own market share, with customers buying only individual tracks rather than whole albums of popular artists. The increased sales of some products have been offset by reductions in sales of other similar items.

We shall return to Amazon's success later with a more detailed look at e-commerce and consider the role of market cannibalization in the section on product portfolios (page 91).

SLEPT EXPANDS INTO STEEPLE: THE ADDITION OF ENVIRONMENTAL AND ETHICAL FACTORS

NOTE FOR TEACHERS

During the last 10 years due to a combination of factors, firms have had to consider their environmental and ethical responsibilities.

In keeping within the spirit of the IB philosophy, a full discussion is not offered here as the reasons fall outside the syllabus of the Business and Management course. Students should investigate these reasons themselves and use other Group 3 subjects of their package such as geography or economics or cross-curricular options such as STS offered under Group 4.

DVD resource

The interested reader may like to consider two excellent DVDs which highlight these concerns and provide compelling evidence of the need for a business strategy to consider these external factors.

- **An Inconvenient Truth by Al Gore.** Oscar-winning documentary on the inevitable impacts of global warming.

- **Enron: The Smartest Guys in the Room.** This is an excellent review of one of the most famous examples of unethical behaviour by a major corporation leading to one of the biggest US corporate insolvencies of all time. The film also contains some superb analysis and examples of autocratic management style and Theory X motivation.

TOK

Of course a good reflective IB learner would not take these videos as pure truth. A number of commentators have argued that Gore vastly overstates the case and timing for global warming. On the environment question in particular, it is imperative that the student adopt a holistic approach to the issues and not just be swayed by one person's view.

OPPORTUNITIES TO USE A SLEPT OR STEEPLE ANALYSIS

A SLEPT analysis should be presented as a tool for decision-making for the Business and Management Internal Assessment assignment, especially for Higher level.

In order to guide preparation for Paper 1 – the pre-issued case study for both HL and SL – it is also recommended that a STEEPLE analysis is undertaken.

You could now undertake question 5, page 35.

1.6 Organization planning tools (1)

Failure to plan is a plan to fail. (Anon)

THE IMPORTANCE OF PLANNING

The importance of planning in a business context (perhaps in any context) cannot be overstated. This would be true especially for new business start-ups. Planning will allow an organization to:

- Identify the best use of scarce resources such as time, capital and labour

- Communicate clearly to stakeholders, especially investors, the aims of the business and its vision

- Anticipate potential problems, both financial and non-financial, and suggest, where possible, pre-emptive action

- Aid in the preparation of contingency plans (see unit 2.8)

ELEMENTS OF A BUSINESS PLAN: EXAMPLE – COFFEE REPUBLIC

In 1995, Bobby and Sahar Hashemi decided to set up a coffee and espresso bar. Without any previous business start-up experience, they described their 'journey' in a best-selling book, *Anyone Can Do It*. Their business plan which was put to their bank and to prospective investors ran to 20 pages.

They identified a number of key elements that a business plan should have:

- Aims of the business must be clearly stated

- Details of existing and potential competition

- Amount of funding required with a time line illustrating how the funding would be used

- Funding requirements under different scenarios if the external environment changes

- Time lines for implementation and action to review aims if forecasts are not met

- A marketing plan

- Projected profit and loss account and cash flow forecast

The type of plan presented will of course depend on satisfying a particular objective. In the case of Coffee Republic, the need was to secure funding to launch the first coffee bar. The Hashemis also had plans to open other bars if the first one was successful. All of this was documented and, crucially, the plan was audited by a third party to ensure it was realistic.

Students should note that the above example was for a new business start-up. Other business plans drawn up by existing organizations may be driven by different objectives, for example, to change an existing strategy or to look to restructure operations, and in fact a whole range of other possibilities. The elements contained in these plans will need to be adjusted accordingly.

NOTE FOR TEACHERS: SWOT ANALYSIS

An important tool in planning and decision-making, the SWOT analysis has become a critical component for organizations looking to review strategic direction.

For HL students in the Internal Assessment (IA) Report or even in the Extended Essay for Business and Management, a SWOT analysis (or other appropriate planning tool) should be included at the beginning of the assignment to determine how a new strategic path was identified.

As a moderator of IA projects for a number of years, the author has noted two worrying trends:

- Students place the SWOT analysis in the middle or end of their report, to recommend a certain course of action be taken rather than identifying one.

- Once the SWOT has been created, it is not analysed. It is not enough just to write down the strengths, weaknesses, opportunities and threats. Further analysis, investigation or research is required to try and measure the magnitude of each of the variables to determine whether a new opportunity is to be pursued or threat eliminated.

1.6 Organization planning tools (2)

SWOT IN ACTION: DISNEY COMPANY IN THE LATE 1970s

Background to the SWOT

After the death in 1966 of its founder, Walt Disney, the Disney Company found that its family films and animated cartoons had lost some of their appeal; audience numbers had matured. With revenues falling in the mid 1970s, the company launched a thorough overview of its operations and conducted a SWOT analysis. An interpretation of the findings is given below.

Strengths (internal)

- Very strong brand identity with family and children's movies with a positive moral message since the 1930s
- Industry leader in animated cartoons and movies
- Theme parks had created a total entertainment package and for some a once-in-a-lifetime opportunity

Weaknesses (internal)

- Run by the Disney family since creation
- It was accused of a lack of fresh thinking in a changing industry
- Labour-intensive methods of production leading to very high costs of production for animated movies and time taken to produce

Opportunities (external)

- Themes parks in other countries
- Move into adult action movies, away from family-orientated films?
- Turning a once-in-a-lifetime visit to a theme park into perhaps once-in-a-year visit?

Threats (external)

- Competition from new film companies such as Lucas Film (*Star Wars*) and established industry giants such as Universal, Paramount and MGM. The science fiction genre had mostly been ignored by Disney.

- Threat of home video. The Disney family had long resisted the idea of releasing its valuable back catalogue of films onto video. It was viewed by some members of the Board of Directors as 'cheapening the brand'. Disney regarded themselves a movie production company and not in the home entertainment business. (See Levitt's thoughts on this in unit 4.1, page 81.)

After a number of high-profile casualties on the Board of Directors, the company over the next 15–20 years designed and implemented a long-term strategy:

- Built Tokyo Disney (1983) and Euro Disney (1992)
- Bought an independent movie company – Miramax – to distribute more adult-only movies. First production was Quentin Tarrantino's *Pulp Fiction* in 1993/4
- Reduced the output of animated films but focused on quality with more subtle adult humour or special effects – *Aladdin* and *Beauty and the Beast*
- Launched the back catalogue of classic movies on video from 1981 and created division for Disney to produce its own 'non-Disney' movies. This new sub-brand was called Touchstone Pictures
- Animated sequels launched direct to video without release in the movie theatres
- A joint venture with Pixar, leading to *Toy Story*, *The Incredibles*, etc.

With hindsight it can be recorded that the strategy was successful. It guaranteed the survival of the company although there were significant cultural difficulties in bringing the Disney brand as a theme park to Europe, and changes in senior management.

(Interested readers may wish to follow the events after these changes in the long but informative book by Michael B. Stewart entitled *Disney War*.)

THE MOVE TO DECISION-MAKING

In order to ensure that the SWOT analysis is presented objectively, a number of companies invite management consultants to undertake a SWOT analysis for them to avoid bias. (As an individual would you be honest and objective about your own weaknesses?) The next stage, in common with a SLEPT analysis, is to investigate the magnitude of the respective strengths, weaknesses, opportunities and threats and then decide on a suitable course of action.

However, before we can look at the decision-making framework which has been used effectively by businesses to decide on a suitable course of action, given a number of alternatives, we need to remind ourselves about the impact of internal and external constraints.

Internal and external constraints on decision-making from the student's perspective

Some decisions are straightforward for an individual studying for an IB Diploma.

- A student must decide to take Theory of Knowledge, undertake creativity, action and service (CAS), and submit an Extended Essay.
- The consequence of not doing CAS is that the student fails the Diploma.
- We would all agree that this would not be a rational decision.

However, a student's decision to study business and management as part of their IB package will be governed by a number of other influences.

(continued)

1.6 Organization planning tools (3)

Internal and external constraints on decision-making from the student's perspective *(continued)*

- Some of these will be within your control (your interests and objectives, for example).

However, a number of factors which will influence your decision will be beyond your control.

- We call these factors internal and external constraints.

Internal constraints may include:

- Whether your school offers business and management at both HL and SL

- Staffing levels (Do you have any teachers of business and management in your school?)

- Are there enough students opting to study this subject to justify running this option?

External constraints may include:

- The supply of business and management teachers in your country or region

- The impact of your parents or friends on your decision

- The current state of the jobs market and its impact on your subject choices

- The admissions policy of the university you are thinking of attending after you finish your Diploma

Decisions made by an organization are more difficult, given the large number of stakeholders involved and the greater range of internal and external constraints. We have already looked at a number of these external factors during our investigation into STEEPLE analysis (pages 17–18). Internal constraints will be considered in more detail when we consider operations management problems in topic 5.

THE DECISION-MAKING FRAMEWORK

This model for making decisions is considered to be generic, i.e. it can be applied in any situation where a decision needs to be made, whether it is one to be made by an organization as in business and management or by an individual in purchasing a new mobile phone.

The model assumes that decision-making is a *scientific* process, and is useful in that it can be applied in a number of business and management contexts.

The model in outline

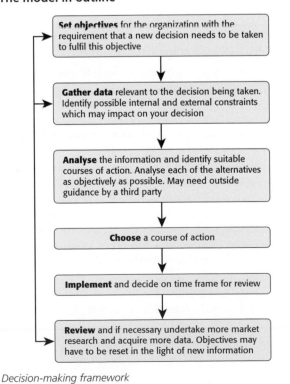

Decision-making framework

- Should a firm introduce a new product into its portfolio?

- Should a firm introduce 'management by objectives'?

- Should a firm change to a 'total quality' culture?

- Given the Ansoff matrix, which growth strategy should be pursued?

- Should a firm remove an old product from its product mix?

Once the decision has been made it is critical to review it.

Depending on the decision which has been made, a firm may wish to:

- Look at sales figures to see the outcome of a new marketing strategy.

- Consult stakeholders to see the impact of the decision and whether initial objectives have been satisfied.

- Possibly analyse the impact of a change in working practices if TQM has been introduced or a change in management practices has occurred.

- Conduct additional market research, both primary and secondary, to view the perception of the firm if it has entered a new overseas market.

Failure to review the final decision may leave the firm looking foolish in the eyes of stakeholders (especially shareholders), especially if mistakes have been made, or sales or profit forecasts do not meet expectations.

However, there may be a more fundamental reason to review performance.

If the company has made a mistake, it would be perceived as irresponsible for the firm to repeat it. Failure to plan once may be an oversight but to do so twice and not learn from mistakes made in the past would be unforgivable.

1.6 Organization planning tools (4)

SCIENTIFIC VERSUS INTUITIVE MANAGEMENT

The generic model of decision-making has served its time very well and under the 'umbrella' term of scientific management has provided a systematic and 'rational' way of decision-making.

Intuitive decision-making

Intuitive decision-makers and those working in club cultures (see unit 2.6) such as Sir Richard Branson (Virgin) and Steve Jobs (Apple) view the decision-making process differently. They regard scientific management as too inflexible and time-consuming and, consequently, a firm may miss out on profitable opportunities.

'Zeus' leaders in club cultures are frustrated by conventions, data, rules and regulations, and regard 'Apollo' cultures with a degree of suspicion. Club cultures clearly would not be loud supporters of scientific management processes.

Intuitive decision-making in these cultures relies on gut feelings, instinct, confidence and experience rather than hard evidence, facts or detailed examination of data.

To back up their views, we must note that both Richard Branson and Steve Jobs have been tremendously successful in their respective industries and thus their views on decision-making and management have been afforded much attention.

However, as we shall discover in the section on market research, Virgin's failure in a high-profile venture – the launch of Virgin Mobile in Singapore – could have been averted if they had conducted some thorough market research, paid attention to detail and not simply relied on the charisma, drive and personality of their leader.

DECISION TREES: THE BENEFITS

A decision tree is regarded as a quantitative decision-making technique.

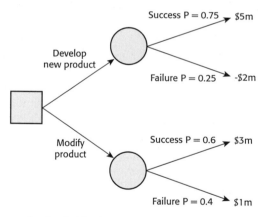

An example of a decision tree

Squares (**decision nodes**) are points where a choice has to be made between different courses of action, e.g. develop a new product or advertise more widely.

Circles (**probability nodes**) are points where there is a chance event which may lead to success or failure. **P** is the probability of success (how close is it to 1?) or failure (how close is it to zero?).

A decision tree allows firms to:

1 Visually represent alternative courses of action (in our example, new product development or modify product)

2 Quantify the outcomes of each action in terms of revenue expected

3 Identify individual probabilities of success or failure

4 View the costs of implementing each course of action

5 Decide on an appropriate course of action based on *quantitative factors only*

DECISION TREES: THE PROBLEMS

The previous points can all be regarded as benefits of using the decision tree to help organizations make decisions. However, we can note three significant issues:

• The probabilities which are integral in calculating the expected values can seem sometimes to come out of thin air. How were they calculated and on what basis? Some managers use experience or perhaps secondary data to calculate these probabilities but how can we objectively measure the probability of success or failure?

• External and non-financial factors are not included in the analysis.

• Finally, the decision tree does not take into account the attitude to risk of the entrepreneur and by

assumption the level of intuitive management present in the organization. For example, Richard Branson was warned repeatedly that setting up an airline to compete with British Airways on the popular transatlantic route between the UK and the US was futile, especially given the low prices Virgin was charging and small predicted revenue streams.

• The decision-tree approach would most likely have suggested that Branson should not enter this market. He did, and was tremendously successful.

You could now tackle question 6, page 35.

1.6 Organization planning tools (5)

FISHBONE OR ISHIKAWA DIAGRAM

This technique is slightly different to the previous models in that it does not offer quantifiable or qualitative solutions to decision-making problems. Instead its purpose is to identify causes of a problem which may exist in an organization, and it is often referred to as a cause-and-effect diagram.

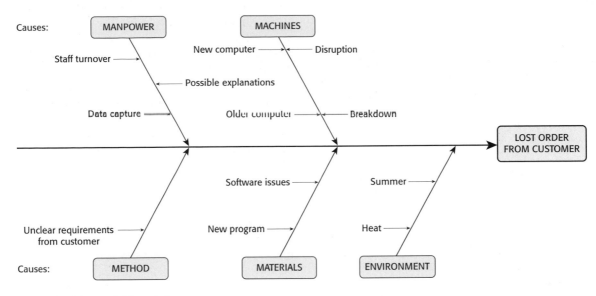

An example of a fishbone (Ishikawa) diagram

The diagram is constructed as follows:

- The name of a basic problem of concern is entered at the right-hand end of the diagram of the main 'bone'.

- 'Brainstorming' is typically carried out to add possible causes to the other bones and typically categories such as materials, machines, manpower and methods are used to classify the possible causes of the problem.

- The causes can be subdivided to add greater detail and information but the intention is for the diagram not to become too cluttered.

- When the fishbone is complete, one is left with a complete picture of all the possibilities about what could be the root cause for the identified problem.

- Further discussion takes place, usually within a group, to ascertain the most likely root causes of the issue.

The fishbone diagram is a useful visual tool and if made available to the group can provide a shared opportunity to help identify causes of a particular problem. Once a final root cause has been determined, it will be up to the manager to test a hypothesis using data to see if it is a statistically significant cause.

1.7 Growth and evolution (1)

After a very poor financial performance for 2008, we need to return to our core competencies and do what we do best; coffee and innovation. We have lost our edge.

Howard Schultz, CEO Starbucks, reporting on Starbucks' first loss and halving of share price in 15 months (November 2008)

GROWTH

Business textbooks have assumed that all firms should try to grow and evolve.

- A much larger organization with greater financial muscle can withstand changes in the external environment much more easily than a smaller firm.
- Greater risks yielding potentially much higher rewards can be taken.
- Increased profitability can not only provide security but also entice additional investors and capital, thus reinforcing the upward spiral of success.

Or so it seems.

Currently, serious questions are being asked about the virtue of being a large organization. Issues of management control, communication and hubris are now being voiced by some of the biggest and most successful industry leaders. (Howard Schultz's comments are typical of the current mood sweeping through a number of corporate boardrooms.)

An evaluation of small firms versus large organizations

First we need to define what a small firm is. The legal definition of 'small' often varies by country and industry.

In the US a small business is one which employs fewer than 100 employees, in the European Union the figure is 50 employees, and in Australia, fewer than 20.

We shall stick to the US measure as our definition but we must be aware that other indicators of size, such as **market capitalization** and **sales revenue**, could also be used.

ARGUMENTS FOR BEING LARGE

The arguments in the box on growth (above) make a strong case for being a large organization. A very important concept used to explain the advantages of being a large organization is the existence of **economies of scale**.

Definition: As the scale of operation changes, firms can benefit from reductions in long-run unit costs of production. These reductions can be obtained internally as the individual firm grows or externally if the whole industry expands.

Types of economy of scale	Internal (I) or external (E)	Example
Financial	I	Cheaper finance costs through increased collateral and lender confidence
Purchasing	I	Bulk-buying of raw materials
Risk-bearing	I	Ability to risk entering new markets and finance prototypes of products which may or may not be successful
Marketing	I	Advertising in media with larger customer reach such as satellite television lowers unit costs dramatically
Research and development	E	As an industry grows, firms can share research facilities, reducing costs of new product development
Training labour and pool of available labour growing as industry expands	E	As an industry grows, local labour migrates to areas and becomes skilled through training colleges or by work experience

A number of large firms such as telecommunication companies or, until recently, car manufacturers have been seemingly able to experience almost unlimited economies of scale. Small firms with their limited initial start-up capital and perceived lack of brand loyalty cannot hope to match these cost advantages.

1.7 Growth and evolution (2)

ARGUMENTS FOR REMAINING A SMALL ORGANIZATION

Many larger firms have experienced periods where long-run unit costs actually increase, giving rise to the phenomenon known as **diseconomies of scale**. The arguments here can be technical and feature principally in economics textbooks but we can note that as a firm grows:

- It can become harder to control and manage effectively. Additional layers of management are required or spans of control may grow; mistakes and quality problems may arise, raising unit costs.
- Communication becomes more difficult with longer chains of command. This can lead to worker confusion and isolation, again perhaps leading to errors and quality control concerns. This can also raise unit costs.

Remaining small: the impact of globalization and outsourcing

A second development which we will explore in greater detail in unit 1.9 is that some firms have decided to remain small because they can take advantage of the benefits of globalization and outsource elements of their operations. They could, for example, subcontract production to other suppliers in perhaps lower-cost countries, or outsource customer service functions while keeping control of their intellectual property creation and strategic direction. Improved global ICT opportunities have encouraged this process.

Satisficing and forgoing additional growth

A number of small organizations such as Scholastic and Lavazza have decided to remain focused on a few key markets and have ignored potential growth opportunities.

The reasons seem principally to stem from the need to keep control and retain the original vision of the company, free from outside (or non-family) interests and outside interference which might occur if additional capital or shareholders were sought.

Profits are still an important driver for taking risks in these companies (every publisher apart from Scholastic turned down J.K. Rowling's original *Harry Potter* story) but a key factor determining the size of the organization is the original vision of the founding members. It is hard to argue with the success of family companies that have had this continuity of ownership, such as Lego, Ferrari and Illy.

ACHIEVING GROWTH

Growth for an organization can be achieved in a number of different ways.

A business can decide to grow organically (internal growth) by trying to capture a bigger slice of total market share by selling more of its existing products.

Second, it can try to grow inorganically (external growth) by becoming involved in:

- joint ventures and strategic alliances
- mergers and takeovers

We will also consider growth strategies such as franchising (page 27) and look at alternative strategic options models such as the Ansoff matrix (page 28).

Finally, in the HL extension section we will look at Michael Porter's generic strategies that will allow a business to build a competitive advantage. However, we shall also consider a new way of thinking about strategy which has recently gained a great deal of attention, by looking at a study by Chan Kim and Mauborgne.

NOTE FOR TEACHERS

This section requires the students to undertake a great deal of evaluation. In order to avoid duplication of material in this section, we summarize some key elements which can be used to help students discuss and evaluate a specific strategic decision. This 7C framework can be applied for all discussion and evaluation questions.

THE 7C FRAMEWORK

- **Cost:** Whether a firm decides to grow internally or externally, the financing of the new strategy will have to be considered. Will the firm have to borrow or can it use retained earnings? What will be the impact on gearing?
- **Control:** Clearly, the larger a firm grows the more difficult it will be to manage. Will the structure of the organization have to change? Will spans of control have to rise?
- **Conflict:** How will change be managed? Will there be any resistance from internal and external stakeholders to the new strategy? If two firms combine, will there need to be redundancies to avoid duplication of roles?

- **Compromise:** Will the vision of the company be compromised by growth? Second, if the firm needs to attract more capital to finance this strategy, they may have to give up elements of ownership with resulting impacts perhaps on objectives and vision. We have already noted some firms such as Scholastic which have refused to dilute ownership because they do not wish to compromise the vision.
- **Communication:** As the firm grows, can we ensure that communication channels will be effective to ensure that everyone is aware of the process of change?

(continued)

1.7 Growth and evolution (3)

THE 7C FRAMEWORK (continued)

- **Culture clash:** Finally, can we assume that, if we grow externally by either joint venture or merger, the combined organizations will be able to work together? As we shall see later when we consider Charles Handy's work on cultural imbalance in unit 2.6, it is important that culturally the two organizations fit. The disastrous merger of Time Warner and AOL is a classic example of the problems which can occur if they do not.

- **Confusion:** In the case of joint ventures and mergers, clear lines of accountability and responsibility need to be drawn so that subordinates know who they are to report to. This is especially true when the expansion involves moving into international markets and firms operate over a number of time zones. This point is especially important if we consider some of the culture clashes that could occur if one organization is used to operating in an 'Apollo' culture and the other is more Athenian in nature (see page 57).

Judgment

A key evaluation tool is time. How long before we can judge the success of the strategy? Do we need to focus on sales profits or costs? Do we need to consult with our stakeholders 6 months after the strategy has taken place? What will be the nature of the external environment in 6 months?

These are difficult questions to answer, but important if we are utilizing a sensible decision-making framework and evaluating a chosen course of action.

JOINT VENTURES AND STRATEGIC ALLIANCES

Definition: An agreement for two or more firms to enter into a project to share risks, capital and expertise in order for both firms to benefit. Not surprisingly, joint ventures usually occur between firms in the same industry. Strategic alliances are effectively the same but a little less formal in structure. There is no transfer of ownership.

If a firm wishes to enter a foreign market, it may well form a joint venture with a firm already situated in that country in order to take advantage of local knowledge of the market or labour expertise. There could be considerable savings in cost and time from forming a joint venture with firms that are already established in their markets or regions.

MERGERS AND TAKEOVERS

These terms are used by some commentators to mean the same thing. However, mergers normally imply some mutual agreement to join together whereas a takeover can occur involuntarily; an acquisition can take place even if one firm does not wish to be taken over by another.

There are usually three types of merger.

- **Horizontal:** The deliberate decision to acquire the intellectual property (products or successful brands) of a rival company operating in the same industry. To acquire instant additional market share (subject to government approval), economies of scale and, it is hoped, the creation of 'synergy'. (Synergy refers to the argument proposed that in the case of large mergers huge 'gains' would be made; the so-called 1 + 1 = 3 scenario.)

- **Vertical:** The need to control the supply chain process either forwards (towards the customer) or backwards (to monitor and secure raw material supplies).

- **Conglomerate:** The deliberate attempt to acquire a new firm in an unfamiliar market or industry, thus eliminating the need for costly research or development or spending vast sums of money on developing a new brand.

MERGERS: THE EVIDENCE

If we take into account the 7C framework for evaluating mergers and takeovers and then look at examples from the business world, it has to be said that mergers have not been as successful as we would like to believe. Shareholder value has not necessarily increased. When senior managers from one or other of the merged companies have little experience in the industry or product markets they are now managing in the newly created, enlarged merger company, things can go badly wrong. Hubris (overconfidence) on the part of the senior management has been observed in a number of high-profile mergers, with disastrous effects for stakeholders. This was particularly true in the case of the Time Warner/AOL merger. (Students are encouraged to research other high-profile mergers and takeovers to see if the author's assertions are correct.)

1.7 Growth and evolution (4)

FRANCHISING

It might be tempting to focus purely on the most successful franchising company, McDonald's. We would see how the franchising strategy can prove to be rewarding for the company selling the idea (the **franchisor**) and the entrepreneur who wishes to put up capital in order to obtain the intellectual property rights in delivering the good or service (the **franchisee**).

The McDonald's business model however is not typical, and it would be wrong to assume that all franchises work in the same way. It would be a fruitful exercise for the individual student to investigate for themselves a franchise model which operates in their own country.

We can note a few generic ideas about the effectiveness of the franchise model of growth.

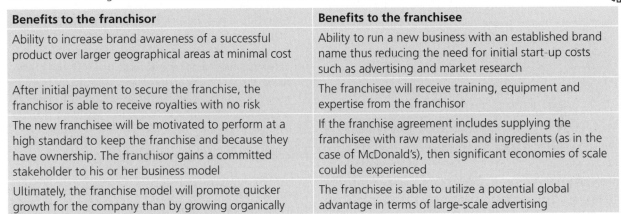

Benefits to the franchisor	Benefits to the franchisee
Ability to increase brand awareness of a successful product over larger geographical areas at minimal cost	Ability to run a new business with an established brand name thus reducing the need for initial start-up costs such as advertising and market research
After initial payment to secure the franchise, the franchisor is able to receive royalties with no risk	The franchisee will receive training, equipment and expertise from the franchisor
The new franchisee will be motivated to perform at a high standard to keep the franchise and because they have ownership. The franchisor gains a committed stakeholder to his or her business model	If the franchise agreement includes supplying the franchisee with raw materials and ingredients (as in the case of McDonald's), then significant economies of scale could be experienced
Ultimately, the franchise model will promote quicker growth for the company than by growing organically	The franchisee is able to utilize a potential global advantage in terms of large-scale advertising

Of course there will be drawbacks to the franchise model, mostly dependent on the type of agreement which has been signed between the two parties. Some franchise agreements are relatively flexible while others allow for very little entrepreneurial initiative on the part of the franchisee (the McDonald's agreement is quite restrictive in this respect).

A McDonald's franchise in the UK shows visitors a 45-page document, illustrating how a Big Mac should be 'assembled'. Apparently the procedure has to be followed to the letter. It is interesting to note that many of McDonald's most successful ideas such as the Big Mac, the Egg McMuffin and the McChicken did not originate from McDonald's itself, but from franchisees.

Evaluation of franchising

We can highlight a few drawbacks to this model apart from those relating to the agreement.

- Franchising encourages standardization of vision, service and product development which some entrepreneurs may after time come to regret.
- A poorly performing franchise in one area can impact on the reputation of others locally. This point could also be extended to the problems of trying to establish a consistent reliable global brand.
- The Starbucks model of clustering franchises, for example, has actually led to competition between franchises, to the detriment of the franchisee. One franchisee cannibalizes the market share of others, with some ultimately being eliminated.

1.7 Growth and evolution (5)

Judgment and links with other topics

Students are advised to look back at the 7C evaluation model (page 25) and apply this to the role of franchising.

- The domination of franchises (the franchise business is worth an estimated 1 trillion dollars in 2008) and the ubiquity of the stores in high streets and malls around the world has been a symbol of globalization which a number of stakeholders have taken objection to. We will look at the issues surrounding this aspect in unit 1.9.

- The steadily rising trend in franchising is a recent phenomenon.

- Some franchise businesses such as Subway have enjoyed superlative growth.

- Others have found this growth hard to control and are currently rethinking their strategy (see quote from Schultz, page 24). For the sole trader, the risk associated with running a franchise (despite the initial huge fees which have to be paid) is smaller than that for starting a business of their own, but entrepreneurial innovation will be limited.

You should now attempt question 7, page 35.

ANSOFF MATRIX

We now undertake a brief study of the Ansoff matrix.

- We use the matrix to see how a business could identify a number of different strategies to pursue further growth, either within existing markets or, taking a riskier route, looking at potential future markets.

- Students are only asked to explain and apply the matrix to a strategic decision, and not to evaluate.

	Existing products	New products
Existing markets	Market penetration	Product development
New markets	Market development	Diversification

- **Market penetration:** Aiming to increase market share. Least risky of the four routes, but limited growth. Once market reaches saturation another strategy is required.

- **Market development:** Targeting existing products to new market segments such as new geographical regions. More risk than penetration.

- **Product development:** Firm develops new products targeted to existing market segments. Good strategy if the company enjoys strong brand loyalty from its customers. A good example would be Sony and their recent success over the Blu-Ray DVD format.

- **Diversification:** The most risky strategy of the four. One writer has called this the 'suicide cell'. The company is stepping out of its comfort zone and perhaps moving away from its core competencies. Nokia has been a notable success story. On the other hand, the Virgin Group has been criticized for having an unfocused portfolio: air travel, music, soft drinks and mobile networks (although this has been reduced in the last 5 years).

Practice question on applying the matrix

This question is from the IB examination of November 2007.

Question: Using Ansoff's Matrix, explain the growth strategies used by Toyota.

Suggested answer:

- Market development: through the export of cars to overseas markets. Toyota has also deliberately used foreign direct investment to develop a presence in many countries.

- Product development/modification: the production of new models every two years. Toyota has produced 60 models in Japan and has adapted many to the American and European markets.

- Market penetration: increasing market share in Japan and other countries after establishing a foothold as described above.

1.7 Growth and evolution (6)

PORTER'S GENERIC STRATEGIES AND THE FIVE FORCES

Michael Porter's model of generic strategies has been used extensively by businesses to develop a competitive strategy within an industry, given the existence of 'five forces' which determine and shape the competitive nature of that industry.

The five forces which determine and shape the competitive nature are:

- entry barriers
- threat of substitutes
- rivalry
- buyer power
- supplier power

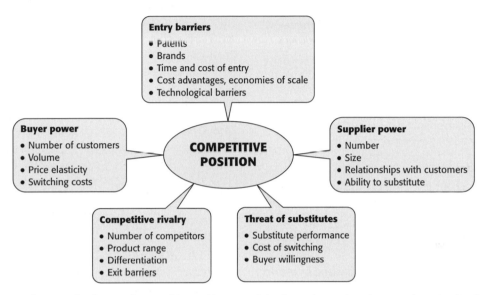

Summary diagram of Porter's five forces of competitive position: a tool that is used to analyse the attractiveness of an industry structure. Based on five forces competitive position model.

Porter proposed three generic strategies which can be used to counter the five forces to maximize opportunities for the firm.

These are:

1 Cost advantage

- Efficiency of production
- Outsourcing
- Vertical integration

Example: Wal-Mart's significant competitive position within the retail industry has been driven by close attention to these factors.

2 Differentiation

- Added value in the eyes of the consumer through product attributes leading to effectively a unique product.

Example: The Apple iPod. It retains enormous market share despite being more expensive than most of its rivals and offering less functionality for the same price as rivals such as Creative and Sony.

3 Focus

- Strategy based around customer loyalty with lower volumes and targeting on specific segments.

Examples would be the luxury car segment such as Ferrari and Rolls Royce.

Evaluation

Porter's generic strategy model is not without its criticisms.

- Competitor firms can attempt to match cost advantage strategies. This has been seen by the recent growth in offshoring. Competitors can easily imitate.

- A number of writers such as Trout have argued that the options for differentiation based on price and quality are limited. Interested students should investigate his excellent book, *Differentiate or Die*. We will cover some aspects of Trout's thinking in later chapters.

1.7 Growth and evolution (7)

A NEW WAY OF THINKING

A more recent of criticism of Porter's thinking is that finding competitive advantage in a maturing or saturated market is increasingly becoming too difficult.

- In their recent book, *Blue Ocean Strategy*, Chan Kim and Mauborgne argue that a successful strategic position is not about competing in existing markets (a Red Ocean strategy).

- The key is to develop a new Blue Ocean strategy: one attempts to make the competition irrelevant.

- They provide a compelling example of Blue Ocean strategy success by using the example of Cirque du Soleil.

Cirque du Soleil was launched at a time when the external factors surrounding the opportunities for circus-style entertainment were very unfavourable.

External factors

- Competing entertainment options such as home video, DVD and games such as playstations.

- Decreasing revenue and profits being earned by the incumbent firms such as Ringling Brothers and Barnum & Bailey.

- A dramatic change in social attitudes and increased ethical concerns about animals being used in circuses.

- The circus market was aimed at children with parents, who found the cost compared to other forms of 'entertainment' prohibitive.

The key was that Cirque du Soleil did not try to compete with the existing firms in what was clearly very limited market space. *They instead made the competition irrelevant* by creating a new experience featuring acrobats and human performers who catered specifically for adults, and the lucrative corporate client market, at a price several times higher than traditional circuses.

The authors argue that the success of Cirque du Soleil and its founder, Guy Laliberte, was remarkable because *it was achieved in a declining market with limited potential for growth and a set of unfavourable external factors.*

Chan Kim and Mauborgne identify the key ideas behind a Blue Ocean strategy compared to the Red Ocean (which is similar in many ways to Porter's generic strategies).

Red Ocean	Blue Ocean
Compete in existing market-place	Create an uncontested marketplace
Exploit existing demand	Create and capture new demand
Choice of either differentiation or low cost	Differentiation and low cost
Beat the competition	Make the competition irrelevant

Interested students may wish to look at the classic case studies of Southwest Airlines (US) and Yellowtail Wines (Australia) as examples of other successful Blue Ocean strategies based on differentiation and cost.

Next you could tackle question 8, page 35.

1.8 Change HL (1)

NOTE FOR TEACHERS

The reasons for change and the process of change is designated as a Higher level only topic.

We shall look at Lewin's model of force field analysis and use an example of how this model could be used to help an organization change and adopt a new strategy. In this unit there will be links with other topics such as human resource management and motivation. As change impacts on the whole organization, and in order to avoid duplication, the reader may just wish to review these sections and key terms first before proceeding.

There have been few specific questions in the examinations about change. Instead examiners see this topic as more of an analytical tool to help us perhaps evaluate a course of action a firm is taking or discuss the implications of switching strategies. Some of the issues discussed in this section would find a good home in an Extended Essay in Business or a Higher level Internal Assessment project. Good students may also find some of these ideas useful when preparing to analyse the pre-issued case study.

CAUSES OF CHANGE

HL

There could be a range of reasons why a firm wishes to change:

- The threat of new competition and a saturated market
- A change in a number of the STEEPLE factors
- Shareholder impatience with the current senior management

Let's assume, following a decision-making model as discussed in unit 1.6 (page 21), that the business has carried out either a STEEPLE or a SWOT analysis to gauge the magnitude of the opportunities or threats before it, and has decided to review operations and make a change.

If the firm decides that only **tactical changes** are required then this could launch a further investigation into one aspect of the organization. Tactical changes could include but are not limited to:

- Price changes to some of the products in the portfolio
- A new promotional campaign to raise the brand awareness of the company
- A decision to manage liquidity by offering discounts to debtors for early payment

If, however, the firm uses an Ansoff matrix or Porter's generic model to look at a significant **strategic change**, then the recommendations for change might be:

1 Transferring all operations to a new country to reduce production cost

2 Splitting the company into profit centres and/or geographical regions

3 Divesting or de-merging one part of the company to concentrate on a key market

In this section we will be focusing on strategic changes.

RESISTANCE TO CHANGE

HL

With any new strategic move there will always be resistance. This resistance will mostly stem from fear about not exactly knowing what the changes may mean for various stakeholders.

Clearly, it would seem natural that in order to effect change, a senior management team or whoever is entrusted to implement the change in strategy must work on allaying these fears. Not all will be satisfied but, by weakening the resistance, there is more likelihood that a new change strategy will succeed.

Stakeholder	Resistance due to
Line workers	Fear of new working practices, threat to Maslow lower-order needs such as **security**, **love** and **belonging**
Customers	Fear of losing a product that they were loyal to
Suppliers	Fear of losing a place in the supply chain. Job losses and lost revenue
Management	Fear of having to implement change and dealing with adverse reaction

1.8 Change HL (2)

LEWIN'S FORCE FIELD ANALYSIS

This analysis regards an organization as one which is comprised of competing forces which can push an organization in one direction to achieve a goal (**drivers**) to be met with resistance by those forces not wishing to move (**restrainers**).

- Driving forces try to establish a new equilibrium or status quo.
- Restraining forces try to restrict a new equilibrium being achieved.

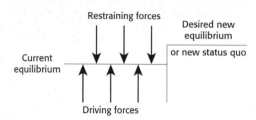

Lewin's force field analysis

In order to effect change the driving forces need to be able to move the organization to a new status quo and reduce the power or influence of the restraining forces.

This is easier said than done. A number of operational tactics will need to be utilized in order for successful implementation.

Dearden and Foster (1994) argue:

- The team charged with implementing change must have authority to implement change, which is understood by those affected by change.
- The board of directors through the CEO must indicate that change is necessary and extol clearly the virtues of this change for the whole organization.
- The change process including contingencies must be clearly communicated to all stakeholders early, including (as accurately as possible) timelines for implementation.
- Early successful outcomes of the change must be clearly communicated and celebrated.
- A constant reminder of the goals and objectives of the strategy change must be highlighted prominently around the workplace.

It would seem that clear effective communication plays a crucial part in the change process.

We will now look at a typical example (adapted from www.mindtools.com) of a strategic change within an organization and use force field analysis to help us understand the competing forces.

The change

- An organization looking to reduce unit costs of production to become more competitive and reduce errors and defects decides to introduce new technology in the workplace to boost productivity and raise quality.

The process

The board of directors instruct a senior management team to investigate additional drivers to move the company to a new equilibrium while recognizing that restraining forces will exist. The senior management team is to rank the magnitude of the forces, with 1 being weak and 5 being strong.

Drivers

- Customers looking to generate higher value at lower prices   4
- Speed of production   2
- Productivity increases   3
- Control of maintenance costs   1

Restrainers

- Loss of overtime for line staff   3
- Fear of new technology   3
- Disruption: time for implementation   1
- Cost of transfer of technology   3
- Environmental impact   1

Moving to a new equilibrium

A number of the restrainers affect the workers directly. Human resources may become uncooperative if change is forced upon them so a key tactic in the change strategy is to try and weaken the restrainers rather than force the drivers through.

- By training staff (increase in costs) fear of technology can be reduced.
- Board can convince staff that the changes are necessary to ensure survival and security for the majority. (Maslow need: security and safety?)
- Staff could be encouraged by the prospect of upskilling. (job enrichment?)
- Increase in productivity could lead to wage increases as long as the competitive objective in the new strategy is not undermined.
- The environmental impact of the change to new technology may satisfy local community concerns.

You could now tackle question 9, page 35.

1.9 Globalization (1)

NOTE FOR TEACHERS

Students are advised to regularly update their knowledge in this area as the arguments surrounding globalization and the impact of multinational activity on stakeholders have been subject to considerable discussion and debate. With the growing financial crisis and credit crunch taking hold, there have been recent calls for more 'protection' of local economies and less openness – effectively calling for more regulation; the perceived enemy of globalization.

At the time of writing, unemployment is rising in many developed economies and in the media there seems to be a growing discussion that we may have to review our thinking on the role of open markets and the free movement of capital, labour and resources. The concept of globalization is being carefully scrutinized.

THE MULTINATIONAL CORPORATION

Key terms

Globalization: The growing integration, interdependence and general connectedness of the world through markets, labour mobility and capital transfer.

Multinational corporation (MNC): one which operates, owns and controls resources outside its country of origin. A company is not considered an MNC if it merely sells abroad.

WHAT DOES A TYPICAL MULTINATIONAL COMPANY LOOK LIKE?

A typical MNC may own research and development facilities to generate new intellectual property ideas in the host country as well as advertising, marketing and strategic direction but may allow customer service operations or manufacturing overseas (offshoring). Local managers may also be transferred frequently around the different international markets to increase knowledge and experience.

REASONS FOR THE GROWTH OF MULTINATIONAL ACTIVITY

Surprisingly, there is considerable debate as to when globalization became a new paradigm of business thinking. Nobel Prize-winning economist Paul Krugman argues that, even in during the 1960s and early 1970s, many firms were reluctant to move operations overseas despite enormous cost savings in labour and materials. It was the widely held view that it was better and more efficient to produce at home.

And then something happened to create a 'perfect storm' which allowed globalization to flourish:

- A significant fall in airfares with an increase in the number of routes available. Greater competition in the airline industry.

- Increased opportunity to spread tax liabilities around the world hence boosting profitability to shareholders. And to take advantage of generous government assistance in helping to attract MNCs.

- The increase of and availability of international schools to help with the relocation of families. (Growth in the popularity of the IB?)

- Dramatic falls in the cost of communication. The cost of a telephone call between the US and India fell by 80% between 2001 and 2003. The simultaneous use of VOIP tools such as Skype has cut these costs even further. The increased use of video conferencing.

The impact of the Internet and other events

The ubiquity of the Internet clearly has a defining role to play in explaining the upward trend in MNC activity.

In his popular book, *The World is Flat*, Thomas Friedman identifies a number of factors where the Internet has levelled the competitive playing field and driven the move towards globalization.

- 9 November 1989: Fall of the Berlin Wall (world balance of power shifting towards more open economies and markets).

- Netscape IPO 9 August 1995 (sparking interest in fibre-optic cables which allow much faster transfer of data).

- Power searching on the Internet through Google and other search engines allowing greater transparency and allowing individuals to build up a personal 'supply chain of knowledge' of the world.

- Wireless technology increasing mobile and personal communication opportunities.

- Open-source software facilitating a greater degree of online collaborative workspaces, e.g. Google Docs and Wiki spaces.

The reader is encouraged to discuss these topics or investigate these areas further, and the increasing changes in technology, and perhaps challenge some of the above ideas or introduce new ones.

1.9 Globalization (2)

THE IMPACT OF MULTINATIONAL COMPANIES ON THE HOST COUNTRY

Benefit to the host country	Discussion
Creation of new jobs, employment opportunities	Jobs created may be lower down in the hierarchy with limited senior management positions for local workers
Revenue-raising opportunities for the host government	Some MNCs will be able to repatriate funds offshore due to the increasing ability of tax free havens
Importation of new technology, skills and management techniques	A strong benefit especially in Asia which has become the largest outsourcing market: • India and software • China and manufacturing
Increase in choice of goods and services available for host country citizens	Will local consumers be able to afford these goods and services bound for western markets? Unfair competition for local producers may increase unemployment in some industries

FURTHER RESEARCH: THE CASE OF IRELAND

Interested students are encouraged to investigate the experiences of the Irish economy which went through a significant transformation by encouraging MNC activity. The consequences have been both positive and negative.

You may now like to tackle questions 10, 11 and 12, page 35.

REGIONAL TRADING BLOCS

Learning Objective: Explain the impact on a business of a country that is a member of a regional economic group/bloc.

Students are encouraged to investigate their own regional trading bloc and compare the results with another bloc which is geographically close and one further away to see if there are any similarities or differences in the impact on firms.

More generally we could identify:

• Firms inside the bloc may be able to avoid tariffs and quotas which will be applied to some non-member countries' firms.

• Strategic alliances may be more possible within a bloc.

• If we examine a PEST framework there may be other compelling political, social and technological factors which may benefit a firm being a member of a trading bloc. This could be a fruitful place to start for a student to investigate the possibility of a company looking to relocate its operations inside an economic bloc for an Internal Assessment project, assuming that currently the business operates outside the bloc.

Exam questions on Topic 1

1 **a** Explain how the BMW Group could implement in practice the following two policies:

   • A reduction in its environmental impact

   • An increase in its attractiveness as an employer.

   b Evaluate the view that the BMW's move to greater social responsibility will lead to
   commercial success. (November 2006)

2 With reference to the Walt Disney Company, analyse the potential effects on stakeholder
groups of a global conglomerate investing in China. (November 2007)

3 Assess the effects of moving jobs overseas on four stakeholder groups. (May 2005)

4 Analyse why BP might find it difficult to satisfy all its stakeholders. (May 2004)

5 To what extent is the external environment an important influence on the number and
size of mergers and takeovers? (May 2008)

6 **HL Goal plc** is a South American football club. Although the players are highly motivated
and united as a team, they have won very few games. Loyal supporters and shareholders are
worried about relegation to a lower league and a significant fall in revenue and potential cash
flow problems as a result. The management team is considering three possible options to
improve the team's performance and attract more spectators.

The expected returns from each option depend on the prevailing economic conditions. These
economic conditions and the probability of each occurring are shown in the table below.

	Expected return ($)		
	Improved	**Unchanged**	**Worsened**
	20%	**50%**	**30%**
Option 1. Buy new players from top European teams. Cost $2m	5m	4m	1m
Option 2. Build a new modern stadium on a nearby underdeveloped site. Cost $3m	6m	5m	(-1m)
Option 3. Renovate the stadium and the training facilities. Cost $1m	3m	2m	1m

Construct a fully labelled decision tree. (Show all your working) (November 2007)

7 Examine the potential problems that Subway may face as a result of its planned rapid expansion. (May 2006)

8 Using a model such as Ansoff's matrix, evaluate the strategic options available to companies
seeking future growth in saturated markets. (May 2005)

9 **HL** Analyse the driving and restraining forces on MNCs that are considering globalizing their
sales, manufacturing and operations. (May 2006)

10 Evaluate the extent to which globalization is encouraged by the development of new ICT. (May 2004)

11 Discuss how leadership and motivation in MNCs will be affected as they become
increasingly global. (May 2006)

2.1 Human resource planning (1)

INTRODUCTION

In previous chapters, we highlighted the fact that businesses face an increasing number of pressures forced on them by changes in the external environment, the growing onset of globalization and the impact of de-industrialization.

An area of the organization directly affected by these developments is the planning and management of human resources. With slowing birth rates in the developed world, the increased ageing of the working population, the trend towards migration of workers and the new 24/7 economy (especially in the service sector), firms have had to rethink their workforce planning requirements.

This unit will try to analyse some of these external factors and the implications for recruitment, training and appraisal. We will also briefly look at some inevitable consequences if there is a significant deterioration of the external environment by looking at retrenchment and restructuring.

DEMOGRAPHIC CHANGES IN THE DEVELOPED WORLD

- The service sector (known as the tertiary sector) represents the biggest employer and the biggest contribution to overall output.

- Male participation in full-time work has decreased relative to female participation.

- According to OECD figures, the number of hours worked by full-time employees has fallen by a third but the number of workers participating in the workforce has risen by a third (a good indicator of the growing importance of part-time work).

- A fall in domestic birth rates with an ageing population (raising the retirement age is being considered by a number of countries to avoid a pensions crisis).

- The increasing importance of immigration to cover both short-term and long-term gaps in human resources outlined above.

- Some firms are simply unable to recruit workers in some primary or secondary sector roles due to de-industrialization.

In developing countries, the impact of these changes has required the development of a number of new strategies designed to prepare for future human resource shortages.

- Online recruiting of workers from other countries.

- The increasing use of overseas employment agencies to find key workers.

- With the lower cost of operating in overseas countries, a number of firms have taken the decision to outsource some or all of their operations.

Changes in work patterns and practices

In addition to changing demographic factors, we can note that traditional working practices are also changing, mostly in response to changing societal conventions. For example:

- Extended opening hours in the retail sector including weekend shopping leading to job-sharing and the creation of additional part-time opportunities.

- A culture of the 24/7 service sector with online retailing growing in importance.

- The end of the 9am to 5pm convention of the 'normal working day'.

- The growth of childcare services allowing both adults in a family to work.

The employer's response

Faced with rising overhead costs, seasonal and fluctuating demand for goods and services and the increasing use of remote Internet connections, employers have also contributed to the paradigm shift in working patterns by:

- Allowing employees to undertake flexi-time arrangements

- Enabling employees to work from home via technology

- Replacing permanent positions with contract workers to release temporary workers if there is insufficient demand.

You could now tackle question 1, page 62.

Conclusion

There has been a fundamental shift in perception as to what constitutes the trading and working day. The key is that employers especially are trying to make more effective use of human resources, given the enormous changes in demographic and social factors outlined above, signalled by the phrase 'flexible working' which has created opportunities and threats for all employees. Human resource planning has never been so important and we now turn to this aspect of business organization by looking at recruitment, training and appraisal.

2.1 Human resource planning (2)

RECRUITMENT, APPRAISAL, TRAINING, DISMISSAL AND REDUNDANCY

The process of recruitment has become increasingly important in the new competitive environment. Mistakes made in the recruitment of line managers or senior managers can create significant opportunity costs for a firm; as time passes these 'wrong appointments' can turn into significant financial and human resource problems. The objective of recruitment is to employ the right worker at the right time for the right job and allow him or her to be productive. This is not an easy task.

Moreover, recruitment methods are changing. The traditional job advert and interview are now supported by the following innovations:

- Jobs advertised on the Internet
- Specialized global recruitment agencies
- An increase in social networking with jobs offered before they are advertised
- Psychological profiling and psychometric testing of potential candidates
- Interviews which may stretch over a number of days rather than hours.

All of the above methods are designed to minimize the chance of a poor appointment.

Recruitment has a number of different purposes

- Looking for workers or new managers in addition to current staff
- Covering contingencies such as staff illness, leave, sabbaticals or seasonal factors
- Promoting line managers or heads of department or divisions

External and internal recruitment

External recruitment:

- Can be time consuming.
- Can remove a significant amount of work for the firm and minimize disruption.
- Can be an expensive process.

Internal recruitment:

- Can be a powerful motivating factor for young managers wishing to move up the hierarchy.
- Can be cheaper than external recruitment but may encourage firms to be too inward-looking and not employ new people who bring fresh ideas and perspectives to the firm.
- Can become a 'hot topic' for employees and encourage informal networks and groups that champion their own selections.

APPRAISAL

Many workers fear appraisal as they assume that it is merely a way of judging performance. This narrow view does not take into account the fact that if appraisal is carried out effectively it can become a very motivating process for both the employee and the employer.

When appraisal is carried out efficiently it will have the following positive consequences:

- The employer has the opportunity to restate objectives and vision for the company (especially important for senior managers).
- The employer can praise high-performing workers and reaffirm their role in the future of the organization, thus aiding the retention of key workers.

- The employee may get a chance to voice concerns about the organization's direction, giving them an opportunity to channel frustration. Management hear about 'grass-roots' problems and are able to pre-empt future conflict.

Many companies leave the appraisal process to the end of the financial year. Some companies take a more flexible view and encourage employees to discuss issues with managers more regularly. How appraisal is carried out will depend a great deal on the culture of the organization (see unit 2.6).

2.1 Human resource planning (3)

TRAINING

A notable and worthwhile outcome of appraisals is to identify areas where an employer can help an employee develop new skills to enhance productivity. Training or professional development is a key topic and we will return to it both in the motivation sections of human resource management and in some aspects of operations management.

Training is usually identified within three areas:

- Induction training
- On the job
- Off the job

There are benefits and drawbacks to all three. (The disadvantages of off-the-job will look very similar to the advantages of on-the-job.)

Type of training	Benefits to employer	Benefits to employee	Issues/problems
Induction	Allows employer to set expectations of the new employee right at the beginning of the employment period	Clear guidelines as to culture, role and expectations. Allows the employee time to settle	Can be costly and diverts senior managers away from important tasks
On the job	Cost is lower than off-the-job. The training is specific to the needs of the firm.	Minimal disruption to the working day. Skills learned can be readily put into practice	Lack of outside training may narrow experiences of employee. Too inward looking. Not a good way to train in fast-moving technological industries
Off the job	Expensive and cover needed for staff who are absent	Being away from the workplace for a day may allow perspective and sharing of best practice. The firm creates external outside networks	Skills learned may take time to be put into practice in the firm. Too much off-the-job may lead to resentment by employees who have to cover absences

The amount of training a firm offers will depend on several factors:

- The cost
- The amount of disruption the firm is prepared to experience
- The nature of the industry. Firms in fast-moving technology industries may require their employees to constantly keep up to date with the latest industry developments
- Employer motivation towards training. Some employers may be reluctant to train externally for fear of workers being 'poached' by rival firms.

2.1 Human resource planning (4)

DISMISSAL AND REDUNDANCY

There is a great deal of confusion about these two terms and some students use them interchangeably. Given new management buzzwords which were introduced into our vocabulary during the 1990s such as downsizing, retrenchment, disestablishment and financial reengineering, some confusion on the part of the student may be understandable.

Dismissal

Possible reasons for dismissal:

- An employee has been advised that their performance is below expectations (perhaps during an appraisal meeting) and continues to perform below expectations.
- An employee may not have followed company rules and regulations on issues such as hours or rest breaks.
- An employee may have a pattern of poorly explained absenteeism.
- Other issues which contravened the employee's work contract.

In order to satisfy the requirements of employment legislation laid down by the government in a particular country, the employer would normally issue both verbal and written warnings.

The employee must expect that if they ignore these warnings their job will be terminated by their own negligence and refusal to comply. If, however, the employee feels that dismissal was unwarranted and can prove that there may be other mitigating factors, then claims of **unfair dismissal** may be possible (legal rights and standing on this issue vary from country to country. Students may wish to investigate the legal position in their own country).

Redundancy

Redundancy occurs through no fault of the employee. A redundant worker is not replaced. A worker's position may simply disappear due to the following reasons:

- A sustained fall in demand for the company's products
- The need to restructure due to changes in the external environment (a change in one of the SLEPT factors such as new technological innovations)
- Strategic decisions to move some parts of the operation overseas or to outsource a particular job.

When redundancy occurs an employee will normally be entitled to a redundancy payment based on the number of years' service to the company. However, redundancy payment arrangements differ widely between companies and countries. Firms that have made large numbers of workers redundant may offer counselling and training to affected workers to help them find new jobs. These out-placement services however are not cheap and therefore not universally offered.

RETRENCHMENT AND DOWNSIZING

Faced with a combination of limited sales revenue growth in saturated markets, challenging economic trading conditions and increased pressure by shareholders to deliver ever increasing profitability, a number of large companies, most notably in the US, began a new trend of workforce planning in the late 1990s called downsizing. In Asia the term most commonly used was retrenchment. It was a brutal policy of removing whole layers of middle and line managers from organizations.

Downsizing was justified as a way to guarantee the organization's survival, maintaining profitability by slashing costs. In some famous examples, firms which retrenched tens of thousands of workers found their share price rising. However, given the extent and nature of the human resource cuts, downsizing was challenged as an effective way to manage the workforce.

- First, with whole layers of management stripped out, how could the organization continue to provide effective operations and customer service?
- Second, what would happen to those workers who remained in the organization after the restructuring?

Who would manage these workers? And if training was required would this not raise costs? (As a number of firms have indicated, the actual process of restructuring can cost millions of dollars. Ironically, in the short term, retrenchment could actually cost more than the other option of keeping the status quo.) There were also concerns that motivation levels in the workers left behind would be reduced as they fear the increased workload and perhaps the next round of human resource cuts.

- Third, a large number of firms retrenched line managers who had acquired enormous industry experience. Some of these experienced workers were then rehired by competitors.
- Finally, what would happen when economic conditions became more favourable? Would there not be gaps in the management process?

As a way of managing human resources downsizing has with hindsight been regarded as a classic example of 'short-term' thinking. There was an acknowledgment by stakeholders that in the short term, faced with changing external conditions, restructuring and job losses were inevitable. However as the rate of change of downsizing grew faster some of the reasoning behind the retrenchments seemed very arbitrary at best and to some extent morally questionable.

2.1 Human resource planning (5)

HANDY'S SHAMROCK ORGANIZATION

Charles Handy has become well regarded in the business world for his work on organizational culture and management. His is particularly well known for his vivid use of engaging metaphors and examples. Students are encouraged to read excerpts from *Gods of Management* and *The Empty Raincoat*.

One of Handy's contributions to workforce planning was his insight into the roles of workers required in the new demographic and social changes outlined in Unit 2.1.

Handy identified the need to have a flexible workforce to allow firms to adjust faster to changing external environments.

He identified core, contract and peripheral workers and developed the idea of the 'shamrock' organization.

- **Core:** Full-time employees with trusted experience and small in number.
- **Contract:** Employed on a short-term basis for a specific task. Examples of these tasks are the recruitment of senior managers or the installation of a new data management system.
- **Peripheral:** Flexible workers employed on a part-time basis for reasons identified earlier such as seasonal shifts in operations.

Traditional inflexible 20th-century organization with core full-time staff

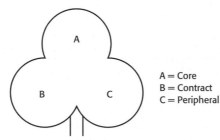

A = Core
B = Contract
C = Peripheral

Shamrock organization

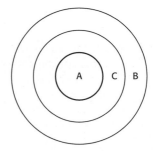

New flexible 21st-century shamrock organization

The implications of Handy's work should be clear. Given the significant changes in working patterns and external social and demographic changes outlined earlier, fewer full-time workers are necessary. The Shamrock organization has important implications for leadership, management, motivation, communication and culture.

2.2 Organizational structure (1)

NOTE FOR TEACHERS

This unit and subsequent units rely heavily on the student understanding a large number of terms and definitions. It is 'jargon heavy'. Students are advised to check carefully their understanding of these terms. We will also be making reference to some of the themes investigated in unit 2.6 on organizational culture as this has a significant influence on **communication, leadership, motivation** and **organizational structure**. Standard level students are encouraged to read unit 2.6 before unit 2.2 even though **organizational culture** per se is not on the Standard level syllabus. It will significantly enhance their understanding of the topics mentioned above.

DEFINITIONS

Subordinate: Workers who have to report to and are answerable to a manager.

Delegation: The process of entrusting a subordinate to perform a task for which the superior retains overall responsibility.

Span of control: The number of subordinates under the control of a supervisor. In your class the span of control is the number of students directly supervised by the teacher.

Levels of hierarchy: The number of levels of formal authority from the top to the bottom of an organization. To a large extent the choice of a particular span of control will dictate the number of levels. This interaction of span of control and levels of hierarchy gives the following two hierarchical structures:

- **Tall:** small span of control and many levels
- **Flat:** larger span of control and fewer levels

Chain of command: This is usually depicted on an organizational chart as a vertical line of authority enabling decision-making or responsibility to be passed down through the layers of hierarchy. The chain establishes the formal communication channels.

ORGANIZATIONAL CHARTS

Activity: Before you embark on the analysis of organizational charts and structures, you should try to draw an organizational chart of your school or college. Avoid names and personalities and focus on roles. Ask a classmate to do the same thing and if possible ask a third party who may have a strong association with the school to do the same. Then compare your results.

Areas of discussion

Are the diagrams similar in terms of levels of hierarchy and span of control?

If you show your diagram to a stakeholder who was at the school a few years ago, do you think he or she will find there have been significant changes in structure? Has the hierarchy become flatter or taller?

If as expected the school has grown in size, have spans of control become wider? This exercise should generate some fruitful discussion.

THE DIAGRAMS

We now present a number of standard diagrams to illustrate how organizational charts can be drawn.

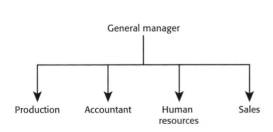

Typical structure for a business organized by function

Typical structure for a business organized by geography

Typical structure for a business organized by product/profit centres (HL only)

2.2 Organizational structure (2)

THE DIAGRAMS *(continued)*

The table is used to analyse the different methods of structuring.

Structure	Benefits	Issues/Problems
By function	Clear lines of communication and responsibility are established. Good for new stakeholders especially employees to see how the organization is structured. Encourages specialization leading to economies of scale	This type of structure may encourage departments to view themselves as isolated and set own goals and objectives. Relies heavily on the success of the General Manager to communicate and manage effectively
By geography	Gives autonomy to local managers to allow more accurate local decision-making. Closer to local markets to gain updated research such as customer feedback	Given geographical location or time differences, potential loss of control of overall objectives. (With the onset of communication technologies this may not be such a big issue.) May have to set local goals and aims
By product or profit centre (HL)	Allows expertise in specific products and markets. Rapid decision-making and objective ways of measuring centre performance. Greater flexibility for growth and expansion. Additional centres can be added without affecting the operations of the other centres. Good if a takeover or acquisition has been made	Conflict and competition between centres. Some duplication of function such as accounting, marketing and human resource management. Allocation of overhead crucial in influencing pricing strategies of individual centres (see Absorption pricing, page 96)
All		Informal communication channels and groups are not revealed

Henri Fayol

The origins of formal organization theory can be found in the work of Henri Fayol. Fayol's approach was driven by scientific management (in the same way as Frederick Taylor's theory on motivation was) and designed to allow organizations to maximize efficiency and, more importantly, establish the link between organizational objectives and performance.

Dearden and Foster (1994) stress the importance of this point:

The most appropriate structure for a business will be that which best helps it to achieve its objectives.

2.2 Organizational structure (3)

For HL students

'Zeus' cultures prefer to concentrate the power of decision-making in the hands of a selected few with fellow workers becoming followers. 'Apollo' cultures stick rigidly to rules, roles and regulations and strongly endorse formal channels of communication. Here in lies the essence of **centralization**.

Clearly the opposite of centralization is **decentralization**, with perhaps Athenian and Dionysian cultures taking a greater role in decision-making.

In this extension unit, we will be looking at a number of alternative structures from the orthodox ones studied in the first part of the unit.

The reader is invited to decide for themselves which structure is the most appropriate for an organization, having considered the crucial point which ended our analysis in the previous unit. Given its critical nature, it is repeated here for emphasis.

The most appropriate structure for a business will be that which best helps it to achieve its objectives.

HL

A SUMMARY OF ISSUES CONCERNING CENTRALIZATION AND DECENTRALIZATION

To summarize some of the issues already presented, centralization:

- allows consistent policies to be applied throughout an organization
- ensures that quick decisions can be made without consultation
- may avoid duplication in decision-making and is essential in times of crisis.

But centralization also:

- reduces the input of subordinates who are keen to show initiative and share ideas, leading to demotivation
- risks demoralizing department managers who may feel powerless and mistrusted, especially if there is minimal delegation.

FROM CENTRALIZATION TO DECENTRALIZATION? MCDONALD'S MARKETING MIX IN THE 1990s

The McDonald's Corporation, famously a centralized company in the US, decided that, in order to increase its global market share, it would allow a greater degree of decentralization in marketing outside the US. It would encourage franchisees to try new menu items that would satisfy local tastes, effectively allowing variation in the marketing mix. This has been enthusiastically taken up by a number of countries, for example:

- New Zealand: the Kiwi Burger contains beetroot
- South Korea: the Pork Burger

- France: alcohol is served in French restaurants
- Japan: the Chicken Teriyaki Burger
- Saudi Arabia: a halal McArabia
- Singapore: regularly introduces new menu items for short periods as line extension strategies, e.g. McPepper, McCrispy and Fish Dippers.

Readers are invited to add their own country favourite to the list and to discuss how the marketing of fast food from outlets such as McDonald's is altered to take into account local tastes and cultural preferences.

2.2 Organizational structure (4)

FLEXIBLE STRUCTURES: HENRY MINTZBERG   HL

The traditional approach to organization structure outlined previously, whether by function, geographical location or product (profit centre), is defined on a hierarchical basis – from the top where the CEO and the Board sit, downwards towards the lowest-level subordinate.

A number of new approaches have now emerged to take into account new theories in motivation and communication. It is considered that formal hierarchical models need updating, to which we now turn. We shall be using the work of Henry Mintzberg to help us understand these new structures.

Mintzberg called for greater flexibility and derived a grid which identified four types of organization classified by complexity and various stable or dynamic states. Based on the work of Robert Waterman, Mintzberg developed his own type of organizational term called adhocracy to illustrate his preference for flexible, adaptable organizations.

	Simple organization	Complex organization
Stable	A Machine Bureaucracy	B Professional Bureaucracy
Dynamic	C Entrepreneurial Start-up	D Adhocracy

Source: Russell-Walling (2007)

- **A:** Mintzberg called these **bureaucratic structures** (technostructures). Apollo-like cultures with an 'army of accountants, analysts, managers and planners (technocrats)'.

- **B: Professional bureaucracy.** Highly trained professional organizations with individuals working relatively independently. Firms set the rules of work but performance is dictated to by external professional standards. An example of such an organization would be hospitals.

- **C: Effectively a Zeus club culture.** Highly centralized but low on technocrats. The leader and managers have control and direct supervision but, as in club cultures, empathy and loyalty are driven by a common enthusiasm. Mintzberg argues that most firms in their early years of start-up could be classed as C.

- **D: Adhocracy.** Examples include dynamic Athenian cultures such as advertising and media agencies and ICT companies. Responsibility is devolved down to workers in informal groups or ad hoc teams (hence the term 'adhocracy'). A process of 'mutual adjustment' is advocated to decide on the make-up of each informal group. Mutual adjustment includes the need for a group to create respect, tolerance and teamwork. With these present, adhocracy can be achieved.

The work of Mintzberg has led some writers to discuss openly the possibility of an inverted pyramid structure with customers at the top of the hierarchy and ad hoc teams made up of key workers to follow, with the Board relegated to the bottom. The argument is that the customer and the market in general are now the most important aspect of the organization, with frontline workers who interact with these customers being best placed to advise managers and ultimately the Board on the strategic direction the firm should take. Students are invited to discuss in greater detail the implications of this inverted structure.

2.2 Organizational structure (5)

MATRIX STRUCTURE AND PROJECT TEAMS HL

The idea behind the matrix structure is that traditional functional and department boundaries are ignored when a project team is selected to work on one 'problem' for which the members' individual qualities are ideally suited. Dearden argues that IBM used this technique when developing the original personal computer.

Once the problem has been solved the team is usually broken up and individuals return to their functional roles or departments.

The matrix system has been used enthusiastically by the Japanese in their creation of **quality circles** and **kaizen** although in Japanese management the matrix is viewed as being very much a long-term commitment and not just for one-off projects. They regard project terms as being a very powerful motivating force in terms of teamwork and breaking down barriers which may exist between departments working in the formal organization.

However, it should be noted that an important aspect of the matrix system which needs to be addressed at the beginning of the project is that with individuals joining from different departments, clear lines of authority need to be established indicating who is overall in charge. This could be undertaken as suggested by Mintzberg by 'mutual consent'.

This is a good opportunity to try and answer question 2, page 62.

THE ROLE OF THE INFORMAL ORGANIZATION HL

Dearden defines the informal structure or an organization as the structure which acknowledges the employees to be individuals with differing personalities, free to join social groups and have particular friendships, rather than regarding them as holders of particular roles. These groups do not meet regularly in the working day but may form and develop in staff canteens or other break areas.

The informal organization principally sprang from dissatisfaction with formal lines of communication where perhaps worker X in department Y, feeling demotivated, sought advice from worker A in department B, although no formal link existed according to the prevailing organizational chart. Clearly therefore there is a very strong link between the informal organization and informal communication, which is discussed in unit 2.3.

Dearden is unequivocal in his support for the 'grapevine' although he acknowledges the issues of controlling gossip and rumour. He writes: 'many problems undermine the formal structure and tend to encourage the use of the grapevine. The notion of a formal organization structure underpinning *all* activity should be severely questioned.'

Students are encouraged to think about the role and importance of formal and informal groups in their own institution.

OUTSOURCING, OFFSHORING AND MIGRATION OF HUMAN RESOURCE FUNCTIONS HL

Given the recent deterioration in the external environment, and the rise of unemployment in many developed countries, the process of offshoring in particular has become a very contentious issue. The following article adapted from the *New Zealand Herald* concerning a recent announcement by NZ Telecom to move 250 contract call centre jobs to the Philippines, perfectly captures the current mood of the stakeholders affected.

TELECOM TO MOVE 250 MORE JOBS OVERSEAS

Wednesday Feb 04, 2009

Telecom is proposing to move about 250 contact centre positions from this country to the Philippines during the next 18 months.

The company said today that when the process was complete, it would have around 1600 contact centre positions in this country and 700 positions outsourced in Manila.

The move followed almost a year of trials and research which looked at the impact on customer experiences from moving several Telecom contact centres overseas.

*The outcome is that Telecom is proposing to retain its largest contact centre operations, 123 and *123, in New Zealand, mainly in Hamilton, with the approximately 250 positions being moved from a range of other contact centres in this country.*

*"In the case of 123 and *123 the trial data did not show us the consistent performance we needed to see in order to be comfortable with a large-scale offshoring of that operation, in which a detailed knowledge of an extremely varied set of products and services is all-important," Mr Gourdie said.*

"In other areas, where specific, technical knowledge was particularly important, offshore staff have delivered strong results for the New Zealand customers they dealt with."

The proposal would see further moves of Telecom's broadband support helpdesk to its outsourced partners, where it had been found it was easy to recruit technically-skilled staff.

Telecom Retail chief executive Alan Gourdie said that due to the length of the timeframe involved the number of redundancies was expected to be "very limited".

(continued)

2.2 Organizational structure (6)

OUTSOURCING, OFFSHORING AND MIGRATION OF HUMAN RESOURCE FUNCTIONS (continued)

If the proposed model were confirmed then Telecom would work hard to ensure affected staff would be redeployed within the company or offered support to find other roles, he said.

Engineering, Printing and Manufacturing Union national secretary Andrew Little said the union represents about 20 workers affected by the move.

He said with New Zealand's economy heading into a "difficult time", Telecom's decision is "unfortunate".

Mr Little said the country needs all the spending power it has and jobs moving off-shore will not help.

He said there could be more businesses moving jobs overseas this year as they review their businesses practices.

Mr Gourdie acknowledged the past year had been a time of uncertainty for staff in Telecom's New Zealand-based call centres, particularly those at the Hamilton operation.

"We have communicated openly and regularly with staff throughout the trials. Feedback on the proposed structure will now be sought over the next two weeks, with a final contact centre structure to be confirmed by early March."

We shall use this article as a source document to help us understand some of the issues which will arise in the remainder of this unit and unit 2.7.

Definitions

- **Offshoring:** moving part of a company's operations to another country
- **Outsourcing:** A business function or operation performed by a third party either **onshore or offshore**

Reasons for and a discussion of the benefits of outsourcing and offshoring human resource functions

To avoid duplication the reader is advised to first re-read unit 1.9 which provides generalized arguments for the recent growth in globalization and multinational corporation activity. This unit will focus on offshoring as outsourcing is covered in more depth in Topic 5 when we consider make-or-buy decisions and supply chain management.

In the specific case of human resource management (HRM), the article from the *Herald* amplifies the point that, in the telecommunications industry, offshoring of customer service centres has become not only economically desirable but also illustrates that any quality assurance concerns which may have been raised have been quickly dismissed. One is inevitably drawn to the conclusion that Telecom customers soon after the switch of call centres has been made may not be able to detect that they are speaking to someone in Manila. Interestingly, this article appeared in the same newspaper the following day.

Telecom's call-centre workers in the Philippines will be trained to talk like New Zealanders, learning slang words and mastering the Kiwi accent as part of a move to outsource 250 jobs.

To continue the discussion on offshoring:

- The growing use of the Internet, ICT applications on a global scale and the creation of the 24/7 business model have made the use of offshoring almost a given now for many firms in HR areas such as customer service and software development. According to figures from *Business Miscellany* 80% of the offshore market is now located in India.

- The problems of offshoring have been quickly minimized as staff training and cultural awareness courses have enabled workers in India to offer the same level of service as offered in the host country. As we have seen, quality control concerns have also been allayed by piloting and testing service levels before they have been introduced.

- The dilemma is that offshoring may become the victim of its own success. As demand for workers in India rises, local wages will grow and, if sustained over a long enough period, then the competitive position of the firm offshoring could be undermined or they may seek an alternative location which will involve significant increases in set-up costs.

Now is a good time to tackle question 3, page 62.

2.3 Communication (1)

In order to 'communicate' the information as clearly and concisely as possible, we shall use a table to classify accepted methods of communication.

Method or channel of communication	Example	Discussion
Oral	A manager asking a subordinate to work overtime at the weekend	The manager is able to gauge instant reaction and feedback through verbal and non-verbal means but it can be time consuming if undertaken repeatedly
Written	A memo or report is displayed on a notice board	If clearly seen can reach a large number of people. A hard copy can be kept for future reference in case of confusion or disputes. However, hard to gain any feedback or reaction to sensitive issues unless further communication is arranged. Can be viewed as impersonal management if used repeatedly
Visual	A warning notice or signpost indicating danger or direction to be followed	Research has shown that this is the most cost-effective way to communicate; this is why warning signs are in red. Visually appealing signs will have lasting impact
Non-verbal	Body language/ facial expressions communicating without speaking	Not an effective way to communicate as body language is open to individual interpretation and thus may cause confusion or offence. There are a number of cultural issues here. (see below)
Formal	Communication using established channels of communication as highlighted by the organizational chart	See section on Organization structure by function, geography and product in unit 2.2 for more detail
Informal	The grapevine or the rumour mill. Channels of communication established by the employees themselves perhaps without full management knowledge	Information is passed around the organization quickly and as in the game 'Chinese whispers' messages may be distorted or exaggerated leading to inaccuracies. In some firms, employees are not allowed to speak to outside parties such as the media without the CEO's consent (see crisis and contingency planning, unit 2.8, HL only)

CULTURAL ISSUES AND INFORMAL COMMUNICATION

The Economist's *Business Miscellany* (which is an excellent companion to the Business and Management course for teachers and students especially) highlights a number of business etiquette conventions from around the world which amplify the need for a clear understanding of cultural sensitivities and informal communication.

Examples include:

- The importance of 'saving face' in Asia cannot be underestimated. Embarrassment and loss of face can lead to confusion and impact considerably on business planning.

- Tactile displays of emotion (hugs) and kissing on both cheeks are quite acceptable among businessmen in Saudi Arabia and the Gulf.

- Indians and Singaporeans dislike saying no (link to saving face). Body language will often provide more clues than what is actually said.

- Falling asleep in meetings is not uncommon in Japan. Silences – pauses in communication – are also an important part of business etiquette.

- Students may wish to think about their own 'cultural' etiquette conventions and those of their peers if studying in an international school.

2.3 Communication (2)

Barriers to effective communication

We have already noted the impact of cultural differences on the success or failure of non-verbal communication. We can also identify some other sources of communication breakdown. In each of the following situations, effective communication between sender and receiver is reduced due to:

- **Jargon:** Industry terms or 'buzzwords' which may confuse the receiver.

- **Noise:** Taken as a metaphor for vague imprecise language used especially when the sender is trying to cover a good deal of information in a short space of time.

- **Emotional impact:** A number of companies have now sent managers on training courses to guide them in the process of passing on sensitive information such as redundancy or dismissal. This needs to be handled carefully. In one apocryphal story an employee left a manager's office thinking that he had a promotion when in fact he was being retrenched.

- **Hierarchical barriers:** Subordinates may be unwilling to speak openly to managers about key issues for fear of generating ill-feeling or at worst dismissal. This problem may be exacerbated in tall hierarchies where subordinates on the lowest levels may have no opportunity to engage regularly with senior managers and may feel intimidated. Again there are cultural issues at work. In Japan, such discussions between workers and senior managers are welcomed, even encouraged, especially in a total quality culture. In other parts of Asia, it may be regarded as inappropriate to openly discuss issues with a senior member of the Board.

Evaluation of solutions to communication failure

The solution to eliminating ineffective communication will depend on the type of communication barrier present.

- We have already highlighted the fact that many companies now include training for senior managers to handle sensitive communication issues, for example the downsizing and retrenchment of some workers. This will inevitably lead to an increase in costs but will allow the firm to counter any unwelcome publicity or media attention if claims of unfair dismissal are raised.

- Cultural awareness exercises can be used to also reduce some of the problems identified in communicating sensitive information.

- A number of firms operating in global markets have gone further and decentralized operations to be closer to markets, local managers and other stakeholders to reduce the possibility of cultural misunderstandings. Again these strategic moves will increase short-term costs significantly and will take time to implement.

- The increased use of ICT has long been mooted as a solution to communication failure. We will examine this issue in greater detail in the next section.

Some writers such as Herzberg (whom we will meet in our section on Motivation) have argued that businesses try to communicate far too much, which leads to confusion and not surprisingly dissatisfaction. Have the relatively recent leaps in communication such as mobile technology, e-mail and the introduction of Voice Over Internet Protocols (VOIPs, such as Skype) increased the quality of communication as well as the quantity?

Learning Objective: Identify types of ICT and discuss the effect of new technologies on the effectiveness of communication within and between organizations and their stakeholders.

NOTE FOR TEACHERS

This is a vast topic and one where knowledge can date rapidly. Answers to questions in examinations on new technology have recently referred to the telephone, air travel and the Internet as 'new'. While this may be reasonable for the Internet which has only become commercially available as a communication medium to millions since the mid 1990s, it may not be true for the first two. Students need to update themselves periodically with knowledge as to what is considered 'new'. As of 2009, the author proposes that mobile and wireless technology, Internet chat rooms, social networking sites such as DoCoMo or Bebo, VOIP applications and growing virtual Internet communities such as Second Life should be considered 'new'.

Effectiveness of communication with the new technologies

Given that we have identified that there are new technologies, we can highlight some implications for communication for organizations and their stakeholders.

- Some concerns have been expressed about the amount of communication which ICT generates within organizations.

- Linked to this point is the fact that there is growing concern about the increase of organizational spamming (junk mail) and phishing (tempting receivers of e-mails to reply to e-mails of dubious origin).

- Mobile global communication which is reliable and secure is not a reality in *all* parts of the world. A number of countries (New Zealand included) have yet to fully upgrade their ICT systems to be able to offer full 'roaming' capabilities. This is also true about the lack of wireless coverage at an affordable price even in central business districts of other developed countries. Both of these elements can lead to considerable frustration for senior managers who need to communicate while on the move.

- Video conferencing and VOIP opportunities such as Skype have provided organizations with a valuable way to save time and money, especially in organizations which are structured by geographical region.

(continued)

2.3 Communication (3)

Effectiveness of communication with the new technologies *(continued)*

- We will note when we come to the marketing topic (page 84) that ICT provides a crucial link between organizations and customers. This has been achieved by introducing loyalty programmes in marketing, for example, where customers are invited to communicate feedback on new products or promotional campaigns. Organizations clearly wish to communicate with their customers on a regular basis, as illustrated by the need to 'contact us' which is posted now on most company websites.

- Pressure groups have used ICT to try and raise awareness of ethical and corporate social responsibility issues either by indirect action through social networking sites such as Bebo and Facebook or through direct action by communicating with the organization themselves.

Communication methods

It was noted by a number of writers that as significant protests by the Anti-Globalization movement gain momentum, the chosen method of rallying support and organizing demonstrations has been through increasing use of the mobile phone and the Internet; the very symbols of the move towards greater interdependence and ironically globalization.

The reader is also invited to discuss the value and appropriateness of e-mail communication, for example, within their own workplace.

You should now attempt question 4, page 62.

COMMUNICATION NETWORKS

HL

To explain how different types of communication networks influence the effectiveness of communication we shall use the work of Alex Bavelas.

CENTRALIZED NETWORKS

DECENTRALIZED NETWORKS

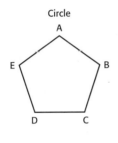
Circle

Chain

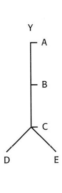
Y

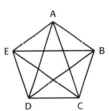

Communication networks

Bavelas identified two types of network: centralized and decentralized, analysed each type and measured the effectiveness of each using the following criteria.

	Centralized networks	Decentralized networks
Speed of learning new procedure	FAST	SLOW
Speed of solution of simple problems	FAST	SLOW
Speed of solution of complex problems	SLOW	FAST
Originality of ideas e.g. Brainstorming	LOW	HIGH
Number of messages sent	FEW	MANY
Satisfaction/morale	LOW	HIGH

Source: Dearden and Foster (1994)

Taking the results as a whole, the decentralized networks were less efficient with straightforward tasks but not surprisingly much more creative and effective in problem-solving of complex tasks.

Morale and satisfaction were measurably much higher. The implications for effective communication under decentralized networks with the above conclusions should hopefully be clear to the reader.

2.4 Leadership and management (1)

LEADERSHIP STYLES

There is still a good deal of confusion as to what effective leadership actually looks like. Peter Drucker's 1966 definition has stood the test of time.

The foundation of effective leadership is thinking through the organization's mission, defining it and establishing it, clearly and visibly.

We can use Drucker's definition as a hypothesis to test the effectiveness of some of the leadership models which follow below.

- Leadership style model
- Trait or personality (HL only)
- Situational (HL only)

Leadership style model

Leadership style is closely linked with organizational culture. Although not on the Standard level syllabus, all students are advised to review the material in unit 2.6 before looking at and evaluating the effectiveness of the following accepted leadership styles.

Leadership style	Description	Discussion
Autocratic	The decision-making process is determined solely by the leader or chief authority figure. There is little or no consultation. For example, the armed forces or organizations with tall hierarchies	Can be demotivating for some workers not to have an input into the process. Autocratic leaders can be effective in crisis situations
Democratic	The decision on what is to be done and how it is to be carried out is taken after group discussion and consultation. Examples can be found in media industries especially advertising and public relations	Increased motivation and productivity for some key skilled workers. Decision by committee can be time-consuming and expensive. May not be an effective way of decision-making in a crisis situation
Laissez-faire	Effectively there is no leadership. Groups are unsupported and left to decide for themselves. Charles Handy has argued that many universities operate under laissez-faire conditions.	Given no formal leadership, new employees may find the workplace environment confusing as they will lack knowledge of workplace conventions. Setting overall organization objectives may be difficult without formal leadership

If we apply Drucker's definition to each of the three leadership styles:

- Laissez-faire leadership needs to ensure that the mission is clearly articulated and understood by all workers.
- Many students of business assume that democratic leadership is always best, and the 'fairest' method of decision-making. However, too many people in the process may lead to problems with clarity.

- Although unpopular and unfashionable in today's business environment, an autocratic leadership style may actually be closest to Drucker's intention.

This is only a brief analysis, and the reader is invited to investigate business leadership styles from successful CEOs such as Jeff Bezos from Amazon, Jack Welch of GEC or Steve Jobs of Apple.

HL

For HL students

It is unlikely that a leader will be 100% autocratic or 100% democratic in all decision-making taken as a whole. The **Tannenbaum Schmidt continuum** highlights that many leaders adopt a range of styles. This work complements the study by **Blake and Mouton** who developed the **managerial grid** approach.

To preserve clarity a full investigation is not given here. Students are advised to review these models themselves and decide after analysing them whether they add significantly to our knowledge of leadership styles.

2.4 Leadership and management (2)

TRAIT OR PERSONALITY LEADERSHIP

This is the oldest method of classifying leadership and has its origins in the work and writings of Plato. Leadership here is defined by the leader who has a number of key characteristics or traits that distinguish them from others.

The 'great man' theory or the personality approach held that it was the personality characteristics of an individual which made it likely that he or she would become a leader, irrespective of the circumstances. These qualities would enable 'domination of the situation', thus causing others to follow his or her direction. These qualities would be in the hands of a select few.

In this model, leadership qualities include:

- Intelligence
- Reliability
- Determination and single-mindedness
- Physical presence and energy
- Ability and being respected for that ability in the eyes of others
- Extrovert in nature
- Charisma
- Decisiveness

This model has clearly had some longevity and the reader is invited to think of historical figures who have demonstrated these qualities, and more.

However, the issue is not that clear cut. Subsequent research revealed that many famous leaders, when examined closely, lacked many of the desirable qualities listed above and the ' trait' model began to break down. New approaches were proposed leading to the last of our three models: situational leadership.

The situational approach: Frederick Fiedler

A full investigation of Fiedler's work is not possible here. But we can note that the basis of situational leadership is that it takes the view that it is the situation in which the leader is trying to lead that is important, rather than any character attributes the leader may have, or any dominant style which may be used.

The situation in which the leader is trying to lead may be a function of the characteristics of the organization, the nature of the task itself and the 'group atmosphere' which exists. Fiedler attached a great deal of importance to this last point. The leader is followed and obeyed not because of rank or power but due to positive group emotions such as loyalty, liking, trust and respect.

Again students are invited to think of examples both past and present of leaders who have demonstrated a leadership style based on the above analysis.

- Manpower planning including recruitment and selection
- Motivation to achieve goals
- Controlling performance

Some key thinkers

Additional ideas on management which are explicitly mentioned in the HL syllabus are summarized below (adapted from *Business Miscellany*).

Peter Drucker: Drucker focused the bulk of his research on how to make managers more effective and pragmatic. He has contributed significantly to the development of management thinking by encouraging greater use of decentralization and the idea of management by objectives (MBO).

Henri Fayol: Fayol separated the tasks of management into four categories: planning, organization, co-ordination and command. He was in favour of very short spans of control and each employee being answerable to only one person.

Charles Handy: We will see in unit 2.6 Handy's substantial contribution to culture and management. He wrote what is considered to be the first dedicated book on management in the UK, *Understanding Organisations*. His writing is clear and his use of metaphors has endeared him to many students of business.

THE KEY FUNCTIONS OF MANAGEMENT

There is some confusion as to the difference between leadership and management. A succinct quote from Russell-Walling tries to highlight the difference:

Leaders do the right thing; managers do things right.

Some writers separate management into administrative and operational roles.

- The administrative function of the manager co-ordinates the functions of finance, marketing and production by planning and defining procedures, the procedures and objectives of the organization having been decided by the Board and the senior executives.

The operational aspect refers to the implementation of these plans.

Gabriel (1998) identifies five key functions:

- Planning a suitable course of action
- Organizing the human and material resources

2.5 Motivation (1)

MOTIVATION THEORY

In the early 1970s, F. Herzberg gave a presentation called 'Jumping for the Jelly Beans' to a group of British businessmen, which can be watched in two segments on YouTube. Below is a selection of quotations:

*What is Motivation? Motivation is when you **want** to do a good job rather than having to.*

*The more someone can do, the **more** they can be motivated to do.*

The key motivators which will motivate someone to play the piano are:

- *Can I play the piano? (Ability)*
- *Is there a piano for me to play? (Opportunity)*

There are many theories concerning motivation. Four well-known theorists on the topic of motivation are:

1 F.W. Taylor: Scientific management or economic man approach

2 Maslow: Hierarchy of needs

Maslow's hierarchy of needs (updated 8-stage model)

3 D. McGregor: Theory X and Theory Y

Diagrammatic representation of Theory X and Theory Y attitudes to work

4 F. Herzberg: Two-factor theory of motivation

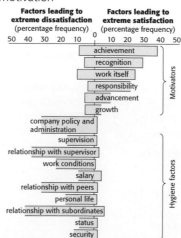

Herzberg's motivators and hygiene factors

A detailed examination of all their theories is not given as they are available in business textbooks.

2.5 Motivation (2)

Some misconceptions

For study purposes it may be useful to highlight a few misconceptions which can lead to poor understanding.

- We have already noted in unit 1.6 that students generally feel that Taylor's approach to scientific management has no place in the new millennium. However, there is nothing 'wrong' in adopting these approaches. As we shall see in the next unit and later under operations management, it may be totally appropriate to adopt more autocratic and bureaucratic forms of leadership to enhance worker motivation and to improve productivity.

- Herzberg's hygiene factors are not motivators but it would be wrong of employers to neglect them. If appropriate hygiene factors such as a market wage or supportive working conditions are not in place, then the worker may be dissatisfied. Hygiene's presence allows the motivators to work.

- We must not forget that the above theorists did most of their research on American companies, and the samples used in the investigation were small. We must also remember that there may be specific cultural factors which may impact on worker motivation.

- Struggling artists or musicians (or teachers!) may sacrifice lower-order Maslow needs such as physiological or security (by refusing to take a higher-paying job) in order to have the time and space to attempt to achieve self-actualization through their passion.

- Note that McGregor's work on Theory X and Y principally comprises a model of leadership as it analyses how leaders might view their employees rather than offering guidance on how to motivate.

- Interested students may wish to investigate Ouichi's Theory Z.

APPLICATION OF MOTIVATION THEORY

We shall now try to apply these theories to given motivational situations. Below are examples of workers' actions analysed in the light of the theories.

A worker wishes to learn new skills in order to gain promotion

- Maslow **self-esteem** needs are to be satisfied with a desire to professionally grow, as advocated by Herzberg.

A manager is requested by the Board of Directors to achieve higher sales targets. Higher bonuses will be paid if the targets are met

- The Board is using **scientific management** to encourage middle managers to be more profitable.

Workers in a call centre are threatening to walk out over poor conditions and long hours

- **Hygiene** factors perhaps are absent, which will not allow the motivators to function, in addition to Maslow's **security needs** not being met.

EXAMINER'S HINT

The key is **to analyse the situation and identify the nature of the motivational problem** and then suggest the **most appropriate motivation theory** to help explain the behaviour. More than one theory might fit each situation.

MOTIVATION: PRACTICE

Financial motivation

Taylor's scientific management principles were put quickly into practice in the early part of the 20th century and a number of industrialists began to make huge profits, especially Mr Henry Ford, whose Model T Ford soon became the symbol of this new management style. Taylor has been viewed by many students as the enemy of the worker and the theorist who said that man will only work for money. Few realize that his underlying philosophy was that he wanted scientific management to produce 'a bigger cake for *all* to share in'. Ford certainly saw the value in Taylor's ideas but we cannot blame Taylor for Ford's failure to pass on and share some of the gigantic profits to the workers.

Peter Drucker argues that Taylor deserves a place alongside Darwin and Freud in the making of the modern world. F.W. Taylor's work is worthy of a second look and readers are encouraged to investigate his contribution to management in more detail.

2.5 Motivation (3)

Methods of financial motivation: rewards packages

The issue of financial motivation is a complex and controversial issue. After the collapse of a number of high-profile companies and subsequent financial bailouts of the banking sector in 2008, the media spotlight has focused on the huge financial packages offered to some CEOs and senior executives despite record corporate losses.

This unit will focus on the learning outcome of the evaluation of reward packages including:

- Wages
- Salary
- Commission
- Profit-related pay
- Share options or company share ownership schemes
- Fringe benefits

Question: Evaluate alternative financial reward packages and the impact on job satisfaction, motivation and productivity.

NOTE FOR TEACHERS

In the opening pages of this book, we have mentioned that the word 'evaluate' is generally very poorly understood by students. Many will be able to tell the examiner what a wage is and whether the wage is high enough to attract workers but may be unable to discuss and judge whether one type of reward system such as a monthly salary is a more appropriate way to raise productivity and worker motivation than a profit-related pay scheme.

In the scenarios below we will identify a financial reward method and then try to evaluate its effects on worker motivation and productivity.

Scenario 1

Question: Evaluate a firm's decision to increase the pay of its entire staff by 10%.

On a **positive** note some possible answers include:

- Worker retention may be improved.
- Staff morale is enhanced as all workers are seen to receive a pay rise.
- With morale and retention increased, productivity may rise, leading to a fall in unit costs of production. (A pay rise will increase total costs but leads to a fall in average or unit cost if spread over a higher number of units.)

On the **negative** side, however,

- The pay rise may increase costs, and prices of finished goods may rise. Revenues may fall in a competitive market and the firm may begin to incur losses.
- Workers on higher salaries (those higher in the firm's hierarchy) will receive a larger increase in their pay packet than those on lower salaries. This may cause resentment in the workplace and may affect morale.

- Why is the firm paying 10% more? If the root cause of the workers' problems is not about higher wages (we speculate) then motivation may be unaffected, especially if Theory Y management is being utilized or if some of Herzberg's motivators are being neglected.

The key is that the student has evaluated and shown both sides of the argument. To complete the evaluation, students will be expected after analysing the issues to make a final judgment and suggest a suitable answer to the question.

Scenario 2

Question: Discuss a firm's decision to introduce performance-related pay.

Suggested answer (written in 20 minutes):

Performance-related pay is a reward system which tries to give workers additional remuneration above their basic salary or wage if the management of the firm believe that the worker has performed above some target value or expectations. An example could be a salesperson who exceeds sales forecasts or receives excellent feedback from his or her clients, and the management wish to reward this additional effort.

Hint: Even though a definition has not be asked for, it is good practice for students to define terms in a discussion question.

The basis for awarding additional payment will usually be discussed between the worker and the senior management at an appraisal meeting at the end of the year in order to set targets for the following year. For some theory X workers this may act as a powerful motivation to work harder, leading to additional cost savings through increased productivity. There may also be benefits for the recruitment and retention of key workers, especially given recent demographic trends in the developed world where the number of adult skilled workers is declining.

However, there are problems introducing change of this kind in the workplace. If the output of the worker or team is not easily measured (how would you put a true value on additional customer service, for example?) then it may be difficult to identify additional 'performance' and reward it accordingly. Some stakeholders such as trade unions or pressure groups may view the process as unfair or unethical. Two industries which typically find it difficult to agree on a 'fair' system of performance-related pay are education and health. We all value the work of a nurse, but how do you really measure performance?

Finally, there is the interesting question: if a worker or team is guilty of 'poor performance' as defined by the profit-related pay criteria, then would this imply that the worker should take a pay cut? One could envisage that if carried out there could be a great deal of individual worker demotivation, especially if the team's performance as a whole is being assessed.

Now you could work through questions 5 and 6, page 62.

2.5 Motivation (4)

NON-FINANCIAL MOTIVATION

There are a number of non-financial methods of motivation. We present them here in a table to explain the link between job satisfaction and productivity. A discussion of these methods is an HL topic only and will be separated from the explanation. In the HL extension material alternative theories of motivation from Mayo, McClelland, Vroom and Adams are reviewed and applied.

Method of non-financial motivation	Explanation
Job enrichment	Sometimes referred to as 'vertical loading' where an employee is offered more challenging work with increased levels of responsibility to motivate them
Job enlargement	Sometimes referred to as 'horizontal loading' where an employee is challenged by performing more tasks at the same level of responsibility. The argument is that the variety of tasks stops boredom and creates improved satisfaction as the employee is able to participate in the whole production process
Empowerment	The individual is given more control over their daily work routine with minimal supervision. This creates a sense of trust in the organization which can be motivating for some and can lead to productivity increases
Teamwork	This motivating factor can take many forms depending on the nature of the team, the task and the reward offered. Motivational research has found strong increases in productivity for those who work consistently in teams rather than individually

JOB ENRICHMENT PROGRAMME

HL

McGregor and Herzberg have been two key figures in the development of this school of thought on motivation. The YouTube clip we referred to earlier has a number of examples from Herzberg himself as to the virtues of job enrichment. We can group these into two areas.

- Job enrichment allows personal or 'psychological growth' of the individual. ('The more someone can do the more they can be motivated to do.')

- Meaningful work and self checking of this work via the job enrichment programme provides the opportunity for the individual to be responsible and motivated. Herzberg argues that you must not make somebody to be a 'responsible idiot'. They must perceive that they are contributing 'meaningful work' to the organization's overall effort.

Problems of the job enrichment method

- Herzberg notes that training is a key element in the process and this will cost money and take time to bear fruit in an organization.

- Management will need to ensure that 'meaningful work' is available and possible for the worker to complete. Herzberg argues that the two key functions of motivation are ability (enhanced through training) and the opportunity for the individual to put into practice what they have learnt. Otherwise demotivation will occur.

Criticism of job enlargement and empowerment

- Some writers have argued that job enlargement is really just offering workers 'more of the same' and is not really an opportunity to develop talents. Others have gone further to suggest that job enlargement is merely a ploy by the organization to boost productivity by asking fewer employees to do more.

- For empowerment, the argument is extended. Empowerment is viewed as a simple way to cut costs and remove management layers. Without sufficient training, some workers may be unable or unwilling to be responsible for their daily routine, preferring instead to work in areas with clear lines of communication and responsibility.

- This argument has been strongly put forward by critics of TQM (see page 118) who argue that the costs of empowerment and time taken to develop a quality culture can outweigh the gains. They also argue that, in a Theory X or Apollo culture, empowerment may be impossible to introduce.

2.5 Motivation (5)

TEAMWORK

The motivational impact of employees working in teams has very strong support from a number of motivational theorists. We have also seen that flexible structures in organizations such as those proposed by Mintzberg (page 44) can also be powerful influences. One is left with the impression, backed up with strong evidence from companies such as Nissan, Volvo and Toyota, that teamwork should be introduced wherever possible into the workplace.

However, in one of his last interviews before his death, Peter Drucker was sceptical about the benefits of teamwork. He writes:

It is generally assumed today that there is only one kind of team – call it the jazz combo – where

each participant does his or her own thing but together they make great music. Actually, there are perhaps a dozen types. Different teams each with its own area of application and its own limitations and difficulties and each requiring different management.

Unless we work out and fast, what a given team is suited for, and what a given team is not suited for, teams will become discredited as just another fad.

(**Source:** Peter Drucker quoted in *Forbes Magazine* 5/10/98, "How to prosper in the new economy")

OTHER THEORIES OF MOTIVATION

HL

We conclude our investigation of motivation theory by highlighting some other contributions.

Content theories: Mayo and McClelland

Content theories of motivation mainly focus on internal factors that energize and direct human behaviour and that influence how much effort is put into a given task. Mayo's groundbreaking study conducted during his experiments with groups of manual workers, which led to the 'Hawthorne Effect', should be well known to students. A key finding in the analysis which challenged the Scientific Management orthodoxy of the day was that workers are committed to completing a task as a group especially if they have had some input into the decision-making process. The Human Relations School of Motivation was born.

McClelland's work focused on research that suggested what motivates people (which they learn from early childhood) is that certain types of behaviour and life experiences will determine individual needs. These needs he classified as **achievement, affiliation and power.** The key for the business to motivate workers is to be able to identify the need present in the worker and design opportunities around these to meet those needs:

- High need for **achievement** workers should be given challenging projects with reachable goals. Frequent feedback should be given to ensure that the individual is on task to achieve.

- High need for **affiliation** workers will perform best in a cooperative working environment with the opportunity to share ideas.

- High need for **power** workers will seek opportunities to manage others and must be allowed to do so wherever possible.

Process theories: Vroom and Adams

Process theories of motivation provide an opportunity to understand the thought processes that influence human

behaviour. Vroom's work in common with McClelland assumes that individuals will try to achieve goals and in doing so aim to satisfy their needs. However, individuals will only act to achieve their goals if they feel that there is a chance of success. The **expectancy theory** argues that high levels of expectancy will lead to high levels of motivation, with the reverse being true for low levels of expectancy.

One is tempted to argue that the reason why so many people are motivated to enter reality TV competitions such as *American Idol* is that individual competitors have a high expectancy (and confidence) of success, when in fact the opposite is true, given the many thousands who audition. This may explain why so many performers react with disappointment when told that they have not moved on to the next 'round' even though expectancy theory should have told them in the first place that they have little chance of success.

Equity theory

John Adam's work here is worth investigating as it raises a number of interesting discussion points. The key element in equity theory is that motivation is a function of a worker perceiving that the reward he or she is receiving for their efforts fully reflects their contribution to the organization. If he or she feels that their contribution is being recognized then motivation to stay will be high, and vice versa.

Workers' contribution cannot always be measured objectively but firms who use equity theory have discovered that, for example, giving a worker time off for compassionate reasons or allowing flexible working for part-time workers can create an environment of 'fairness', which can be very motivating.

Students are invited to discuss the implications for equity theory of the 'fairness of awarding senior managers large bonuses in loss-making organizations', which have recently been the recipients of government assistance.

2.6 Organizational and corporate cultures HL (1)

NOTE FOR TEACHERS

Although this unit is not on the core syllabus, Standard level students are advised to read these notes as they provide useful additional information for an understanding of leadership and motivation. The culture of an organization will have a direct impact on appropriate strategies to deal with poor leadership, management and/or worker motivation.

ORGANIZATIONAL CULTURE

HL

Definition: The culture of an organization is defined as the attitudes, beliefs, experiences, norms and values which determine working relationships between internal stakeholders and ways of interacting with external stakeholders.

Classification of cultures

We shall first consider the work again of Charles Handy (1995). The following table is adapted from his book *Gods of Management* where he assigned a classical figure to each of the four possible absolute cultures present in an organization.

First we must note that:

- There is no cultural purity within an individual. We are composites of all four cultures depending on the situation we may find ourselves in. What is important is our dominant culture.

- All cultures have strengths and weaknesses. No culture or mixture of cultures is 'bad or wrong' in itself, but it may be inappropriate to its circumstances.

	Zeus	Apollo	Athenian	Dionysus
Culture	Club	Role	Task or problem-solving	Existential or based on Individualism
Example of organization	Family business	State services, local government	Media companies	Universities
Example of Individual in this culture	Richard Branson. Seems to be the epitome of Zeus	Accountant or immigration officer	Advertising executive. Prefer to work in matrix structures	Groundsman in a school, ICT specialist, teacher, nurse
Leadership style appropriate to culture	Paternalistic	Autocratic, bureaucratic	Laissez-faire/flexible	Anti-management. Does not wish to be managed
Ways of describing typical individual in this culture	Charismatic, impulsive, hardworking, aggressive, optimistic	Gets on with the job, thoughtful, reliable, rational	Sociable, responsive, extrovert, anxious to solve problems	Rigid, introverted, reserved but loyal
Ways of motivating	Power and Influence. Money acts as an enabler to take more risks. Values networks and connections. Likes to be able to influence others	Clear career path offered. Promotion based on work ethic. Visible signs of recognition e.g. Corner office and company car	Training giving new skills with opportunity to use these new skills in a dynamic problem solving environment	Allowed to get on with their job with minimal interference. Professional respect from colleagues because of talent
Issues/Problems	Hates to be constrained by rules and regulations	Can be too inflexible. Hates change. Perceived as rather dull but can be excellent in a crisis	Expensive form of decision-making and can be indecisive in crises. Irritated by certainty and stability	Can be viewed as selfish. The organization is viewed as helping the individual and not the other way around

Student exercise

In Handy's book, there is a questionnaire by Dr Harrison whom Handy credits with the original analysis on differences in culture. Interested readers may wish to answer this questionnaire to determine their own cultural viewpoints and those of their organization.

There are a number of cultural and personality profile exercises which can be downloaded from the Internet and used to determine the student's dominant culture.

Culture clashes

From the table on the previous page, we can predict that there will be cultural clashes between individuals within an organization.

- Zeus may be become irritated with Apolllo's insistence on sticking to rules.
- Athenians need to be challenged or may become bored.
- Dionysians may be perceived as impossible to manage.
- Apollos appear to be dull and inflexible.

Students are encouraged to think of other potential clashes and discuss how to resolve them (if possible).

In any organization, the key is to manage these differences so that some equilibrium can be achieved (see force-field analysis, page 32, and leadership and management, page 50).

This issue is particularly relevant when we consider culture clashes when organizations merge. The Time Warner (Apollo) merger with AOL (Dionysian) already mentioned (page 26) appears to have been jeopardized from the start without a significant review of how two such opposing cultures were to remain in balance.

Now is a good time to attempt question 7, page 62.

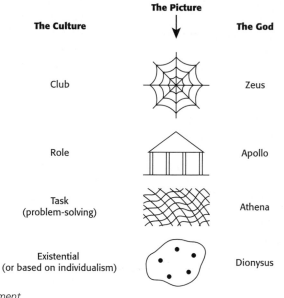

The Culture	The Picture	The God
Club		Zeus
Role		Apollo
Task (problem-solving)		Athena
Existential (or based on individualism)		Dionysus

Charles Handy's four gods of management

2.7 Employer and employee relations HL (1)

NOTE FOR TEACHERS

With the threat of unemployment rising in the developed world, as the global slowdown begins to bite, the nature of the relationships between the employer and the employee becomes critical. It is around this context that we will build our analysis in this extension topic.

During difficult times employees especially need to be realistic as to the extent that they can bargain for wage increases. A job with a modest pay rise for all workers may be preferable to some workers receiving a higher rate and the firm having to make compulsory redundancies. Environments driven by conflict and confrontation need to be tempered with conciliation and co-operation.

This unit investigates the nature of the dynamic relationship between employees and employers and their representatives. This relationship will be different in every country depending on the cultural environment and the prevailing legal framework which governs industrial relations law. In this guide we cannot cover every country's situation and thus our analysis will be presented in generic terms. The student is encouraged to research the current legislation which exists in the country in which they are studying.

HL

METHODS BY WHICH THE EMPLOYEE AND THEIR REPRESENTATIVES PURSUE KEY OBJECTIVES

We can identify a number of methods a trade union or similar organization which has been elected to act as a representative on behalf of the employees may use in order to promote collective objectives. These include maintaining the level of current level of employment in an organization or improving pay and conditions for its members.

- **Negotiation:** the trade union or employee representative begins a period of 'negotiation' or bargaining with the employee, usually face to face.

- **Go-slow:** employees are instructed by their representatives to work at reduced speeds without jeopardizing the production process.

- **Work-to-rule:** the employee deliberately works to the letter of their contract and withdraws 'goodwill'. Goodwill in this context refers to the unpaid additional duties workers gladly take on although they are not normally included in their formal job description. Examples include ambulance drivers who could reluctantly withdraw goodwill if their contract demanded that they finish at a certain time and not drive an emergency patient to hospital. This argument can be extended further to the public sector, especially in sectors such as nursing and teaching, where the removal of goodwill would have profound effects on stakeholders.

- **Overtime ban:** many public service providers rely on workers working overtime during weekends and unsocial hours. The introduction of an overtime ban could impact on these sectors and services considerably.

- **Strike:** this 'weapon' is usually treated by the employees as a last resort. If negotiations have broken down and there is a clearly an impasse or in the extreme an unbridgeable gap between the two sides, a strike or prolonged stoppage may be called by the employees' representatives.

However, in many countries a strike can only be sanctioned after a ballot of members has taken place. Otherwise the strike may be deemed unlawful. This is important for two reasons:

- If the strike is unlawful, workers may not be entitled to receive 'strike pay' which is intended to support them while they are not working.

- An unlawful strike may generate a lack of stakeholder support for the strike and lead to a loss of public sympathy for the cause. This may weaken the position of the representatives if negotiations resume.

DVD resource

I'm alright Jack is an outstanding movie made in 1960 about the whole issue of strikes, unions and the sometimes difficult relationship with employers. It is a comedy but lurking beneath the humour is a not-so-subtle satirical look at working practices, scientific management and the 'them and us' approach to industrial relations which dominated industrial democracy during this time.

Data on strikes

It is interesting to note that according to the Economist *Business Miscellany* guide, the number of strikes recorded (many go unrecorded as they may last only a few hours) as a function of working days lost in a whole range of countries from Canada to the US, is at an all-time historical low. Given the recent prevailing external environment, this position is unlikely to change.

2.7 Employer and employee relations HL (2)

METHODS BY WHICH EMPLOYERS TO PUT PRESSURE ON EMPLOYEES

The student is invited to reread the article on page 45 concerning Telecom's decision to offshore 250 jobs to Manila, and we repeat part of it here.

> Engineering, Printing and Manufacturing Union national secretary Andrew Little said the union represents about 20 workers affected by the move.
>
> He said with New Zealand's economy heading into a "difficult time", Telecom's decision is "unfortunate".
>
> Mr Little said the country needs all the spending power it has and jobs moving off-shore will not help.
>
> He said there could be more businesses moving jobs overseas this year as they review their businesses practices.
>
> Mr Gourdie CEO acknowledged the past year had been a time of uncertainty for staff in Telecom's New Zealand-based call centres, particularly those at the Hamilton operation.
>
> "We have communicated openly and regularly with staff throughout the trials. Feedback on the proposed structure will now be sought over the next two weeks, with a final contact centre structure to be confirmed by early March."

From this brief article, it is clear that the company has tried to be fair with the timing of this announcement and has consulted 'openly' with the workers. This behaviour by employers is becoming more commonplace. This contrasts starkly with the behaviour of some employers who, during the 1990s at the height of downsizing, gave little warning of the removal of whole layers of management.

Employers are not limited to negotiation, there are also a number of methods or 'weapons' open to them in order to achieve their own objectives. We must note, however, that these moves are considered aggressive and likely to inflame employees and their representatives, especially if there is no end to negotiations in sight. In some countries, some of the following practices may be unlawful:

- **Threat of redundancies:** some firms may announce that redundancies are inevitable if the union presses ahead with its industrial action. This may attempt to blunt the union's move even if the threat is not as large as the company claim.

- **Change of contract:** Given a downturn in an economy an employer may announce that changes of contract are required to keep the organization in business.

- **Lock-out:** faced with mounting tension a firm may lock workers out of the workplace. This is a difficult and dangerous tactic. The publicity surrounding a lock-out may create poor public relations and sympathy may shift from the employer to the employees, especially if some workers wish to work and earn a wage.

- **Closure:** the last resort option.

CONFLICT RESOLUTION: AN EVALUATION

HL

Given the inherent tensions which may exist between employee and employer during an industrial dispute, a number of conflicts have been decided instead by a third or outside party in a process of **conciliation** and then **arbitration**.

Once the conciliation process, the decision of the third party (the arbiter) is final and both sides who decide to enter into conciliation must abide by the outcome. However, the process of deciding the outcome can take time and is costly.

Other employers have tried to use other tactics such as **no-strike** or **single union agreements**.

- Employers may offer a union a deal where in return for not striking an employer may automatically allow a dispute to go conciliation and the arbitration third party.

- Single union agreements allow the employer to avoid negotiating with three or four unions which could delay final resolution and lead to competition between the unions for the best deal.

- Time, lost production and goodwill could all be saved through unnecessary bargaining.

In extreme cases a firm may offer a **no union deal**.

- Workers for 'Wal-Mart' are treated as 'associates' and not employees and through employee participation programmes are encouraged to participate in a form of industrial democracy giving workers rights collectively over the resolution of key issues.

- This model has been employed with enthusiasm in Japan which has the lowest recorded number of strikes, measured by working days lost (where reliable statistics exist), and has led to significant improvements in morale and productivity.

DVD resource

Unfortunately, this model has its critics with Wal-Mart being the most famous example of a company that did not allow union activity within the company or its supply chain. Recent criticism by pressure groups has softened Wal-Mart's perceived hard-line stance; see the documentary *Wal-Mart: the high cost of low price* on DVD.

Conclusion

With changes in legislation making strikes more difficult and the need for employees and employers to work together a new era of workplace relations may be upon us. Clearly, recent changes to the economic environment have aided this process.

Now you could attempt question 8, page 62.

2.8 Crisis management and contingency planning HL

INTRODUCTION **HL**

The term crisis is sometimes overused by the media. However, the impact on a company of a public relations embarrassment, a product recall due to safety concerns, or simply that the company may have been found guilty of false and misleading advertising, cannot be underestimated.

Interested students are invited to research the case of two young New Zealand students (Anna Devathasan and Jenny Suo) who in their own classroom experiments found that claims by GlaxoSmithKline that Ribena contained four times the vitamin C of orange were false. GSK had been running a misleading campaign for many years and had to retract their advertisements, offer apologies to customers and pay a substantial fine.

Given these potentially damaging consequences, a number of organizations have generated contingency plans to try and pre-empt or plan for events which may not actually happen. There is debate as to whether firms should divert time, resources and management to a situation which might not occur.

CRISIS MANAGEMENT

This term is believed to have been coined by US Secretary of Defence, Robert McNamara, after the Cuban Missile Crisis of 1962, to describe a way of dealing with crises as they arise, without undertaking any long-term strategic planning.

Crisis management assumes that because the actions of others cannot always be predicted or planned for, crises have to be dealt with when they happen.

Some examples

Examples of crises affecting an organization could be with actual companies affected in brackets.

- Financial (Enron)
- Industrial accidents (the Bhopal tragedy)
- Industrial action (the screenwriters' strike in 2007 effectively halted film and television production in Hollywood)
- Environmental problems (Shell and the Brent Spar oil platform)
- Product recall due to safety concerns, e.g. children's toys
- Public relations (Nestle and contaminated milk powder)

Students are invited to investigate their own examples and also to discuss how possible it is to plan for a crisis.

CONTINGENCY PLANNING **HL**

Recently two well-known companies (Wrigley's and Kellogg's) experienced a public relations crisis when celebrities associated with the companies tarnished their image through inappropriate behaviour. Both companies were quick to disassociate themselves from these individuals. One is tempted to suggest that, given the unpredictable nature of some celebrities who are paid to sponsor or promote a product, thus generating media coverage, firms should have an action plan in place to deal with any potential crises before they occur. This process is known as contingency planning.

Benefits

- Contingency plans can be drawn up in a number of different areas of an organization including finance, human resource management and operations. This is especially important for potential liquidity or staffing problems influenced by external factors that can change very quickly.

- As we shall see through the work of Jack Trout, the perception and positioning of the company or product is a defining factor in determining the success of the marketing effort. Contingency plans can be used to try and protect brand image in the eyes of stakeholders.

Costs

- It has been estimated that the contingency plans created to cope with the problems of the millennium or Y2K computer 'bug', which apart from a few minor incidents failed to materialize, cost the world economy over $300bn in 2000. It is debatable whether problems over Y2K were averted due to these contingency plans or whether it was just a colossal waste of money.

- Time and resources are working capital tied up in contingency plans which could be successfully employed elsewhere.

Exam questions on Topic 2

1   A growing number of companies are complaining that they are finding it harder
    to recruit people. An international survey for the Corporate Executive Board in 2006
    found that 62% of senior human resource managers are worried about company-wide
    talent shortage. Managers face a dilemma. How do you recruit and retain employees
    when there is a shortage of skilled labour? How do you reward and motivate people who
    can easily move elsewhere?

    The world supply of workers is contracting. By 2025, the number of people aged 15 to 64
    is projected to fall by 7% in Germany and 14% in Japan. In addition the retirement of the
    'baby boom' generation will lead to the loss of many experienced workers. Demographic
    and social change means that companies will find it harder to find suitable replacements
    domestically. They will have to develop their employees' talent through training and be
    prepared to consider changes in work patterns and practices.

    Comment on how management may adapt work patterns or practices in response to the
    demographic and social change identified above.   (May 2008)

2   **HL** Explain two advantages and one disadvantage of moving from an existing tall hierarchy
    to a matrix structure.   (November 2006)

3   **HL** Evaluate the financial rewards and methods of payment that will enable firms to recruit
    and retain skilled workers.   (May 2008)

4   Explain how a flat management structure could lead to more 'open and informal'
    relationships.   (November 2007)

5   Explain two disadvantages and one advantage of introducing a piece rate system at Fish
    Packaging Limited.   (May 2008)

6   Using appropriate motivational theory, analyse how Jaguar (a car manufacturer trying to
    introduce Just-in-Time production) has managed to increase the pride and commitment
    of its employees.   (May 2005)

7   **HL** Examine the potential problems of integrating the corporate cultures of two large firms
    such as Kmart and Sears.   (May 2007)

8   **HL** Examine how a call centre trade union could affect employees.   (May 2007)

3.1 Sources of finance (1)

NOTE FOR TEACHERS

With the recent 'credit crunch' or 'crisis' still fresh in the media and the minds of stakeholders as of March 2009, the importance of finance to the business community has been brought into sharp focus.

Second, given the globalization and interdependence of the world's financial system, new models of sourcing finance have been created. It is now possible for even very small business start-ups in the developing world to obtain finance through organizations such as the Grameen Bank and the Acumen Fund. Such was the impact and success of the Grameen Bank and its founder Muhammad Yunus that the organization was awarded the Nobel Prize for Peace in 2006.

Finally, after the financial horrors which accompanied the dot.com boom and the collapse of Enron in 2002, there has been greater attention from media commentators and governments on the role of accounting and finance. The mood is now that stakeholders should focus attention not just on the figures themselves but seek greater clarification and understanding of the 'stories' behind the numbers.

INTERNAL AND EXTERNAL SOURCES OF FINANCE

Source of finance	Description	Discussion
Internal		
Profits	Firm uses retained earnings to finance projects	There will be no interest to pay and no dilution of ownership (see below). May be viewed positively or negatively by stakeholders depending on their objectives
Sale of fixed assets	Firm disposes of 'old assets' for cash	Selling assets reduces productive capacity and weakens balance sheets and shareholder value and thus may be unpopular
Improve the working capital cycle	Reduce stocks, improve debt collection, use of debt factoring	Reducing stocks at a deep discount may create finance but may not be sufficient to fund certain projects. The interdependence of the working capital cycle may make it difficult to improve debt collection from debtors or credit allowed from creditors
Sale and lease back	A new method where firms may sell an asset but then lease or hire it back to use without the responsibility of ownership. An initial lump sump is received to finance other projects	There are a number of complex sale and lease back schemes. Used mostly for large fixed assets or, increasingly, ICT systems. In lease schemes only, firms may be able to update assets periodically to avoid obsolescence. This has become a feature of new outsourced ICT schemes
External		
Sale of shares	A publicly traded company may issue further shares to existing (a rights issue) or to new shareholders to raise funds	Significant sums can be raised in the capital markets but there may be dilution of ownership issues (see debt vs equity trade-off below). In order for the share issue to be successful, a clear growth objective or strategic plan will need to be given to encourage shareholders. Shares may not be purchased if the perception is that the funds are only going to be used to pay off existing debts
Overdrafts Loans	Firm borrows additional funds from a multitude of different financial institutions. Overdrafts are very short term while loans vary in duration from 1 to 30 years depending on the purpose	Overdrafts must be authorized in advance or can be a very expensive way to finance. Interest will have to be paid but there will be no dilution in ownership. Interest rates can fluctuate and impact on interest payments and cash flow. Some sophisticated loan packages have been created such as SWAPS. Creative but complex and controversial
Debentures	Fixed interest loans made by firms or individuals	As above but interest is usually fixed. Debenture holders usually have first claim on a firm's assets if the company is put into liquidation and bankruptcy proceedings are started
Venture capital	Volatile capital made available by individuals or institutions to be put into potentially profitable but risky projects	Venture capital has been cast as a hero (the Grameen Bank has sourced venture capital from the developed world) and villain (fuelling the unsustainable dot.com boom of the late 1990s) Some critics have argued that in the pursuit of short-term profits, venture capitalists may exert too much influence over a firm's objectives

3.1 Sources of finance (2)

APPROPRIATENESS OF SOURCE OF FINANCE

A firm will wish to use a number of different sources of finance depending on the purpose behind the need to acquire more funding:

- time considerations
- the cost to the organization
- and the key issue of the debt versus equity dilemma.

Purpose and time

Firms will have immediate, short, medium and long-term needs for finance. The source they choose will depend on the time frame under consideration.

- For immediate liquidity concerns, an extension to a bank overdraft may be all that is required.
- For short-term finance, internal methods may be quicker to access, e.g. using previous profits or reserves, rather than trying to raise new additional external finance.
- For longer-term strategic uses, a firm may have to conduct a 'financial' SWOT analysis and involve financial institutions or management consultants in order to source the most appropriate, cost-effective method. The fees from such expertise can run into millions of dollars, so it is assumed that only the largest organizations can afford these services.

As a general rule, if the purpose or objective to be financed is considered to be long term (over a number of years) then the most appropriate method of finance will also be long term. If the purpose is short term, then a short-term funding solution should be found. Accountants call this process 'matching'. It is a fundamental accounting concept yet a full explanation is outside the scope of this guide.

Now would be a good opportunity to try question 1, page 79.

Cost

Planning and size are important factors in determining the cost of finance.

- If a firm has inadequate planning and runs short of cash to pay immediate invoices then a hastily arranged overdraft can be expensive with punitive interest rates.
- Loans from financial institutions may also carry high interest rates if the purpose behind the loan is not carefully articulated to the bank or financial institution lending the money. Discussions and the creation of a business plan will be needed at this point.
- Finally, larger firms have the advantage of financial economies of scale over smaller firms and are able to borrow large sums of money at greatly reduced interest due their size and amount of **collateral** they can offer the lender as security.

DEBT VS EQUITY DILEMMA

A critical analysis will need to take place when an organization considers the choice of financing large, long-term projects.

- Do they issue more shares, and as a result dilute ownership (we assume that the shares will be targeted at new potential owners rather than existing ones) but avoid borrowing and paying interest on loans?
- Or does the organization allow more debt onto the balance sheet to finance the purchase of additional fixed assets, but keep their existing level of control among the existing shareholders?

Therein lies the dilemma. Students are invited to discuss this issue in class.

This topic has links to the gearing ratio of a firm which is analysed on page 76.

E-FINANCE: THE INTERNET AS A SOURCE OF FINANCE

Analysis of the 2008 US presidential election revealed that Senator Obama raised nearly 50% of the $603m needed to fund his campaign from donations of less than $200, collected from supporters who visited Obama's website and transferred funds electronically.

Furthermore, the work of the Grameen Bank (and other not-for-profit organizations) in fundraising over the Internet has given considerable weight to the role of the Internet as an important conduit for e-finance.

3.2 Investment appraisal (1)

INTRODUCTION

The most appropriate way to study this topic and cover the requirements of the syllabus for Higher level and Standard level is to work through a recent past examination question (adapted from May 2005).

Lev Yashin and Alexi Kirov are partners and racehorse owners. They are looking to move into new sports activities and have begun to look into the possibility of owning a football team to increase their range of businesses and increase their commercial success.

They have identified two potential teams, both public limited companies which may provide potential takeover and investment opportunities. They have prepared financial estimates of returns and costs of each proposal.

We must assume that the costs of financing the opportunity have been included. We do not know if the two investors have borrowed the capital or are using private funds.

Figures in millions of $	Team A	Team B
Cost of Takeover	200	70
Expected Returns		
Year 1	−30	15
Year 2	−2	18
Year 3	76	21
Year 4	96	24
Year 5	150	30

Calculate the following to two decimal places and analyse your results.

- *Payback*
- *Accounting or average rate of return*
- *Net Present Value assuming that the discount factor is 6% (HL only)*

We shall calculate the values first and then provide some suggestions on how we can use these to help us analyse an investment decision.

INVESTMENT APPRAISAL

This is the process consisting of a set of techniques designed to determine whether an investment opportunity should be taken. In the case of multiple opportunities, investment appraisal can be used to rank projects in order of desirability in quantitative terms only. External and qualitative factors are not considered. The three techniques to guide decision-making are payback, average rate of return, and (HL only) net present value.

Payback

Payback is defined as the time period required before an investment opportunity 'pays back' (recovers) its initial investment cost.

For team A the cost of the takeover is $200m.

Team A will return $290m in 5 years: $(-32 + 76 + 96 + 150) = \$290m$.

It will return −$32m after 2 years and $172m after year 4, a total of $140m.

Hence for team A to pay back the whole $200m, $60m of year 5's $150m is required.

Assuming that this money is received evenly throughout the year, we can expect the $\frac{60}{150} \times 365$ days in 146 days or 4.8 months.

Students are now invited to calculate the payback for team B themselves and confirm the figure of 3 years 243 days or 3 years and 8 months.

- Payback is a straightforward way of looking at an investment opportunity. It assumes that expected returns are received evenly throughout the year and that a dollar received in 1 year's time has the same value as a dollar received today. Both assumptions can be challenged.

- A closer look at the expected returns from each takeover reveals that for team A the majority of returns are expected to arrive later in years 3, 4, 5. The biggest returns are forecasted much later where their value cannot be guaranteed. For team B, the expected revenues arrive earlier in the 5-year investment horizon with only $30 million expected to arrive in year 5. This has important implications for decision-making especially as it is difficult to predict the influence of external factors in 5 years, after the initial decision has been made.

Average rate of return (ARR)

The formula for this calculation will be given to candidates on the formula sheet at the start of the examination.

$$ARR = \frac{\text{average profit per year}}{\text{cost of the opportunity}}$$

For team A, the expected average profit over 5 years $= \frac{290 - 200}{5} = \$18m$.

For Team B, the expected average profit over 5 years $= \frac{108 - 70}{5} = \$7.6m$.

$$\text{ARR for team A} = \frac{18}{200} = 9\%$$

$$\text{ARR for team B} = \frac{7.6}{70} = 10.86\%$$

In common with payback, the ARR assumes that a dollar received in 1 year's time has the same value as a dollar received today. We shall challenge this assumption when we consider NPV and discounting.

(continued)

3.2 Investment appraisal (2)

Average rate of return (ARR) *(continued)*

The ARR and other ratios, as we shall see in unit 3.6, is not useful in isolation. The ARR will need to be compared with other investment opportunities such as a risk-free savings account in a financial institution to see if the additional return given by the opportunity is justified for the level of risk taken. Of course, the attitudes of the investor with respect to risk and the external environment will need to be considered in combination with the calculations.

Analysis in terms of the question asked

From the payback and the average rate of return calculations it would appear that team B should be chosen.

- It has a lower cost and a quicker return of the initial investment. It has a lower overall profit but a higher ARR.
- However, before making a final call, we must consider the time value of money, which both payback and ARR ignore.

NET PRESENT VALUE

Both payback and ARR calculations ignore the time value of money. So far we have assumed that $1 received today from an investment opportunity is the same as $1 received in 1 year's time. In reality, this will not be so.

THE TIME VALUE OF MONEY

A dollar received today can be invested and, assuming an interest rate of 10%, would be worth $1.10 in 1 year's time.

In 2 years' time, assuming that the whole amount is invested again at 10%, a dollar invested will be worth $1.21 (1.1 + 10% of 1.1).

Alternatively, we can find out the true value today of $1.10 received in 1 year's time. This is called the present value of $1.10.

In situations where a firm is receiving future amounts in 1–5 years' time, these amounts will need to be discounted by a factor, to arrive at the present value. These discounted amounts will be compared with the cost of an investment opportunity (which we know at today's value) to calculate the net present value (NPV). In order to calculate the present value of $1.10 received in 1 year's time at an interest rate at 10% we must apply a discount factor of 0.91 to two decimal places, from the discount table which is available in your textbook or the formula sheet which will be provided as the students begin the final examination.

$$\text{Present value} = \$1.10 \times 0.91 = \$1$$

To calculate the present value of $1.21 received in 2 years' time at an interest rate of 10%, we apply a discount factor of 0.83 to two decimal places.

$$\text{Present value} = \$1.21 \times 0.83 = \$1$$

Students are invited to check their understanding by calculating the future amounts of $1 invested at an interest rate of 10% over 3, 4 and 5 years and then discount these amounts using factors from the discounting table.

Towards the final NPV **HL**

NPV = future discounted returns added minus cost of the investment opportunity

From the table, the discount factors over 5 years at an interest rate of 6% are: Year 1 0.9434, Year 2 0.89, Year 3 0.8396, Year 4 0.7921, Year 5 0.7473.

We can now calculate the NPVs for the two investment opportunities.

Full workings are not given. It will be up to the student to check their arithmetic to make sure they understand the process described above. Negative figures are in brackets.

Years	Team A	Team B	Discount factor	Present value A	Present value B
Cost today	(200)	(70)	0 (as this is today)	(200)	(70)
Expected return					
Year 1	(30)	15	0.9434	(28.3)	14.15
Year 2	(2)	18	0.89	(1.78)	16.02
Year 3	76	21	0.8396	63.61	17.63
Year 4	96	24	0.7921	76.04	19.01
Year 5	150	30	0.7473	112.1	22.42
Total of Present Values				21.87	19.23

Analysis

The NPV for team A is higher than for team B. Hence with the time value of money taken into account and assuming an interest rate of 6%, team A will yield higher expected returns than team B as an investment opportunity. This contrasts with the findings from the payback and ARR calculations.

An alternative way of looking at NPV is that both opportunities offer a smaller return than the firm could achieve by putting a lump sum of – in the case of Team A – $200m in a low-risk bank account.

TAKING IT FURTHER

The question that needs to be asked, but is beyond the scope of this guide, is whether the risk reward of $21.87m over the initial cost is suitable to the investors. This will depend on the degree of risk the investors wish to take, which is unknown.

3.3 Working capital (1)

WHAT IS WORKING CAPITAL?

Definition: Working capital is the difference between current assets and current liabilities, and has a number of alternative names such as day-to-day finance or circulating capital.

Its role is to bring the other factors of production such as land, labour and man-made capital into productive use. Without working capital being spent on resources such as raw materials, power or stationery, these factors would be idle and not productive.

Secondly, working capital provides cash and credit opportunities to allow businesses to trade with other firms. (Cash in our context refers to **money which the firm has at its disposal for immediate use**. It could be notes and coins but is likely to be electronic cash transactions or bank transfers.) Many transactions in business are settled in cash but many firms rely on being able to pay for raw materials or finished goods up to 2 months after they have been delivered.

A firm can be a creditor to its customers who have not yet paid and a debtor to its suppliers who have allowed the firm to receive raw materials without paying in advance. Credit is a vital source of working capital.

THE WORKING CAPITAL CYCLE

We shall provide our own version of the working capital cycle of a spoon manufacturer (as featured in the *Balance Sheet Barrier* video) to help students understand the process. We shall also add a comment about the possible cash flow implications for a firm. This will lead us nicely into the importance of cash flow forecasts.

Cycle stage 1

- A firm purchases raw materials such as metal plating for pressing spoons and equips two workers to carry out this work.

Cash flow out or credit received to pay for this.

Cycle stage 2

- The firm processes raw materials (sheet metal) into spoons and begins to take orders. Firm may pay suppliers of sheet metal.

Cash flow out with possible credit allowed to customers as orders received.

Cycle stage 3

- The firm fulfils orders and delivers.

Cash flow in possible from customers and invoices sent to customers with delivered order. Truck hired with driver to deliver. Cash flowing out?

Cycle stage 4

- Firm follows up on unpaid orders. Payment received by debtors. Firm pays creditors. Profit from sale is kept in reserves. New orders are received.

Cash flowing in from debtors and out to remaining creditors. New orders are received and the process begins again.

Too much working capital or too little?

It is hoped that the above simplified example clearly states that enough working capital must be present in an organization to allow production to take place. If a firm has too little working capital then it will be difficult for the company to trade with other companies and inevitably liquidity problems will be the result.

What is perhaps not so obvious is the opposite situation. Having too much capital tied up in raw materials or finished goods with substantial reserves of cash in a bank account may imply that the firm is missing out on potential profitable opportunities. Alternatively, if the firm is holding too much stock, this may create additional costs. This issue is explored in greater detail in unit 5.7 on production planning.

3.3 Working capital (2)

CASH FLOW FORECASTS

A template is give below for a fictitious small firm forecasting cash flow from January to June 2010. The figures are not given as only the structure is being presented. The structure below is just one possible version. There could be variations in the ordering of rows.

Item	Jan	Feb	March	April	May	June
Opening balance						
Cash inflows						
Cash received						
Sale of assets						
Total cash available						
Cash outflows						
Rent						
Rates						
Materials						
Wages						
Total cash outflows						
Total cash available – total cash outflows						
Closing balance						

The closing balance at the end of the month will become the opening balance for the next month.

- Cash flow forecasts are presented at the centre of a business plan for new start-ups.
- Lenders will wish to see if future cash flow issues can be anticipated.
- Liquidity problems will be potentially easier to solve if they can be foreseen.
- Of course the cash flow forecast cannot predict the unforeseen.

Now work through question 2, page 79.

EVALUATING STRATEGIES FOR DEALING WITH LIQUIDITY PROBLEMS

Before discussing this point we need to define what we mean by a liquidity problem and then try to offer a solution. There is some overlap here with ratio analysis which will be covered in unit 3.6.

The table below is focused on four short-term liquidity problems. Longer-term financing issues were covered in unit 3.1.

Liquidity problem	Solution	Discussion
Firm has run out of cash to pay immediate expenses such as wages	Bank overdraft extension to tide the firm over until further cash is received from customers	Using a bank overdraft in this case is a suitable but expensive way to borrow funds
Firm unable to pay creditors	Try to extend the credit period	The business world is interdependent. The firm's creditors may also have debts to pay. Careful negotiation is necessary. The firm may have to pay interest for late payment
Firm is waiting for debtors to pay	Offer discounts for payment but if situation persists may have to employ a debt factor	If the situation is critical then some money received is better than none. With debt factoring only a proportion of the debt is recovered
Firm has unsold stock which is taking up shelf space and tying up valuable working capital	May be left with no option but stock clearout, especially if LIFO* is used and the firm has out-of-date unsold goods	Deep discounting is undesirable as profit margins will be cut. Could affect perception of the firm due to low prices. However, costs of goods going out of date or fashion must be recognized if left unsold

*HL only: LIFO = Last In First Out, effectively the most recent stock is issued to customers first.

3.4 Budgeting HL

HL

THE PURPOSE OF BUDGETS

Students will be familiar with the role of a movie director – the person who creates the scenes, instructs the actors where to stand, how to act and react, in the process transferring the finished script to the screen. What is not so commonly known is the role of the producer. Put simply, the role is to find the finance, hire the key talent (including the director) and make sure that the film meets its budget, which has probably been allocated to the producer by a senior executive unconnected to the film. It is a demanding and stressful role.

This introduces the importance of budgets, their role and relevance to strategic planning, and will also help us understand the concept of variance analysis.

Budgets perform a number of crucial functions for an organization. They can be particularly important if the culture of an organization does not have strong accountability (as opposed to Apollo structures: HL only) and flat hierarchies. With laissez-faire leadership styles, budgets are an essential method of financial control.

Definition: A budget is a financial target or prediction of how much a firm is expected to spend or receive in a given time period.

Budgets have been described as a 'route map' in helping an organization achieve its objectives for a predetermined period.

Budgets can:

- Impose financial discipline on departments and require managers to become accountable for every dollar spent. This process is sometimes referred to as zero budgeting.
- Provide financial motivation (and thus rewards!) to divisions or managers if they are empowered to meet certain targets or forecasts.
- Allow senior management to control and monitor spending and through variance analysis perhaps highlight or pre-empt potential problems.
- Allow senior management to review performance if a new strategic plan has been introduced (see below).

VARIANCES

A variance occurs if a figure such as advertising expenditure for a firm calculated at the end of the financial period is different to the budgeted or forecasted figure.

These differences can be *favourable* (actual > budget in the case of revenue or budget > actual in the case of costs) or *adverse* (actual < budget in the case of revenue or budget < actual in the case of costs).

The following example will help to clarify understanding. (Please note that for the 2009 syllabus specific knowledge of actual variances is not required.)

All figures are millions of dollars.

Cost or revenue item	Budgeted figure	Actual figure	Variance
Sales revenue in host country	42	40	2 Adverse
Overseas sales	17	21	4 Favourable
Material costs	24	21	3 Favourable
Advertising	6	11	5 Adverse

The advertising account has overspent by $5m and it will now be up to the senior management to investigate further the causes of this variance.

BUDGETS, VARIANCES AND STRATEGIC PLANNING

As we saw in unit 1.6, the generic model of decision-making can be used to help firms decide on an appropriate course of action. The decision to be made could be either tactical or strategic.

Once a decision has been made on a suitable course of action, the decision-making framework demands that the decision is reviewed periodically, perhaps in terms of sales increases or cost reductions – whatever the original objective was behind the decision.

The setting of budgets and the calculation of variances could be important elements in this review process to see whether the strategy is meeting forecasts or is in need of adjustment If early indications reveal that the new strategy is not going according to plan.

Possible areas of enquiry

- Were new sales targets met?
- Did the company overspend on above-the-line promotion?
- Has the new strategy resulted in a fall in labour costs below target?

Depending on the nature of the strategic plan, its scope and time frame for completion, budgets and variance analysis can be used to see if the new direction is 'on track'.

If variances in particular look likely to be grossly adverse, immediate corrective action in the strategy could be taken. It would not be sensible for an organization to wait too long before deciding whether to change if the strategic direction is off course.

Jack Trout in his book *Big Brands, Big Trouble* sums up this view on strategic planning very succinctly:

Remember the Titanic. (Trout, 2001)

3.5 Final accounts (1)

INTRODUCTION

In the new course guide, the accounting topics have moved away from calculating transactions (much of which can now be done by computer software) towards analysing how accounting can help organizations make effective tactical or strategic decisions. Accounting has thus become more active and engaging and, through use of the Internet and increased transparency of published company accounts, more accessible.

DVD resource and Internet research

No study of accounting would be complete without a review of one of the bleakest episodes of financial mismanagement in recent years by a large organization. *Enron – the smartest guys in the room* is essential viewing, not too difficult to follow and very entertaining. However, it remains a worrying parable of our times, where greed and inappropriate accounting practices create an unethical and unpalatable mix.

Students are encouraged to research companies of their choice to view real-world balance sheets and profit and loss accounts. The information from these sites is extensive and at times overwhelming but can provide a great starting point in the study of this unit. For example, Nike's website and financial information is accessible and informative.

THE PURPOSE OF ACCOUNTS

The main purposes are:

- To be able to analyse business performance in terms of profitability, liquidity, efficiency and gearing in combination with accounting ratios.

- Given the above, to allow the senior management to make adjustments to a strategic direction where necessary.

- To satisfy legal requirements in the case of publicly traded companies and thus to calculate corporate tax liabilities.

- To provide a degree of transparency on the company's financial position to external stakeholders such as potential investors, lenders and suppliers. This point has become more important since the Enron scandal.

We now consider the use of published accounts and their relevance to key stakeholders.

- **Current and potential investors:** Investors will be especially concerned with the profitability and gearing aspects of the balance sheets. They may also wish to view financial accounts over a time period to build up an overall picture of financial performance.

- **Lenders of funds:** Creditors will be concerned with liquidity, profitability and existing levels of gearing, and perhaps, the amounts of fixed assets for collateral purposes if the firm is looking to borrow additional funds.

- **Suppliers:** Suppliers will interested and concerned with liquidity issues arising from the current assets and liability sections of the balance sheet.

Judgment

Final accounts can provide an invaluable source of information in the decision-making process. However, they must be taken in good faith and accepted on trust. Different stakeholders will view the accounts with different perceptions depending on the stakeholder's objectives and motives.

With any consideration of quantitative information, stakeholders will also have to consider qualitative information as well as the external environment in which the firm operates.

Given the uncertainties surrounding the current economic climate, balance sheet values should be treated with caution, in addition to over-optimistic profit forecasts. The lessons of the unsustainable dot.com boom need to be learnt.

EVALUATING THE IMPORTANCE OF FINAL ACCOUNTS TO EACH STAKEHOLDER GROUP

The final accounts are also called published accounts. Students often make the mistake of thinking that the company is 'giving away secrets' by publishing final accounts. They are not, and it would be impossible to run an organization by using these accounts as they are merely outlines or sketches of the performance of a company.

Internal accounts, sometimes referred to as managerial accounts, are much more detailed and revealing and thus, not surprisingly, are not made available to competitors or external stakeholders.

We must remember that published accounts refer to the past. They should be used with caution when trying to predict future performance. The dot.com boom of the late 1990s provides us with a classic example of investors throwing large sums of capital at Internet start-ups in the hope of achieving what turned out to be fictitious profits based on over-optimistic balance sheets, cash flow forecasts and profit and loss accounts based on only the flimsiest of business plans.

Students are invited to investigate the fate of pets.com, one of the high-profile casualties of the dot.com boom, which lost an estimated $300m in less than two years of trading.

3.5 Final accounts (2)

THE BALANCE SHEET AND PROFIT AND LOSS ACCOUNT

Adjustments to profit and loss accounts: a worked example

Please note that depreciation does not appear on the SL syllabus. The worked example was originally set for HL students. SL students should note the format of the profit and loss account only.

NOTE FOR TEACHERS

We are going to move very quickly through this section to allow us to focus on the 'stories' behind the numbers in unit 3.6. The format and structure of balance sheets and profit and loss accounts is not given here. Students are referred instead to pages 72–73 of the IB *Business and Management Guide* for the template which will be used where balance sheets and profit and loss accounts are given in case studies or in examination questions.

When a student is given a balance sheet or profit and loss account to amend in the examination it is likely that only a few simple changes will be required. Students will not have to prepare a full set of accounts from a Trial Balance.

Forecast financial information for Gemel Ltd for the years 2008 and 2009.

Gemel Ltd's fixed assets were valued at $200,000 on start-up. The assets would have a useful life of 4 years and an estimated scrap value of $40,000.

	2008 ($000)	2009 ($000)
Turnover	485	870
Cost of stock sold	245	450
Expenses	91	138
Non-operating income	11	13
Interest	20	55
Tax	35	60
Dividends	60	75

a *Using straight-line depreciation, calculate the annual provision for depreciation that the accountant omitted. (Depreciation is HL only)*

b *Using the financial information provided for 2008 and 2009, prepare profit and loss accounts for the two years, adjusting the figures in the table above to include the provision for depreciation and re-calculating the tax payment to equal 25% of net profit before tax.*

Solution

$$\text{Depreciation} = \frac{\text{historic cost} - \text{scrap value}}{\text{number of years of useful life}}$$

$$= \frac{\$200,000 - \$40,000}{4}$$

Depreciation charge per annum = $40,000 (HL only)

Revised profit and loss account for 2008 and 2009 ($000)

	2008	2009
Turnover	485	870
Cost of stock sold	245	450
Gross profit	240	420
Expenses (including new depreciation charge)	131	178
Total operating profit	109	242
Non-operating income	11	13
Net profit before interest and tax	120	255
Interest paid	20	55
Net profit before tax	100	200
Tax @ 25%	25	50
Net profit after tax	75	150
Dividends	60	75
Retained profit	15	75

DEPRECIATION

Depreciation is a poorly understood topic. Many students, when asked, reply that depreciation is 'the wear and tear' of using an asset. Although this answer has some merit, it is not totally correct.

Firms depreciate assets because over time assets lose value due to use or because the technology incorporated in the asset becomes obsolete or out of date.

Strictly speaking, however, depreciation is the process of allocating the historic cost (or price paid) of a fixed asset less any residual or scrap value, over the number of years that the asset is deemed useful, also known as 'writing off' the value of an asset.

When charging this expense to the profit and loss account, there is no physical movement in cash. Instead the depreciation charge for the year is set against the profits earned by the company and the book or current value of the asset is automatically reduced.

3.5 Final accounts (3)

DEPRECIATION: REDUCING BALANCE METHOD

We have briefly covered the first method of depreciation which is called the straight-line method. This formula is not given in the formula sheet which is handed to candidates at the beginning of the examination.

The reducing balance method of depreciation is another possible way of spreading the cost of a fixed asset over its useful life. The fixed asset is depreciated by a constant percentage each year, e.g. 20% of the book value.

Let us go back to our previous example from Gemel Ltd and compare the depreciation of the fixed assets under the two different methods.

The depreciation charge on fixed asset costing $200,000 with a residual value of $40,000 over 4 years of useful life is $40,000 per annum.

Let us depreciate the same asset by, say, 40% per year on the remaining book value at the end of the year.

Year	Opening value of asset straight line	Depreciation charge for that year	Book value at the end of the year	Opening value of asset reducing balance	Depreciation charge or that year	Book value at the end of the year
1	200,000	40,000	160,000	200,000	80,000	120,000
2	160,000	40,000	120,000	120,000	48,000	72,000
3	120,000	40,000	80,000	90,000	36,000	44,000
4	80,000	40,000	40,000	44,000	17,600	26,400
5	40,000	0	Asset sold	26,400	10,560	15,840

The table highlights a number of important considerations.

- Straight-line depreciation is aptly named as the book value of the asset reduces by a constant amount. We can show this on a diagram.

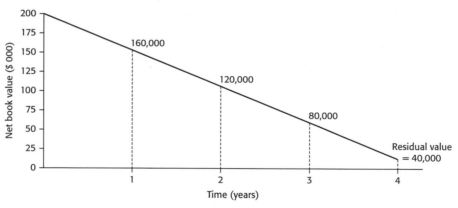

Depreciation by the straight-line method

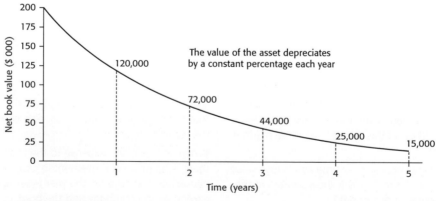

Depreciation by the reducing balance method

3.5 Final accounts (4)

IMPLICATIONS

- We can see that for the reducing balance method the initial depreciation charge to the profit and loss account in the first couple of years of an asset's useful life is higher than for the straight-line method.

- It is impossible to reduce a number by a percentage less than 100% and arrive at zero, so with the reducing balance method it is impossible to 'write off' the value of an asset completely.

- With straight-line depreciation if the residual or scrap vale is zero then it is possible to exactly spread the cost of the asset over its useful life.

- For products which may become technologically obsolete very quickly such as personal computers, the reducing balance method of depreciation is more appropriate.

Finally, for a few fixed assets neither method is appropriate, for example, aeroplanes or other forms of transport which add productive capacity to an organization. Rather than the number of years of useful life of an aeroplane, one should focus on the number of hours the asset is in use as this will have more impact on 'wear and tear'. More complex methods of depreciation are beyond the scope of this guide.

INTANGIBLE ASSETS

An intangible asset is one which cannot be physically touched or seen. However, as we will see in our study of branding, intangible assets are an important component of balance sheets of large multinational organizations, valued in millions of dollars.

In addition to branding, there are a number of other common intangible assets. The two most important are goodwill and patents and copyrights.

Goodwill is an asset which can take a number of forms. It is normally created when an organization changes ownership and the price paid by the acquirer exceeds the book value of a business; it is usually calculated by looking at the balance sheet of a company. The new owner is rewarding the previous owner by paying more than the book value in recognition of their past efforts in establishing a strong brand presence in the marketplace. For example, it is believed that Nestle paid over $1bn more than the book value to acquire Rowntree with its roster of famous confectionery brands including top-selling KitKat.

In the public or not-for-profit sectors where there may be no change of ownership or sale and purchase of a business, goodwill can be identified by the skills of the workforce or willingness to work additional hours for no extra pay (the education or health sectors are good examples). These skills do not show up in the balance sheet but they remain a valuable asset of the organization.

Patents and copyrights and the role of the intangible asset of intellectual property rights will be explained in more detail in unit 5.8.

Valuing intangible assets

It can be difficult to price an intangible asset. Goodwill can only be accurately measured for a business when the business is sold.

However, some attempt must be made to quantify the value that a management style, innovative brand or logo may have to a company if they contribute to the success – as measured by profitability – of that organization.

For example, the Apple share price fell in early 2009 in reaction to reports that CEO Steve Jobs was to take immediate sick leave. Investors felt that, without Jobs at the helm of the company, the organization might lose its innovative edge.

Valuing brands in recent years has been made easier by the work of *Interbrand*, an organization which conducts exhaustive research into the value of this most important intangible asset. Students are encouraged to visit their website.

Just as a guide, here are the top 10 global brand names and their perceived market value in US$ billion in 2008.

1	Coca-Cola	66
2=	IBM	59
2=	Microsoft	59
4	General Electric	53
5	Nokia	35
6	Toyota	34
7=	Intel	31
7=	McDonald's	31
9	Disney	29
10	Google	25

Interestingly, Apple and Sony are in joint thirteenth place with the same market value of their brand.

3.5 Final accounts (5)

STOCK VALUATION

Under the current assets section of a balance sheet, an organization will list those assets which will be used by the organization for less than one year but are an essential part of working capital. They include cash in a bank account, monies still to be received for goods sold on credit (debtors) and stock of goods unsold.

One key question is: what value do we give to this closing stock?

Two current valuation methods are used and need to be studied for HL, namely LIFO (last in first out) and FIFO (first in first out).

These stock valuation methods assume that when goods are dispatched to customers, a firm can choose whether to issue the most recent items produced by the firm (LIFO) or the first to be produced (FIFO). The method chosen will determine the value placed on the balance sheet and, more importantly, will influence gross profit calculations.

Let us take a look at an example from a previous examination question (May 2003).

> Gunwale Surfboards sell boards to predominantly young surfers and sources its stock of boards from local suppliers. It made the following purchases and sales in the first six months of the year.
>
> Please note that it had 12 boards in stock that had cost $156 each to purchase on 1 January.

Month in 2003	Purchases (units)	Cost per unit ($)	Sales (units)
January	140	165	86
February	60	162	93

Stock valuation under FIFO **HL**

Assuming that the firm sold 86 boards in January and purchased 140 @ $165, it would release 12 of the boards held on 1 January and 74 bought during January to customers.

At the end of January, it would have $(140 - 74) = 66$ boards remaining, each valued at $165.

If Gunwale sold a further 93 boards in February and purchased 60 @ $162, it would issue first the 66 held over from last month and 27 from this month to customers to fulfil sales orders.

At the end of February, it would have $(60 - 27) = 33$ boards remaining, each valued at $162, i.e. closing stock = $5,346.

Stock valuation under LIFO

Under LIFO, the same purchases and sales of boards are made. The difference is that Gunwale does not issue the older stock of 12 boards @ $156 first to customers. Instead, the firm will issue the most recent surfboards received from its suppliers.

Hence at the end of January, Gunwale will have 12 boards @ $156 and 54 boards @ $165 left in stock.

In February, all the new boards received in February will be issued to customers. 33 of January's boards will be needed to fulfil orders. This leaves the closing stock for February as:

12 boards @ $156 (the stock at the beginning of the year)

21 boards @ $165 (purchased in January)

Closing stock = $5,337

COMPARISON OF FIFO AND LIFO AND IMPACT ON GROSS PROFIT **HL**

If we assume that, due to inflation, prices on average will rise over the course of the trading year (although this assumption might be wrong – there are deflationary pressures in 2009!) then the FIFO method values closing stock at higher, more recent purchased prices, as the old stock received is always issued first. Any units left over are therefore always valued at the current purchase price.

A higher closing stock will imply a lower cost of goods sold and thus, given the same figure for sales, a higher gross profit than when using the LIFO method.

EXAMINER'S HINT

FIFO and LIFO questions regularly appear on examination papers. They are not too difficult but, under time pressure, attention must be made to the layout of the purchases of stock, units issued and monthly closing values, otherwise a student may lose track of the amount of stock left over each month.

Now work through question 3, page 79.

Which method to use?

This will depend on the type of market the firm operates in, the nature of the product and the costs of holding stock. This latter point will be discussed in unit 5.7.

Stock valuation has important links to other parts of the Business and Management course. In our example above regarding Gunwale, issuing the most recently received surfboards (LIFO) may be an attempt to follow a new trend or fashion which has arisen. FIFO could be used if the firm thinks that surfboards are immune to changes in tastes over such a short period. Either way the firm is taking a view on the state of the market when deciding which boards to issue first to customers.

As a result LIFO stock valuation, which tends to be overlooked in many countries, is becoming a crucial way of managing stock levels in consumer markets where fashions and tastes can change dramatically. With product life cycles increasingly now becoming shorter (page 92), the need for efficient stock control management (page 123) is becoming critical.

3.6 Ratio analysis (1)

PROFITABILITY RATIOS

We will try to keep the analysis brief, focusing on the role each ratio plays in informing stakeholders.

The two key profitability ratios are gross and net profit margin.

Gross profit margin

$$\text{Gross profit margin} = \frac{\text{gross profit}}{\text{sales revenue}} \times 100$$

- **Key stakeholders:** line and senior managers
- This ratio identifies the profit a firm achieves from trading – the buying and selling of goods.
- Assuming that selling prices and purchase prices remain constant over a trading period, this ratio should also be constant.
- If the ratio starts to deteriorate, the implication is that sales are not being transferred successfully into trading profits – a potential cause for concern. Firms may wish to look at their purchases of stock to see if the cost of stock sold is rising.
- For this reason, this ratio can also be viewed as an efficiency ratio.

Net profit margin

$$\text{Net profit margin} = \frac{\text{net profit before interest and tax}}{\text{sales revenue}} \times 100$$

- **Key stakeholders:** senior managers, current and potential investors

- The ratio serves as a signal as to the capacity the firm has to generate profits after overhead or indirect costs have been taken into account.
- The net profit figure excludes interest or tax and is the favoured ratio of managers as the final ratio will be higher than net profit margin after tax, which of course is a compulsory payment to government.
- The ratio should be constant over a trading period. If it starts to fall, it implies that overhead costs are rising faster than sales and an investigation should be carried out.
- Given the above, the company may need to change suppliers or look for alternative insurance quotes to cover premises or vehicles to reduce fixed costs.

An appropriate level of margin per unit sold?

There is an important link between the gross profit margin per unit sold, the industry the firm operates in and the rate of stock turnover (see below).

Supermarkets and increasingly e-commerce retailers can afford to set lower margins per unit given the faster stock turnover these firms experience. In industries where turnover is slower, especially in niche markets, much higher gross and net profit margins per unit sold are the norm.

3.6 Ratio analysis (2)

RETURN ON CAPITAL EMPLOYED (ROCE)

$$ROCE = \frac{\text{net profit before interest and tax}}{\text{total capital employed}} \times 100$$

- **Key stakeholders:** current and potential investors, media groups and the CEO, and the government tax department!
- This ratio is listed in the syllabus as an efficiency ratio because it looks at how efficiently an organization uses its capital or total assets to create goods and services that are in turn used to create profits.
- An alternative way of looking at the ROCE is to consider it as a measure of reward (in the form of profit) for risk-taking by entrepreneurs.

- An entrepreneur has to take the somewhat difficult decision to combine and finance the factors of production such as capital, land and labour into a profitable enterprise.
- The ROCE is the reward for taking this risk, given that an alternative opportunity could have been considered, such as a low-risk investment offered by a financial institution.

LIQUIDITY RATIOS

$$\text{Current ratio} = \frac{\text{current assets}}{\text{current liabilities}}$$

$$\text{Acid test ratio} = \frac{\text{current assets} - \text{stocks}}{\text{current liabilities}}$$

- **Key stakeholders:** lenders, potential lenders and suppliers
- We have already covered a number of liquidity issues in unit 3.3 (see page xxx).

- The acid test ratio is a more stringent measure of liquidity as stocks of unsold goods are not included in current assets.
- Some writers have argued that firms should consider calculating **a 'cash ratio'** where current assets have stock *and* debtors removed from current assets as we cannot guarantee that all monies from debtors will be paid, given the existence of bad debts.

EFFICIENCY RATIOS

Stock turnover can be calculated in two different ways.

$$\frac{\textbf{Cost of goods sold}}{\textbf{average stock}}$$

- This gives the number of times the current level of stock is 'turned over' or sold.

$$\frac{\textbf{Average stock}}{\textbf{cost of goods sold}} \times \textbf{365} \text{ (days in the trading year)}$$

- This formula converts the first figure into a number of days.
- **Key stakeholders:** line managers or heads of department such as purchasing.

- The importance of this ratio will depend on the type of industry the firm operates in and the nature of the good itself.
- In fast-moving consumer goods (FMCG) industries, stock turnover will need to be quick or the firm may find itself with stockpiles of unsold goods. This will be critically important if the firm is supplying perishable goods such as dairy products, fruit or vegetables.

This argument can also be applied in rapidly changing technological markets where the rate of product obsolescence, given Moore's Law, has been increasing.

GEARING

The gearing ratio is measured by observing how much of the firm's capital employed in the business is provided by long-term lenders.

$$\text{Gearing ratio} = \frac{\text{loan capital}}{\text{total capital employed}}$$

- The figure is usually expressed as a percentage.
- A 'high' gearing ratio such as 50% of capital employed, perhaps compared to other firms in the industry, indicates that the firm is vulnerable to changes in interest rates or external factors which may make credit more difficult to obtain.
  The latter is particularly relevant during 2009, with the credit crunch at its height.
- If the firm has sufficient liquidity to pay short-term interest costs, then a high gearing ratio may not be a major

concern to some stakeholders. A number of high-profile takeovers have been instigated and financed by new owners (for example, in the takeover of English premiership soccer clubs) taking on additional borrowing collateralized against the newly created company's assets.

- However, if we return briefly to our point in unit 3.2 about the debt vs equity dilemma (page 64), we must be tempted to ask the question whether other stakeholders would be concerned about the level of gearing and the degree of ownership of the firm. Do we wish for a company to be predominantly controlled by the firm's management or by long-term lenders such as financial institutions?
- **Key stakeholders:** current and future lenders of funds, shareholders

3.6 Ratio analysis (3)

ADDITIONAL EFFICIENCY RATIOS

Debtor and creditor days

$$\text{Debtor days ratio} = \frac{\text{debtors}}{\text{total sales revenue}} \times 365$$

$$\text{Creditor days ratio} = \frac{\text{creditors}}{\text{total sales revenue}} \times 365$$

- **Key stakeholders:** suppliers and creditors, department heads
- The relationship between these two formulae is critical and has important implications for working capital and liquidity. We have already noted in unit 3.3 the degree of interdependence between credit received from creditors and credit allowed to debtors. It is important that these two cycles are matched as closely as possible with, in a perfect world, debtor days being smaller than creditor days. This would imply that our organization on average receives payment for goods sold before we have to pay our suppliers.

ADDITIONAL SHAREHOLDER RATIOS

Earnings per share

$$\text{Earnings per share (EPS)} = \frac{\text{net profit after interest and tax}}{\text{number of ordinary shares}}$$

- This ratio is of particular interest to shareholders as it can reveal the after-tax profit available for distribution.
- However, this does not mean that all the net profit will be distributed to shareholders in the form of dividends. The company directors at the annual general meeting will have to decide how much of this profit will be paid to them directly as dividends and how much will be kept and held in reserves as retained profit. This could be used to finance future investment opportunities and provide a boost to longer-term shareholder value.

Dividend yield

$$\text{Dividend yield} = \frac{\text{dividend per share}}{\text{current market share price}}$$

- This is a kind of individual return or profit from owning one share of a company. Dividend yield is important to potential investors who may be looking to secure an annual income. They could compare the yield from an organization with an alternative savings scheme such as one offered by a financial institution.
- However, if the company is perceived to be performing above expectations, the current market share price will rise, reducing the yield to potential investors.

FINANCIAL RATIOS AND STAKEHOLDERS

We have seen that the key stakeholders involved in using ratios in decision-making processes are current and potential shareholders, lenders, suppliers and senior managers.

We stress again that a single ratio in isolation without comparison to other firms or the current state of the external environment or over time is not a basis for making a considered financial decision.

TOK

We could consider other stakeholders not yet covered.

First, the lessons from the collapse of Enron, in particular, reveal that huge importance has been attached to a firm's ability to deliver increasing profits. It would appear to many that profitability is the only important measure of performance.

Even when in the case of Enron, these profit figures were mere fantasy, stakeholders such as the financial media, potential investors and financial institutions continued to believe the illusion. There are a number of important TOK issues here which would provide the basis for a good discussion. (If the financial figures look too good to be true, then they probably are.)

Second, the increased need for greater transparency of company financial reporting (lessons learned from the Enron collapse?) has allowed consumers to access information such as gross profit and net profit margins, regional sales figures, etc.

This new knowledge should be used to try and inform customer decision-making especially when there have been concerns about the high prices which some brand-driven companies charge for products such as fashionable clothing or footwear. The ease of acquiring this new information quickly and at little cost has been a key driver in the growth of ethical and socially responsible consumer behaviour.

3.6 Ratio analysis (4)

EVALUATING POSSIBLE FINANCIAL AND OTHER STRATEGIES TO IMPROVE THE VALUES OF RATIOS

HL

In summary:

Ratio	Possible strategies with discussion to improve the value, and links to other topics
Gross margin	If ratio is falling the firm may have to look at stock control and purchasing decisions. If the cost of stock sold is rising, managers may have to consider alternative supply chain management strategies (unit 4.6). There may also be significant marketing factors to consider such as the effectiveness of the current promotional mix (unit 4.5), although, of course, altering this could raise costs.
Net profit margin	If the ratio is falling, the firm will have to look at its overheads and indirect costs. Could the firm outsource some production to reduce overhead costs? (unit 5.7)
Current and acid test ratio	See section on dealing with working capital and liquidity issues (unit 3.3)
ROCE	A fall in this ratio relative to competitors over time may signal discussions among senior management into pursuing a new strategic direction especially if the fall is sustained, to try and regain lost market share (unit 1.3) Firm may also consider downsizing and restructuring (unit 2.1) to try to reduce variable costs
Stock turnover	The rate of stock turnover needs to be appropriate for the industry and for the nature of the product, and has links to gross and net profit margin Firm may need to review pricing methods and the marketing mix in general if stock is consistently not being sold (unit 4.4)
Creditor and debtor days	See section on dealing with working capital and liquidity issues (unit 3.3)
Gearing ratio	Further borrowing may transfer some control away from shareholders, towards financial institutions. The firm may need to compare its gearing ratio with competitors and take appropriate action if it is deemed too high. Firm may have to look at asset sales or introducing sale and leaseback schemes (unit 3.1)
Earnings per share and dividend yield	If there is shareholder concern expressed at the AGM about dividend yield and EPS, then the firm will have to look again at changing strategic direction, although this will not bring a quick fix and the focus may need to be on new tactical objectives to demonstrate a commitment to change (unit 1.3)

Before you move on topic 4, you should attempt questions 4, 5 and 6 on page 79.

Exam questions on Topic 3

1 Evaluate the potential sources of finance for a small business like Gemel Ltd to fund the purchase of the following:

  i stocks of finished goods for resale

  ii delivery vans

  iii land and buildings   (November 2007)

2 **Coffee-Cool** has provided the following cost and revenue information for July to December 2006.

Revenue	$4000
Cost of buying and holding stock (coffee beans)	$700 per month from July until October $400 per month in November and December
Cost of ordering stock (coffee beans)	$100 per month from July until October $200 per month in November and December
Own drawings	$1200 per month
Opening balance for July	$400
Promotion	$200 per month
Electricity	$800 per year to be paid in equal instalments every January and July
Rates	$600 to be paid in January every year
Finance charge (interest paid)	$100 per month for three years
Repayment of loan	$2500 per payment to be paid in September and February for two years

  a Construct a cash flow forecast for Coffee-Cool for each month from July 2006 to December 2006 assuming a loan is taken for renovation.

  b Comment on Coffee-Cool's liquidity position.   (May 2006)

3 **HL Jetstream Hot Tub** sell models of hot tubs designed for use in homes. Their premium product is the Premier 12. It sells for $8500.

  At the beginning of July 2005, Jetstream had 8 Premier 12 hot tubs in stock that were valued at $6200 each.

  The following purchases and sales were made during the last 6 months of 2005.

Month	Purchases (units)	Cost per unit	Sales/issues
July	20	6300	25
August	35	6150	32
September	28	6400	30
October	20	6300	18
November	52	6200	50
December	54	6500	56

  Using both LIFO and FIFO methods of stock valuation for the Premier 12, calculate the following for the period of July to December 2005:

  a the value of the closing stock

  b the half-year gross profit.   (May 2006)

4 **HL** Define with examples, intangible assets and explain how these benefit businesses like Shell.   (May 2003)

5 Evaluate the potential sources of finance available to developers of innovative products, such as the Segway (a hi-tech, environmentally-friendly scooter).   (adapted from May 2005)

6 Examine reasons why new firms, especially those set up by younger people, find it difficult to raise start-up capital.   (adapted from May 2005)

4.1 The role of marketing (1)

NOTE FOR TEACHERS

Marketing is the most popular topic in the Business and Management syllabus. Students as consumers are active stakeholders in this area and readily engage with the subject.

However, in terms of understanding, application, analysis and evaluation, especially in final examinations,

students' performance is consistently below expectations, particularly when evaluating a marketing strategy.

Students are advised to learn the following marketing definitions, apply them in context to the question asked and provide necessary balance when discussion is needed.

INTRODUCTION: 'THE TYRANNY OF CHOICE'

Students are encouraged to read Jack Trout's work which discusses in some detail how difficult marketing

has become given the explosion of choice in almost all markets both on a national and global level.

Product	Number of items in US market early 1970s	Number of items in US market late 1990s
Sports utility vehicle (SUV) styles	8	38
Software titles	0	250,000
Bottled water brands	16	50
Milk types	4	19
Mouthwashes	15	66
Dental floss	12	64
Over-the-counter pain relievers	17	141
Contact lens types	1	36
KFC menu items	7	14

Source: Trout (2008)

Trout also highlights that:

- An average US supermarket has 40,000 items.
- An average US family gets 80–85% of its needs from only 150 of those items.
- They will routinely ignore the other 39,850 items.

Clearly with this 'tyranny of choice', a good deal of marketing effort is going to waste. Even in niche markets such as the luxury sports car market which used to be dominated by Ferrari, choice and competition have emerged in the shape of Porsche, Lamborghini, Bentley and Aston Martin, and most recently the Mercedes SLR range.

KEY DEFINITIONS

The following definitions are part of the core knowledge of marketing.

- **Market size:** The total sales of all the producers within a market. Another way of stating this is the total amount of revenue generated. The US personal computer market was worth $15.6bn in the 4th quarter 2008.

- **Market share:** The sales of the individual firm expressed as a percentage of total industry sales.

Market share
$$= \frac{\text{total revenue the firm generates}}{\text{total revenue the whole industry generates}} \times 100$$

US Personal computer sales, market share and market growth

Company	4th Quarter sales 2008 ($m)	4th Quarter market share (%)	4th Quarter sales 2007 ($m)	4th Quarter market share (%)	4Q 2008 – 4Q 2007 growth (%)
Dell	4465.8	28.6	5344.6	30.8	−16.4
HP	4288.3	27.5	4439.5	25.6	−3.4
Acer	2373.9	15.2	1527.3	8.8	55.4
Apple	1255.0	8.0	1159.3	6.7	8.3
Toshiba	1007.7	6.5	900.0	5.2	12.0
Others	2219.2	14.2	3992.6	23.0	−44.4
Total	15609.0	100.0	17363.3	100.0	−10.1

Source: Gartner Inc. from www.macrumors.com

4.1 The role of marketing (2)

KEY DEFINITIONS *(continued)*

- **Market growth** is identified in the last column of the table. It is interesting to note that even in the deteriorating global economic environment some companies have gained market share (Acer, Apple and Toshiba) at the expense of the market leaders.

- **Marketing:** the process of identifying and satisfying consumer wants and needs in line with the objectives of the organization.

- For marketing in the new millennium, a firm should also try to anticipate or even create needs and wants and be able to satisfy them profitably. This will be looked at in later sections when we consider the roles of market research, development and innovation.

LINKS WITH OTHER ELEMENTS OF THE BUSINESS ORGANIZATION

We must not treat marketing in isolation from the other sections of a business.

Consider some of the following issues for a company in the competitive snack food industry:

- The marketing department of a potato chip manufacturer would love to be able to promote a fat-free potato chip and are becoming frustrated by the production department's insistence that it cannot be produced at a low enough cost to make it commercially profitable.

- The finance department have criticized the marketing department for insisting on a new TV campaign to 'buy one get two free', as the company cannot produce such large quantities of stock nor afford the cost of the proposed TV commercial involving a famous media personality.

- The sales director is not enthusiastic about the marketing department's insistence of developing a cheese-and-vinegar flavoured potato chip. His sales team lack enthusiasm for this tactical move.

We could have highlighted a number of other conflicts. The key is that marketing has to fit within the constraints placed on it by the organization and be aware that its actions may have significant implications for other parts of the organization.

MARKET ORIENTATION AND PRODUCTION ORIENTATION

Theodore Levitt (Russell-Walling, 2007) provides an example of the difference between market orientation and production orientation.

> *Movie companies do not make movies but they provide entertainment. In the 1950s, the American movie studios dismissed television and ignored its influence. They lost their customer focus and became too product orientated. ... They have barely recovered from the impact of television. It took them too long to see television as an opportunity for growth and not a threat.*

More examples

Readers may like to remind themselves of the experience of the Disney Corporation in unit 1.6 (page 20).

Similarly, the five major record companies were fearful of the first popular file-sharing site – Napster – which paved the way for the success of iTunes as the biggest source of legal downloads, which many record companies now enthusiastically embrace. The threat has become the opportunity.

A few companies, including Rolls Royce and Apple, are able to operate profitably by concentrating solely on the strength of their product and effectively ignoring the needs of the market (**production orientation**).

Most have to try and satisfy an increasingly demanding consumer base empowered by knowledge and information from the Internet (**market orientation**).

4.1 The role of marketing (3)

MARKETING IN NON-PROFIT ORGANIZATIONS

Our definition of marketing (page 81) was careful to acknowledge that marketing is a process to satisfy needs and wants, to fit in with the firm's objectives. Not all firms are profit maximizers and, as we highlighted in unit 1.3, a number of other corporate objectives exist (pages 12–13).

Maynard (2009) argues that it is important for non-profit organizations to establish a well-defined niche; while most are not selling goods, they are selling their organization's mission, their ideas, their vision and their services. We cannot assume that the non-profit organization (however ethical or socially responsible) will sell itself based on its inherent worth and the goodwill generated in the community. Maynard identifies a number of key points:

- Identify your target audience: define key stakeholder groups.
- Maintain consistent communication.

- Create a strong visual identity: use logos.
- Use message repetition wherever possible: create a slogan.
- Employ multiple communication tactics.

TOK

One is drawn to the conclusion that, given the impact of some of the factors highlighted in our previous STEEPLE analysis, non-profit organizations need to match the tactics used by their profit-generating counterparts. The paradox of the non-profit-making industry acting in a profit-maximizing manner should not be disregarded by the reader and would make a stimulating TOK discussion.

THE MARKETING PLAN

In unit 1.6 we looked extensively at planning and the generic decision-making model. We can add to our knowledge of planning by identifying some additional specific elements relevant to developing a marketing plan.

The plan should include the following elements:

- A marketing budget for above-the-line activities if necessary

- The strategy to fulfil the objectives of the organization
- Tactical methods such as the elements of the marketing mix
- A time frame to review progress of the plan, with a contingency to take corrective action or review tactics if forecasts are not achieved.

SOCIAL AND ASSET-LED MARKETING

HL

Social marketing

The emergence of a more ethical and socially responsible external environment has given rise to a new breed of **'social marketing'**. This has been embraced by both the private and public sectors. The focus here is on communicating the existence of and extolling the virtue of 'merit goods' such as education and health while, for example, raising awareness and aiming to reduce the consumption of demerit products (such as alcohol, cigarettes and 'junk food') given that these products can have significant impacts on the wider community.

Some critics have argued that firms in the private sector may use social marketing in a vague, non-credible manner. However, some organizations such as Nike and McDonald's that have faced increasing stakeholder criticism have responded with positive social marketing messages of their own.

Asset-led marketing

We stated earlier that a very few companies such as Rolls-Royce and Apple are able to be product orientated and focus their operations on producing products with little regard for consumer needs and wants (e.g. launching the new iPhone in many countries at a very high price relative to the competition).

Some companies have taken product orientation to the limit and have created **asset-led** marketing where the competitive position is determined by the firm's individual strengths (or assets!) such as leadership, the quality of the human resource function, the location of its retail outlets or some other intangible asset which other potential competitors cannot match.

Companies such as Volvo (safety), Duracell (long-lasting battery life) and Heinz (ketchup) have been able to asset-lead their marketing by using a technique which some marketing writers refer to as the **dominant attribute**. We shall return to this point later when we review branding in the next section.

4.2 Marketing planning (1)

NOTE FOR TEACHERS

We now begin a number of units focusing on specific marketing issues such as the marketing mix, the product itself, pricing, promotion, distribution, international marketing and e-commerce. The amount of marketing terminology is considerable. It is assumed that students will have access to a textbook for full coverage. The following information here is provided as a guide for study.

A number of questions from previous papers with suggested answers will hopefully add clarity as to the kind of depth and detail required by examiners.

THE MARKETING MIX: 4Ps OR 7Ps?

Students of Business and Management will be familiar with the four elements of the marketing mix (price, product, place and promotion) which are used to develop a marketing plan for a product.

MIX OR STRATEGY?

However, the following may be unfamiliar:

- The marketing mix of a good or service is unique. There will always be a degree of differentiation in each individual mix for each product or service; otherwise one would question why the product was brought to the market in the first place.

- The marketing mix is not the same as the marketing strategy. As we will see in the strategy section (page 93), the marketing mix is a *tool* to effect a strategic plan but it is not the only tool. A firm will have to consider other functions of the business such as finance and human resource management in order to create a strategy.

7Ps

The additional three Ps to the marketing mix were added in the mid 1980s to account for the differences in the marketing of goods and services.

- **People:** As a service is an intangible (you cannot take home the process of getting a haircut), the people delivering the service to the end user (the consumer or the industrial end user) must have sufficient training in order to ensure customer satisfaction.

- The people element in the mix may also include after-sales service. (This element is sometimes applied to the product element in the mix.) As we have seen this element of the mix can be outsourced and off-shored given the substantial improvements in ICT and the spread of globalization (page 33).

- **Process:** A good can be purchased in store and paid for in a number of ways – cash, electronic transfer or credit card. For some services this is not possible. A computer technician installing a new computer system for a company may take many days and is unlikely to be paid until after the work is completed. The process element in the mix looks at how services are consumed and paid for and is crucial in industrial markets when large sums of money are exchanged or large service providers undertake work stretching over many months.

- **Physical evidence:** Some hairdressing salons are able to charge high prices for haircuts. The salon may include special lighting and music to provide relaxing surroundings for the customer. Second, the customer can only tell the outcome of a haircut when it is finished (it may be impossible to start again). Physical evidence in the 7Ps mix tries to cover both these issues. The key is to ensure that the customer feels reassured that the service provider is competent. This could be achieved with demonstrations, reviews or endorsements by previous customers or images of successful styles that the salon has previously undertaken.

TOK

THE ETHICS OF MARKETING

This is a difficult section in which to be objective, given the significant cultural, religious and global differences which exist. It could be argued that all marketing except social marketing is unethical. This topic should, in your class or TOK seminars, result in some challenging and thought-provoking discussions. For example:

- Should all forms of promotion for alcohol and cigarettes be banned?

- Should retailers who market and sell violent video games such as *Grand theft Auto IV* to minors face prosecution, as happens in Thailand?

- Should fast-food companies be more open about the amount of saturated fat in their products, which are linked to obesity and heart disease?

- Was the French government right in January 2009 to ban all mobile phone advertising during children's programming?

Interested students may view the DVD *McLibel* about the legal challenge by two human rights campaigners against misleading and unethical marketing by the McDonald's Corporation.

4.2 Marketing planning (2)

MARKETING AUDIT

This term is often used interchangeably with market analysis.

A marketing audit effectively allows a firm to review its current marketing situation and is a valuable tool to help with planning and effecting change. A marketing audit enables a firm to see if the current marketing strategy is working and to identify any adjustments that may be needed. For example:

- Research into a firm's present 'positioning' in the marketplace will find out whether consumer perceptions of a brand or product align with the intentions of that brand for the company.

- The audit may involve preparing a product life cycle to see at which stage in the life cycle the product currently sits, and this may suggest new extension strategies.

- A review of target marketing and segmentation may check that promotional efforts are being targeted to the right audience.

MARKET RESEARCH

Market research is the gathering, recording, analysing and presenting of information relevant to the marketing process. Our generic decision-making model can be adapted to incorporate market planning.

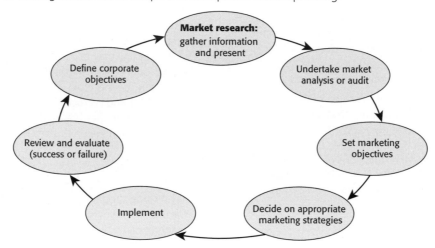

Decision-making model as applied to the marketing process

Sources of market research

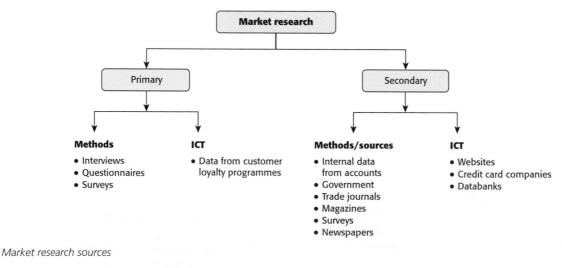

Market research sources

(continued)

4.2 Marketing planning (3)

MARKET RESEARCH *(continued)*

NOTE FOR TEACHERS

Market research is a very popular area for examination questions at both Higher and Standard level. Students are generally successful in defining concepts such as primary and secondary data. However, issues surrounding the analysis and evaluation of market research methods are not well understood and can translate into low marks in the final examination.

In addition, in the Internal Assessment assignments for both levels, students tend to assume that a single questionnaire or a single article from a journal or the Internet is sufficient depth when being asked to research an issue. Both of these do not constitute thorough research and will not allow the student to access the top mark bands for data collection and analysis.

AN ALTERNATIVE VIEW

Jack Trout advises caution over attaching too much importance to the role of market research.

Marketing people are pre-occupied with doing research – getting the facts. They analyze the situation to make sure the truth is on their side. They sail confidently into the marketing arena, secure in the knowledge that they have the best product and that ultimately the best product will win.

It's an illusion. There is no objective reality. There are no facts. There are no best products. All that exists in the world of marketing are perceptions in the minds of customers. The perception is the reality. (**source:** Trout 2008)

Example: Insufficient market research

Let's look at Virgin Group's failed attempt to enter into the potentially lucrative mobile telecommunications market in 2001.

Buoyed by a run of successful entries into new markets, Virgin arrived in Singapore with a provocative advertising campaign and favourable brand awareness (Richard Branson had successfully negotiated the sale of 49% of Virgin Airlines to Singapore Airlines only two years previously).

Unfortunately, due to a number of factors, the mobile service was forced to close just over one year later.

The reasons included:

- Insufficient market research to identify customer attitudes
- Incorrect pricing of call charges
- Underestimating the brand loyalty enjoyed by the incumbent market leader, Singapore Telecom
- Ignorance that its promotional campaign may have caused offence to some cultures
- Unrealistic sales targets which put pressure on the marketing effort from the beginning.

This may be a partial view as Trout also advises businesses to perform market research in order to identify a point of difference from the competition. However, Trout is correct that conducting market research is no guarantee of creating and marketing successful products, if the customer's perception of your product is unfavourable.

You should now be able to tackle question 1, page 109.

EVALUATION OF DIFFERENT METHODS OF MARKET RESEARCH

HL

It was noted earlier that students find evaluating key concepts difficult. Without resorting to a long list of market research methods, a brief framework is given to allow the student to develop evaluation skills. This is a checklist which could be used in a similar way as the 7C framework (page 25). We could call this ORCA.

Objectivity

Given the inherent bias in collecting data, a number of large companies do not collect primary or secondary market data themselves, preferring instead to employ a specialist market research agency to increase the degree of objectivity.

Relevance

If a company is launching a new product in the marketplace, secondary data collection will be difficult to find. Primary data may also be scarce if a questionnaire or interview is expected to reveal how a consumer feels about a product which currently does not exist.

Cost

For small business start-ups, the cost of employing a specialist agency may be high although the time saved could be considerable.

The Internet is a cheap, immediate source of secondary data. But see below for concerns over accuracy.

Accuracy

The above point can also be used to evaluate market research in terms of accuracy. Given that secondary data can date quickly as soon as it is published, especially in rapidly changing technological markets; primary data collection may be more accurate.

However, the number of potential interviewees may be small in niche markets, leading to greater bias.

Judgment

The need for market research cannot be underestimated. To summarize, in carrying out market research a firm needs to balance the degree of accuracy and objectivity required with the cost, purpose and time allowed to collect the data.

4.2 Marketing planning (4)

MARKETING SEGMENTATION AND TARGETING

These two topics are very closely linked.

Market **segmentation** is the process of classifying customers with similar needs and wants within a whole market. The key objective is to allow the firm to focus on their needs more precisely and to avoid waste in the marketing effort. This process is usually described as consumer **targeting**.

Classic segmentation is carried out by segmenting markets according to a number of criteria:

- Age
- Gender
- Geographical location
- Lifestyle to include family background
- Occupation/income levels

Analysis

The benefits of segmentation and targeting are principally built around the ability to focus the marketing effort on a group of consumers who share similar characteristics. However, we can also note that:

- Firms could focus on a segment where there may currently be limited competition or even a need that has yet to be filled, leading to a **market gap**. We will consider this area later when we highlight the role and importance of differentiation and innovation (pages 88 and 122).

- Segmentation may allow specialization and the opportunity to achieve economies of scale which could allow greater price flexibility through reduced unit costs.

- Targeting could create opportunities to develop brand loyalty as the firm tries to establish a 'connection' or 'relationship' with them. This point is given greater detail in unit 4.3 (page 94).

- Loyalty programmes have become a major marketing development in recent years with the introduction of loyalty schemes such as membership cards and privileges. In return for these benefits, the firm is able to receive feedback from customers at minimal cost (usually via e-mail or through data collection) and in turn increase the accuracy of its own research, leading to greater use of **consumer profiling**.

Problems

- Segmenting a market needs to be carried out with care and thought. Considerable problems will occur if a firm tries to segment its market in too many ways. Segments, unless carefully separated from each other with a different product and price – effectively a distinct marketing mix for each segment, may end up leading to the phenomenon of market cannibalization.

We saw earlier, on pages 17–18, with the example of Amazon in 2008 offering the opportunity for customers to download specific songs from their website rather than purchase whole albums on CD, that Amazon were effectively cannibalizing their own market. Increased sales of MP3 tracks were offset by falling sales of albums.

Excessive segmentation?

The 'tyranny of choice' which began our investigation into marketing has also not been kind to segmentation, especially in some markets such as the music and movie industries.

- If you were to enter a music retail shop in the 1970s, popular music would have been classified as just that. There might have been a classical and jazz department but the segments would have been limited. Today, there can be up to 15 different jazz classifications including: traditional, blues, fusion, smooth, avant garde, classic, funky, acid and so on.

- The movie industry has also had to cope with a huge proliferation of genres and styles. Such has been the growth that DVD rental and retail outlets now have to group genres together to avoid creating too complex a store layout. An Icelandic film about fishing and an African documentary are put together in the World Cinema segment, while the Festival segment includes niche or cult movies with small but loyal audiences.

- Readers are encouraged to think of their own examples from their own experiences. Try to segment the popular music industry today.

- Trout in his book *Big Brands, Big Trouble* (2001, pp.17–18) provides an excellent example from the early days of General Motors and their successful and unsuccessful attempts at segmenting the automobile market.

Update 2009

Given the recent difficult trading environment, some companies have reduced product lines, minimized their exposure to some market segments and effectively tried to 'downsize' their market presence. Wal-Mart, currently the most successful global retailer, is rare in competing in many markets (e.g. food, clothing, power tools, to name just a few). Consumers in the UK are currently lamenting the loss of a high-street icon – Woolworths, a popular and famous retail outlet criticized for lacking focus and covering too many segments.

4.2 Marketing planning (5)

POSITIONING AND DIFFERENTIATION

We will begin by quoting one of Trout's most famous maxims:

Marketing is not about a battle between products. It is about a battle of perceptions.

Positioning

Definition: Positioning is the process of creating a consistent and recognized customer perception about a company's brand, product and service or in fact itself.

ATTRIBUTE OWNERSHIP

Some companies, due to a number of differentiating factors which we will come to later, are able to create a perception in the mind of the consumer just by mentioning the company itself. Trout calls this **attribute ownership**.

It is a very valuable quality. A number of examples from the western world are given to clarify understanding. Students unfamiliar with these examples should try to research others more relevant to their culture.

Company/Brand	Attribute
Volvo	Safety
Crest toothpaste	Cavity protection
Duracell	Long-lasting
Toyota	Reliability
McDonald's	Fast food and children's meals
Visa	Ubiquity = everywhere
Evian	Pure water
Gillette	Men's shaving

Some companies have developed their perception so well that the brand has become generic in the minds of consumers and has entered everyday language.

- Xerox (can you Xerox this to head office, please?)
- Hoover (I am going to Hoover the room)
- Kleenex
- Scotch Tape
- GoreTex
- Q-Tips

Positioning maps

Kotler's work in this area has been important. A two-dimensional perception or positioning map illustrates his analysis of the positioning of an instant breakfast drink relative to the variables of the price of the product and speed of preparation.

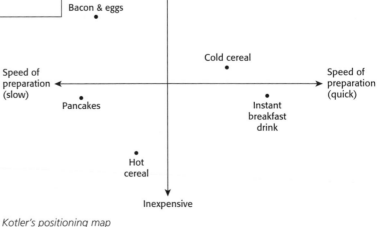

Kotler's positioning map

4.2 Marketing planning (6)

DIFFERENTIATION: A DISCUSSION

All marketing consultants and strategy specialists from Kotler to Michael Porter would agree on the need for a firm to be able to differentiate its products or services away from the competition.

The creator of the art of differentiation is credited to Rosser Reeves in 1960, who in his book *Reality in Advertising* argued the case that advertising should create a USP – a unique selling proposition – for a product to convince a customer to buy a certain brand rather than a competitor's. His ideas on differentiation have been hugely influential.

In the table below we define a differentiating characteristic which students tend to assume must be differentiating (such as price and quality) and then provide a brief overview, suggesting some issues or problems. Interested students are encouraged to read Trout's book to develop a deeper understanding, especially if they are considering writing their Extended Essay on this topic.

Differentiating factor?	Discussion points
Quality	Trout argues that quality is a poor way to differentiate. Consumers expect good quality as standard (which consumers would knowingly accept poor quality?). He stresses that all firms have the same opportunity to implement quality management such TQM, so that 'me-too' products appear in the marketplace all promising the same level of quality. This is hardly differentiating
Customer loyalty programmes (CLPs)	The differentiation impact here has been reduced by ubiquity. CLPs are easily imitated and not always cost-effective. The airline industry with its 'air miles' programme is perhaps one of the most well-known CLPs.
	However, they can
	• Reduce demand for some paid tickets
	• Limit the availability of seats on popular flights which could have been sold at higher prices
	• Irritate loyal customers who cannot 'cash in' their air miles easily
Price	There is the perception that low prices may impact on quality of the finished product in the eyes of consumer.
	Wal-Mart has been able to maintain its low price position by substantial supply-chain power to enforce low prices. This has given them unique cost advantages which a new firm would find very hard to match.
	Trout concedes that a high price differentiation strategy based on more than just quality can be successful if accompanied by a range of other factors such as being first in a market or by obtaining attribute ownership.
	He cites the Apple iPod, Rolex watches and North Face (Gore-Tex) as examples of products which have been successful with high price differentiation
Line extension	The range of products offered can be a differentiation point but size of selection is critical. Toys 'R' Us have been very successful due to their focus and huge selection.
	New line extensions need to counter consumer scepticism that advertised changes may simply be cosmetic and not significantly different
Differentiation based on the company positioning itself as environmentally friendly or socially responsible	Trout argues that this could be a source of differentiation but notes:
	• The firm must find a willingness among customers to pay higher prices to ensure environmental quality
	• Credible information must be available to the consumer at low cost about the environmental and social advantages of consumption

4.2 Marketing planning (7)

SAMPLING

The process of sampling is crucial and it is cost and time saving. It would not be possible for an organization to carry out an investigation of an entire market or population within a reasonable time frame and cost. Instead, a firm may wish to take samples of consumers. There are a number of ways in which these samples could be taken.

Students also have to consider the benefits and costs of each sampling method. To do this the criteria used to evaluate each method will be applied consistently. The **key factors** are time taken, cost, and degree of accuracy required and bias accepted.

A full description of bias and its implications for statistical work is outside the realms of this study guide. However, we should note that researchers try to minimize bias as much as they possibly can.

Sample method	Description	Time taken and cost considerations	Accuracy and bias
Random	In a sample survey, there is an equal chance that any particular respondent will be chosen	Can be time-consuming and skilled interviewers may be required. It potentially can be very costly	Given that there are no preconditions, random sampling has the least bias. For niche or technological product surveys, random samples may not generate enough accurate data as compared to quota
Quota	Respondents are segmented into specific groups which share similar characteristics. The interviewer is then given a target to sample. For example, 10 males aged 18-25 are questioned. Once target is fulfilled no more are asked	Given smaller number of respondents, quota may be cheaper than random. Time will be needed to set up segments	If a company requires that respondents have specialist knowledge, e.g. technological products, then quota may be more accurate than random but bias is increased due to pre-selection of respondents
Stratified	Similar to quota but there are no targets. Respondents are random selected from segments	See quota	See quota
Cluster	Geographical areas are used as the group characteristic. Respondents are then randomly sampled	Again there are similarities to quota	Regional bias may exist especially if there are significant economic and social differences between the regions. Opinion polls based on regions need to be treated with caution
Snowballing	Snowballing is a method of sampling in which existing study subjects recruit future subjects from among their acquaintances. The launch of the premium ice-cream Haagen Dazs in the UK was considered to be a groundbreaking marketing launch and a good example of how snowballing can be used to obtain feedback to help position the brand in the mind of the intended market segment.	The time taken can be considerable. Given the small number of respondents, snowballing can be cost-effective	There could be significant bias in this method as influential stakeholders pass on the information of the product to 'other' influential people. This could generate a very narrow range of feedback but of course this may be what was intended

You could now tackle question 2, page 109.

4.2 Marketing planning (8)

SALES FORECASTING AND TRENDS

NOTE FOR TEACHERS

This area is perceived by some students as difficult. The following excerpt from 'Further clarifications to the IB *Business and Management Guide* (2008)' should allow students to see what they are required to cover.

> In examinations, students will not be asked to calculate sales trends and forecasts using moving-average or other techniques. They must, however, understand the nature of the process in order to be able to 'analyse sales trends and forecasts from given data' (for example a stimulus in an examination) and to be able to 'evaluate the significance for marketing and resource planning'.

Some important definitions

The trend: The underlying movement or pattern of the data presented. In many sales forecasting models, the forecast sales of a product are given over a period of months or even years. This is called a time series. The trend is the underlying pattern of the data of this time series.

The diagram illustrates a set of sales data in time series form, and the trend.

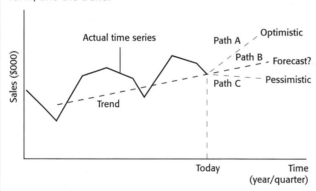

Sales data in time series form, trend, and various forecasts.

Source: Powell (1991)

The trend line can be extended to forecast the future path of sales on the understanding that the trend of external factors will continue into the future (as shown by path B). However, with new information on external factors coming to light, a forecast may need to be adjusted either optimistically (path A) or pessimistically (path C). Whichever path is chosen, it is reasonable to say that the further the trend line is extended the more likely it will prove to be inaccurate.

Seasonal and cyclical variation: The trend may have regular variations. For example, sales of tents and camping equipment may traditionally peak in the warmer months. This is called a **seasonal variation**. However, over a much longer period of years, other variations in camping equipment sales may also be experienced. These longer-term swings are called **cyclical variations** as they depend on the various 'ups and downs' that an economy inevitably goes through.

Random variations: In addition to the regular movements of trend and seasonal factors, there are 'one-off' events which affect data. These could include the feel-good factor generated with the election of a new president or a major sporting occasion such as the Olympic Games. These are termed **random variations**.

The impact of sales trends and forecasts on marketing and resource planning

We shall see in the next unit how the product life cycle can be used to advise managers on appropriate action which needs to be taken as the product enters each individual phase of its 'life'. We will also be able to illustrate how the firm can use extension strategies in order to prolong this life and extend sales when the inevitable competition arrives or simply when consumers have become bored with a product in its current form.

The product life cycle also has implications for human resource planning, cash flow management and production.

Ultimately, as we saw in the decision-making model of unit 1.6, if a firm is using this generic model wisely, then they must systematically review performance and gather data frequently to be able to judge whether a new marketing strategy or human resource decision was justified. Trend and forecast information in this context has a vital role to play in resource planning and to a large extent determines whether a strategic move was the right one, given the information available at the time.

4.3 Product (1)

NOTE FOR TEACHERS

It is unlikely that an established firm will concentrate on marketing and producing only one product. For competitive reasons, a firm may produce a range of products (line extension) to satisfy different market segments or, if the brand is successful (e.g. the Virgin brand), branch out into a whole different range of markets from airlines to soft drinks to weddings (brand extension).

It has often been stated that the product element in the marketing mix is the most important to get right. A marketing mix based on an original promotional campaign backed by an aggressive pricing strategy and a wide distribution network can fail if the product does not satisfy consumer expectations. It is principally for this reason that the IB Business and Management course for both HL and SL pays particular attention to the role of the product, the product life cycle, portfolio analysis and the importance of branding.

THE CLASSIFICATION OF PRODUCTS

Gillespie (2003) identifies five types of consumer goods:

- Staple items – essential everyday purchases
- Emergency – self-explanatory
- Durable – goods which are not consumed immediately but over a period of time, even years
- Non-durable: food items and perishables which will need to be consumed quickly
- Specialty goods – not classified as everyday items but perhaps linked to special occasions or other seasonal factors.

It is interesting to note that the classification used here is determined principally by consumption purchasing behaviour rather than by the goods themselves. A chocolate bar could be a staple item, emergency, non-durable or a specialty good depending on the purchasing intention.

PRODUCT INNOVATION AND TECHNOLOGICAL CHANGE

According to Marketing Intelligence Services Ltd, in 1987 there were 14,254 new products introduced into the United States. In 1998, the number of new products that year was 25,181, or 69 for every day of the year.

Most of these products were neither new nor innovative. Trout (2008) refers to the majority of these as simply adding 'bells, whistles and tweaks' and were effectively modest extension strategies (see page 93 for more about extension strategies).

However since 1998 and the application of Moore's law (see box) there has been an explosion of growth of new technological product aimed at the consumer. Product innovation has become very important to cash flow and even for survival. For example, it was estimated that, for companies such as Hewlett Packard, 75% of global sales in one year were exclusively generated by new products created in the previous year. This imposes a huge burden on companies to be constantly innovative in a rapidly changing technological landscape.

Moore's law

Moore's law states that the number of transistors which can be placed cheaply on an integrated circuit board has increased exponentially, doubling every two years. This has enormous implications for processing speed and memory capability which have also grown sharply. In plain English, it would appear that technological products can do much more for much less every year. Apple and other manufacturers have clearly taken full advantage.

Consider the table below which lists the changes to some of the **product portfolio** of the Apple Corporation since 1998, a company whose philosophy has been built around innovative product design. (A revision is defined as a cosmetic makeover perhaps slightly altering the external features of the product. A re-incarnation is defined as a completely new version of the product with changes made both internally and externally.)

Apple product	First appeared	Number of revisions and re-incarnations
iPod	2001	7
iPod Mini (then Nano)	2005	6
iPod Shuffle	2005	3
iPod Touch	2007	3
iPhone	2007	2
iMac (Desktop)	1998	8
iBook then MacBook (laptop)	2003	5

Source: www.macrumors.com

It is expected that by the time this guide is published, Apple will have added a new updated version of the iPhone and iPod Touch. The MacBook has already had a revision since the writing of this guide began. The iPod Shuffle has been replaced with a smaller voice-activated version.

4.3 Product (2)

PRODUCT RESEARCH AND DEVELOPMENT: A DISCUSSION ON FINANCING ISSUES

This section will be covered in two areas when we look at the role of patents and intellectual property rights (page 121) and the product life cycle which we turn to next.

The product life cycle

It seems obvious that a product is developed, then launched and will go through various stages of growth/ saturation/maturity before it enters the decline phase of the product life cycle. Decisions then will have to be made either to retain or to replace the product. If the latter, the cycle begins again with investment in research and development to create a replacement product.

The traditional product life cycle in an era of limited choice is given below.

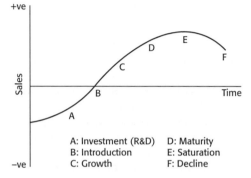

A: Investment (R&D)	D: Maturity
B: Introduction	E: Saturation
C: Growth	F: Decline

Traditional product life cycle (focus on sales)

Relationship of product life cycle to investment, profit and cash flow

The first stage of a product's life cycle is often overlooked. The diagram above indicates that, in the early stages, a product may be a drain on cash flow as the research and development costs need to be paid. This phase is often referred to as the **investment** part of the product's life cycle.

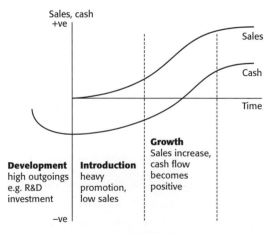

New product life cycle (focus on sales and cash)

Given the traditional shape of the life cycle, we can expect that even after the research and development costs have been paid, the firm can expect cash to be leaving the business until the point when significant growth in sales is achieved. This is because during the **introduction** phase

The reality today is quite different. The traditional product life cycle is only an *observation* of the sales behaviour of a typical product. Some product life cycles experience a very brief existence when goods are withdrawn quickly. Others may take a much longer time to enter the growth phase and the product may experience a dip in sales before regaining market share.

In the new millennium with the 'tyranny of choice' there has been considerable discussion on the shape of the new life cycle but broad agreement that, except for particularly loyal branded items, the life cycle is getting shorter.

the firm will need to support the product with promotional spending, especially on informative advertising.

The cash flow position of a product relative to its product life cycle is given in the diagram below.

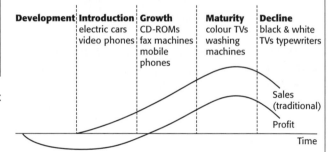

New product life cycle (cash flow and profits)

Finally, assuming that the product enters the growth phase without the company having to use all its reserves of cash to fund the promotional effort, sales of the product will start to rise at an increasing rate. Assuming also that the firm can confidently manufacture the product in larger production runs, the firm should start to experience some economies of scale and, with profit margins rising, the company should start to finally reap the reward for taking the risk of launching the product in the first place – profits.

The amount of profit will depend on the length of the growth phase before the maturity and saturation stages are experienced. It is also important to consider that other competitor firms may be attracted into this market by the thought of making profit themselves. Depending on the nature of the patent (unit 5.6) and other barriers to entry, the original firm may find that it faces competition. This will erode the opportunities for the firm to continue to make large profits.

4.3 Product (3)

THE PRODUCT LIFE CYCLE, THE MARKETING MIX AND EXTENSION STRATEGIES

In addition to researching the product life cycle, interested students may choose to investigate the **diffusion of innovations** model, suggested by Rogers. The language used is technical but it provides an alternative way of looking at consumer behaviour when faced with technological products, and how firms should alter their marketing mixes. Rogers' work is important as it gave us the classic marketing terms **'early adopter'** and **'late majority'**. The early adopter tends to be insensitive to price and is willing to take a risk in order to claim to be the first purchaser of a new technological product, while the 'late majority' tend to be conservative and price sensitive, preferring to wait for the benefits of the new product to be well known before making a purchasing decision.

Summary of the link between the stages of product life cycle and possible adjustments to the marketing mix

The following list is not exhaustive and other appropriate action could be taken.

Stage of the product life cycle	Adjustment to the marketing mix?
Introduction	Heavy promotional spending on informative advertising required Distribution channels may be few Price skimming or penetration. The strategy will depend on the product
Growth	Distribution will need to change if product sales grow rapidly. Price increases may be feasible
Maturity	Sales growth slowdown. Prices may need to be lowered as new competition enters the market. Promotion should focus on differentiation
Saturation	Sales growth has peaked and decision needs to be taken about extension strategies (see below)
Decline	Strategic or tactical decisions need to be made about the future of this product. Price should be at lowest possible. Promotion spending should be reminder orientated. Product repackaging possible although this will add to costs. Some distribution channels will need to be closed

Extension strategies

As a product enters the maturity or saturation stage of the product life cycle (some textbooks combine them both into one classification) a firm may decide to 'breathe new life' into the sales of a product by introducing extension strategies. (An extension strategy does not occur at the introduction or growth phase of the cycle.)

We can highlight some popular extension strategies:

- Modification of the existing product with minor changes such as repackaging or the inclusion of additional new features. This is a classic extension strategy in the DVD retail industry.
- Increase promotional spending or offer reduced prices for a limited time.
- Develop a line extension to complement the existing product to boost sales of both products. (Gillette will add a new shaving cream to boost sales of its razors.)
- Try to find a new market (Ansoff's market development) for the product, perhaps researching overseas markets.
- Repositioning the product. This is risky and examples of outright success are rare. (We can note the success of GlaxoSmithKline in repositioning the health drink Lucozade into a sports/activity beverage.)

Choosing an appropriate extension strategy

Extension strategies should aim to be cost-effective.

- There is little point in spending huge sums of money on a promotional campaign if the profits generated are too small, or if in the process the firm uses up all its cash reserves supporting just one product while neglecting others in its product mix.
- The firm may need to undertake new market research before investing in the extension strategy to identify an appropriate course of action. This will raise costs and take time.
- Trout confirms that there is considerable consumer scepticism about the benefits of line extensions.

Director's cut

Movie companies seem able to make a little go a long way – consider the following DVD repackaging ideas:

- Limited Edition
- Special Limited Edition
- Ultimate Limited Edition
- Ultimate Collector's Special Limited Edition
- Uncut Edition
- 'What the censors did not wish you to see' Edition
- 'Special Edition with deleted scenes now added'

Students are invited to add their own examples.

4.3 Product (4)

APPLYING THE BCG MATRIX TO A GIVEN SITUATION

The Boston Consulting Group Matrix is one the most powerful tools a firm can use to assist strategic decision-making. We provide an example from the author's own experience to see how we can apply this model and satisfy the learning outcome.

An engaging way to apply the BCG matrix in real life is to take a trip to your local DVD or video store and note down the films which are for rent and the shelf space made available for selected titles. A visit to a DVD store north of Auckland, New Zealand, during early 2009 revealed the following:

- **New releases** of very successful films such as the *Dark Knight* seemed to be all rented out. These films charged the highest rental price and took up a huge amount of shelf space. According to the owner, there were 20 copies of this film to rent out, the most of any title. (Star?)

- **Classic movies** released on DVD such as the original *Star Wars Trilogy* from 1977, Hollywood musicals and James Bond films had a few copies available but according to the owner were periodically rented out so that on occasion no copies were left. Shelf space devoted to these titles was considerable and surprising given that some of these films date back to the 1950s. (Cash cow?)

- **Festival** or **world cinema** films (see section on segmentation) had a separate shelf. The films were packaged and recommended heavily by the store with, in some cases, film reviews from local and international papers extolling the virtue of each movie with quotes taken from critics. (Problem children?)

- Finally, shelf space was given over to films priced at the lowest rental cost. The shelf seemed to mostly contain **sequels** (e.g. Son of Mask, Resident Evil 5 or Police Academy 7) with some actors whom the author admits having never heard of. (Dog?)

Applying the BCG matrix:

	High relative market share	Low relative market share
Market growth high	New releases *Star*	Festival/World *Problem Child*
Market growth low	Classic movies *Cash Cow*	Sequels *Dog*

BRANDING

Definition

Defining a brand can be a difficult task. In the 1950s and 1960s, a brand could easily be defined as a product name, a trademark or even just a logo. Trout in 2008 refers to a brand as being:

The sum of all experiences and values associated with a particular product.

A brand now has to encapsulate values, perceptions and experiences in terms of qualities such as health, luxury, quality, reliability and youthfulness. In recent years the Apple iPod has risen to become the 'epitome of cool and belonging', of luxury and necessity, and of acceptance and difference. Branding is a complex and to older consumers sometimes a puzzling topic. It would be interesting for students to have a conversation with an older relative about the role and importance of brands.

There is general agreement that a strong brand identity can create awareness and loyalty, despite the 'tyranny of choice' which we identified at the beginning of this topic.

Other benefits of branding

- Branding can enable companies to charge higher prices and therefore enjoy greater margins.

- Higher margins will impact heavily on distribution channels as suppliers will be eager to stock 'premium priced' items.

- Through loyalty programmes, The company encourages customers to develop a 'relationship' with their brand, thus deepening the 'connection' between company and customer.

- If the brand of an existing product in the same industry has become well established, this reduces the risk of launching a new product under the same brand. Sony has benefited enormously from its association with the Walkman, Discman and PlayStations to increase sales of televisions and DVD players.

- New segments may be created in a market, virtually based on the positioning of the brand. Singapore Airlines' Raffles Class, which is priced above First Class, was created on the strength of the airline's success in niche markets.

- Branding can create powerful intangible assets for a company and increase the value of the company's balance sheet, allowing it to borrow or attract additional funds for expansion.

Trout (2008) succinctly explains the key benefit of having a strong brand identity.

It is better to be first in mind, than to be first in the market. Marketing is not a battle of products. It is a battle of perceptions.

Clearly therefore the power of a successful brand in the minds of consumers cannot be overstated. This explains why many companies spend millions of dollars each year reminding, persuading and reassuring customers that their brand is the one to go for.

4.3 Product (5)

TYPES OF BRANDING

Family branding

A business can use the same brand on a range of products, for example, Heinz beans, ketchup and soup. Some writers have been critical of companies that use brand extension over a range of unconnected products or services in different industries. The often quoted example of overextending the brand is the Virgin Group which has been involved at various times in airlines, soft drinks, property development and real estate, cinema, music, mobile phones, financial services, weddings (Virgin Brides) health clubs and railways.

Product branding

A company produces a generic product and gives each variation on this product a name. Van der Bergh produces Flora, Delight, Krona, Stork, Blue Band and Echo. These are all margarines.

Own branding

A retailer such as a supermarket may ask Heinz or another famous bean producer to purchase beans from a bean processing plant, can them, and, instead of the traditional Heinz label, the supermarket's own label is placed on the can. As we shall see in a later section on contribution (page 112) there may be compelling reasons which encourage the supermarket and Heinz to do this.

Manufacturer's brand

In specialist, niche or industrial markets, the actual manufacturer of the good or service may brand their products which may be unfamiliar to the mass market but familiar to 'insiders' or 'early adopters'. The exclusive end of the hi-fi market in which turntables (Goldmund or Linn) or speakers (Krell or Apogee) can be bought and sold for many thousands of dollars is a good example.

Global branding

A key consequence of the spread of globalization, offshoring and multinational activity has been the creation of the global brand.

A global brand presence for one company can create very high entry barriers against competitors.

The top 10 global brands according to Interbrand contain many household names that enjoy significant global loyalty as of February 2009:

1 Coca-Cola
2 Microsoft
3 IBM
4 General Electric
5 Intel
6 Disney
7 McDonalds
8 Nokia
9 Toyota
10 Google

Maintaining a global brand is not an easy or inexpensive task.

- The consumer's expectation of equivalent brand performance worldwide puts a great burden on firms.

- A poorly performing brand in one region can have a significant impact on the same brand in other countries.

- 'Homogenizing a brand' around the world, given the enormous cultural and linguistic differences which still exist, remains the toughest challenge that a firm wishing to go global can face. There is a sad tale of the Vauxhall Nova which didn't sell too well in Spain (*no va* means 'will not go' in Spanish)!

You could now tackle question 3, page 109.

4.4 Price (1)

PRICING METHODS

There are a large number of pricing methods a firm can employ. The chosen one will depend on a number of factors, i.e. the firm's objectives, the degree of market competition, the nature of the product and the characteristics of the external environment in which the firm is trading.

Although we use the term pricing strategy, strictly speaking a number of these pricing ideas are methods, especially the cost-based ones. These pricing methods are used as part of an overall marketing mix to help guide a marketing strategic direction.

The table lists these pricing methods according to the IB *Business and Management Guide* with summary discussion points.

Method or strategy	Description	Example of appropriate use	Other issues/problems
Cost-plus (cost-based)	Price is determined by calculating cost of individual product and a profit margin is added	Expensive luxury items. One-off purchases in small niche markets. e.g. classic cars	More a pricing method rather than a strategy. Cost-plus ignores market demand conditions
Price leadership	Market leader by market share sets price	Asset-led marketing firms can use this strategy such as British Airways or Singapore Airlines	Market leader may enjoy brand loyalty and may make it difficult for other firms to follow high prices
Penetration (market-based)	Firm tries to undercut existing market firms with lower price	An established firm trying to enter into a new market. Virgin Airlines has offered lower prices on popular routes as part of an entry strategy. Ryan Air and EasyJet are other examples	Need substantial cash reserves to support potential short-term losses. How easy will it be to raise prices once the firm is established without losing goodwill?
Skimming (market-based)	Identify a group/segment and try to target niche customers by charging high prices to attract early adopters	New technological products such as Blu-Ray DVDs. Suitable for innovative products in niche markets to recoup research and development costs	Market growth may be limited until prices are reduced. Problems of me-too competitors from other firms once the patent runs out, impacting on pricing
HL only			
Contribution (marginal)	Set price to cover at least the variable cost of that unit	Hotels in low/off-peak seasons may use contribution pricing to attract customers reluctant to pay full prices. Can offer flexibility to firms in the BCG matrix. See below	Will only cover variable costs and hence not guaranteed to make a profit. When fixed costs have to be paid, contribution strategy may have to be reviewed
Absorption cost and full-cost pricing (cost-based)	Price is set by calculating variable costs and adding a part of allocated overhead. In full costing this allocation of overhead cost such as rent is decided by some accepted criterion such as floor space occupied or number of employees	In the BCG matrix, a firm can allocate the overhead in such a way to allow lower prices on Problem Children and higher prices on Cash Cows. Microsoft could offer lower prices on new software and higher prices on an established market leader such as Office	Full-cost pricing requires a careful consideration of the overhead allocation involving time and resources. Absorption is arbitrary and could be perceived as unfair if some products carry a greater burden of the overhead cost

(continued)

4.4 Price (2)

PRICING METHODS (continued)

Predatory (competition)	A firm sets a very low price with the intention to remove competition from the market	In the print media industry in the UK, News International has been accused of charging very low prices for some of its tabloid papers to try and buy loyalty in a competitive market and to remove rivals. No-frills airlines such as EasyJet and Ryan Air have taken huge slices of market share from British Airways on some routes	Setting very low prices can be illegal in some countries when it is classified as unfair competition. This strategy can lead to price wars, the so-called 'race to the bottom'. There have been some concerns over product quality and safety in the airline industry
Going rate or market pricing	Firms follow each other in a market either voluntarily or involuntarily, offer very similar prices and try to compete on product or other elements in the marketing mix	The fast-food industry seems to follow this price strategy and differentiates on product, positioning and physical evidence	With price differentiation not possible firms have to create new perceptions of their products in the minds of the consumer to create brand loyalty. Expensive and time-consuming for new firms in the industry
Price discrimination (market-based)	A firm charging a range of prices for effectively the same product or service depending on the price elasticity of demand of the end user	A movie theatre offers different prices for adults, students, families and the elderly. (Some have segmented the movie audience market even further by offering reclining beds or couches with waitress service, or 3D IMAX)	The firm must be able to prevent 'leakage' or price discrimination will not be successful. Leakage is the ability of the end user to 'cheat', e.g. a small adult tries to buy a child's ticket. Leakage prevention (such as showing ID) should be low cost or gains from price discrimination will be reduced significantly
Loss-leader pricing (market-based)	Product is sold below cost to encourage consumers into a retail environment who will then hopefully purchase other items with higher margins	The classis loss-leader approach is adopted by supermarkets that offer milk, bread or some soft drinks at below-cost prices	Not a strategy that can continue indefinitely as losses are made. Many loss-leader goods are rotated periodically to maintain consumer interest and to not 'hurt' a brand
Psychological (market-based)	The product is priced to break some psychological barrier to create positive word of mouth or is priced due to cultural factors	The first sub $50 DVD player on the market or the world's first $100 laptop. An Indian company, Tata, has set the price for its base model car at US $2200 in 2009 In Asia prices ending or beginning in 8 are considered lucky, prices beginning or ending in 4 unlucky	Consumer and cultural perceptions may take time to change. Once the psychological barrier has been breached there may be limited opportunity to set a new price point in the short run
Promotional (market-based)	Linked to psychological. Firms may have sales promotions or end-of-stock clearouts to shift older inventory or even to advertise that a retail outlet is closing	2 for the price of 1, extra-large bottles of soft drinks for the same price as regular bottles (e.g. 20% extra free), prizes, cereal boxes containing puzzles or games for children	Consumer annoyance regarding sales promotions (availability, paying delays, queuing). Promotions must be short term and infrequent or consumers will just wait for the promotion and not buy at the regular price. Significant costs of labelling new prices, changing retail displays. Some sales promotions may lead to lower than expected profits

4.4 Price (3)

THE IMPACT OF DEMAND AND SUPPLY ON PRICE

Without resorting to too much economics jargon, it can be argued that if conditions of demand and supply were to change because of a change in the economic environment (influencing demand) and a technological change (influencing supply), firms may need to adjust their pricing methods and strategies discussed above.

For example, a market-based pricing strategy will be heavily influenced by the current state of the economy. During the global slowdown of 2009, some companies will be looking to moderate any price increases. Price-skimming strategies may also need to be reviewed.

An increase in unemployment may allow some firms using cost-based methods to reduce some prices as there may be a fall in direct costs such as wages. Technology improvements may also reduce average costs, allowing companies further opportunities to reduce prices.

If a firm decides to change the price of a product, given some of the issues explained above, the initial concern will be the likely impact on the demand for the good in question. This point neatly leads us to consider the role of elasticity.

ELASTICITY: AN OVERVIEW

For the new syllabus from 2009, an elasticity formulae sheet will be given to all students in the final examinations. The student is directed to their textbook for detailed mathematical analysis.

We include a brief overview of the significance of elasticity for business decision-making and its relationship to the product life cycle and, by assumption, sales revenue.

Factors influencing price elasticity of demand and the role of income elasticity of demand

Three key factors influence the price elasticity of demand for a product and, for business decision-making, the degree to which business can set and influence the price they charge, namely:

- The number of substitutes a product has in the marketplace.

- The degree of 'brand loyalty and power' the product commands in the mind of the consumer.

- The proportion of income that it costs to purchase the product – the lower the percentage, the more price-inelastic the demand for the product

(e.g. a newspaper); the higher the percentage, the more price-elastic the demand for the product (e.g. a new car).

Businesses making or selling relatively high-priced goods will consider income elasticity of demand to see if demand for the product is easily influenced by changes in income; a critical point in 2009 and perhaps the year after.

Cross-elasticity and advertising elasticity of demand

Cross-elasticity and advertising elasticity both have a role to play in influencing business decision-making.

- **Cross-elasticity** is used to see the closeness of substitutes (a high positive figure) or the extent to which a product has a close complement (a high absolute negative value).

- **Advertising elasticity** can be used to look at the responsiveness of demand to a change in advertising expenditure (more detail is provided in the next unit). It is useful to see if changes in advertising or other above-the-line promotional spending can translate into increasing sales.

The relationship between elasticity and the product life cycle

This relationship was the subject of an examination question in May 2003. It is followed by a tutor's answer written in 15 minutes.

Question: Define the term Price Elasticity of Demand and explain why this is likely to change as the product moves through its life cycle.

The price elasticity of demand measures the responsiveness of demand to changes in the price of the product. A product which is very responsive is deemed to be elastic such as a chocolate bar with many potential substitutes. A product which is not responsive to prices changes is termed price inelastic. Examples include basic commodities such as salt or brand loyal goods such as Apple iPods. The price is not considered to be an influence on demand.

As a product moves from the introduction phase to the growth part of the product life cycle, it is likely that the product will be price inelastic. Early adopters of new products are considered to be price insensitive. Assuming the product is innovative and has been supported by a careful promotional campaign, the firm can expect to generate increasing revenue.

As the product begins to enter saturation, sales revenue growth may begin to slow down. Competition may enter the market and the number of possible substitutes will rise. The product is likely to become more elastic and the elasticity value will rise.

(continued)

4.4 Price (4)

ELASTICITY: AN OVERVIEW *(continued)*

The decline phase signals the beginning of a fall in revenue. Prices may have to be reduced significantly to attract late majority consumers. The price elasticity may rise further as the product becomes 'technologically obsolete' and demand falls dramatically. A firm may at this stage withdraw the product from the market.

Students are invited to comment on the depth and detail of the answer.

Contained within this answer is information highlighting the fundamental relationship between price elasticity and sales revenue. The table summarizes the key elements.

	Effect on revenue (inelastic demand)	Effect on revenue (elastic demand)
A significant price increase	Total revenue will rise	Total revenue will fall
A significant price decrease	Total revenue will fall	Total revenue will rise

So a significant cut in price for an elastic product with many substitutes will lead, it is expected, to a large increase in revenue.

On the other hand, inelastic demand implies that a product is not responsive to changes in price. If this is the case, the consumers are clearly brand loyal or perceive that there are few close substitutes. If the product enjoys high market share such as Nokia mobile phones or Microsoft Office, it would not be sensible to cut prices to increase sales.

A final word on elasticity estimates

Elasticity is a vital concept for businesses in their decision-making about pricing a product, especially in an adverse economic environment. An important consideration however is who calculates it? Should the firm calculate it or use an outside agency?

Some writers have argued that elasticity should be calculated by an independent market research agency to enhance objectivity and reliability. This process is costly but it may be a more accurate way of determining value and reducing bias.

4.5 Promotion (1)

INTRODUCTION

Traditional methods of promotion have come under renewed attack. The creation of new media technology has created both opportunities and threats for organizations. The growth of the Internet and the proliferation of media channels through cable and satellite TV have given businesses many new ways to reach and target audiences.

However, some of the new technology has also become a threat. Consumers are becoming irritated by junk e-mail and the practice of 'phishing'. Digital television through facilities such as SkyPlus allows viewers to record TV shows to be watched when desired. The idea of prime-time TV, where advertisers promoted products, ensuring the highest customer reach, is now becoming an anachronism. DVD recorders have been fitted with software which allows consumers to skip TV commercials when they record their favourite programmes.

In our analysis below, we must bear in mind these developments as we discuss the effectiveness of the traditional methods of above-the-line and below-the-line promotion.

ABOVE-THE-LINE AND BELOW-THE-LINE PROMOTION

The author was once asked by a student 'What is the line and where is it?', a valid question indeed. We define **above-the-line** as promotional activities which are directed at consumers through different media such as the cinema, radio and television. They can reach a large number of potential consumers at once, making the average cost of above-the-line advertising small. However, firms are not able to receive immediate feedback from consumers about the virtues or successes of a TV commercial or radio advertisement.

Below-the-line activities are focused on promotional techniques that allow immediate consumer feedback, such as sales promotions in stores, public relations exercises (where there is direct contact with stakeholders), direct mail, store coupons and competitions. Some of these methods of promotion can be successful and cost-effective for small firms that may not be able to afford to advertise by contracting media space. Online e-mail advertising direct to the customer's inbox may be regarded as below-the-line.

We can summarize the key functions of promotion as those actions that inform, persuade or remind consumers about the potential benefits of purchasing a particular good or service. However, there is considerable debate as to the most effective way of achieving this. Promotional effectiveness and the choice of method used will depend on a range of factors such as budget, intended reach, frequency, desired impact and, of course, business objectives. We shall begin by looking at a recent example.

The promotional mix for the race to the White House

On 23 October 2008, just over a week before the US presidential election, the *Guardian* newspaper in the UK published a survey of the spending on promotion by the candidates for the US presidency in order to inform, persuade and remind their potential voters. The table makes interesting reading (all figures in $m).

Candidate	Broadcast media such as TV and radio	Telemarketing and fundraising through direct mail	Print media spending	Internet media spending	Campaign direct mail	Total
Barack Obama	160	24	13	10.3	0.01	207.3
John McCain	111	6.7	0.004	3.01	2.6	123.3

We can draw some conclusions:

- Both candidates spent the largest amount on the same media to promote their candidacy.
- Internet media spending was the fourth most popular method of promotion for the Obama campaign. (We saw the importance of e-finance in the recent presidential campaign, page 64.)
- Print media was hardly used by the McCain camp.
- Direct mailing outlining the policies and intentions of the campaign rated low in the list of promotional activities, but lowest for Obama.

So, despite our earlier comments about traditional methods of promotion being under threat, it turns out that, in perhaps the most important promotional campaign on the planet, TV, radio and cinema were still the most preferred media to convey a message.

4.5 Promotion (2)

THE EFFECTIVENESS OF PROMOTIONAL METHODS

The above example applied to a situation which occurs every four years. We now discuss the more orthodox promotional campaigns which impact on our daily lives as consumers.

Key terms

We shall use the following criteria to analyse the effectiveness of promotion.

- **Targeting:** the ability of the promotional technique to target the right customers to avoid wasting the promotional method and marketing effort.
- **Reach:** the ability of the promotional method to reach the widest audience possible.

- **Frequency:** how often the advertiser wants the message to be repeated.
- **Cost:** measured by average cost per viewer.
- Ability to provide instant **feedback** to the business to gauge impact.

Promotion: when it goes wrong

Students are invited to research one of the most famous promotions which went wrong: the "Buy a Hoover and receive a free flight on an aeroplane" campaign.

Promotional technique	Examples and discussion
Broadcast media	TV, cinema and radio. Can have dramatic impact on a large audience (consider average costs per viewer of advertising during major sporting events such as the Superbowl or the Oscars). Can be too expensive for small businesses or new start-ups. Not able to gauge direct feedback. Under threat from new technology. Cinema has a captive audience and can be segmented by film genre. Frequency can irritate some consumers
Printed material such as newspapers and magazines	Allows close targeting as each newspaper has its own readership profile and audience. Cheaper than TV to advertise with high reach in countries with large populations. Printed material can be used to inform and convey a good deal of information
Point-of-sale material and company newsletters	Cheap to produce and immediate feedback possible if given out in store. Can be specifically targeted and updated quickly. Visual impact limited. Many may be discarded immediately if the consumer is not interested
Coupons, special offers, competitions	Money-off coupons can be very successful and are cheap to produce. Direct contact with the customer. Reach may be limited
Internet	Very cheap with potentially unlimited reach. Spamming and phishing is irritating for consumers. Easy for consumer to delete. Marginal cost is effectively zero
Sales promotions	Need to be short term or the customer will just wait for the sale and not purchase products with higher margins. Sales promotions need to be eye-catching to generate good word-of-mouth. Costs of re-labelling and store design. Overuse may lead to consumer fatigue and scepticism. Goodwill lost if item unavailable or store crowded
Public relations/word of mouth	Sometimes referred to uncontrollable methods of promotion because even with the most tightly controlled media event, the success of public relations exercises depends on the perception of the stakeholders. Staging media events to generate goodwill is not cheap and reach may be limited unless backed up by broadcast media support on TV or radio or in the printed media. This cannot always be guaranteed. Word-of-mouth promotion is something that every company wishes to have but only if it is positive. There is an old saying: *'If a customer has had good service, then they will tell 5 friends. If they have had a bad experience, they will tell 15.'*

4.5 Promotion (3)

GUERRILLA AND VIRAL MARKETING

Although not on the syllabus, students are invited to research for themselves the impact of guerrilla and viral marketing on promotional activities. The creation of social networking sites has provided an amazing platform for companies to promote themselves through word-of-mouth and 'buzz'. This is the general idea behind **viral marketing** although, in keeping with other non-controllable methods of promotion, 'buzz' can be open to different kinds of interpretation and the original message from the company may be lost.

Guerrilla marketing is more controversial. It is designed to be a cheap but provocative risk-taking form of promotion. It includes a mixture of traditional below-the-line methods such as direct mail and newsletters and aspects of viral marketing as described above.

It has been used by start-ups that cannot afford to spend sums of working capital on promotional activities. Some companies such as *Hell's Pizza* in New Zealand have used guerrilla marketing to gain attention but also to push the boundaries of the Advertising Standards Authority to the limit. Older consumers have complained about some of their campaigns while some younger consumers have applauded their efforts to be different and take calculated risks. Students are invited to check out the website and make up their own minds.

4.6 Place (1)

NOTE FOR TEACHERS

This element of the marketing mix is critical for businesses to get right. Unfortunately, it is commonly misunderstood and overlooked by students, especially when asked to evaluate a mix or marketing strategy.

This section tries to provide a straightforward analysis of the main channels of distribution with students being

invited in class to discuss the merits of each channel, given their own experiences as 'end users'. It is also worth noting that future sections on e-commerce and outsourcing have close links to distribution. We will consider in more detail the future of retailing in unit 4.8.

DISTRIBUTION CHANNELS

- **Definition:** The channel of distribution describes how a final good or service passes from producer to end user. The end user is usually a consumer but we must not forget that we can also have industrial markets to supply.

Several distribution channels are open to a producer. The channel chosen will depend on the nature and complexity of the good or service and on whether the target is a mass market or a niche market.

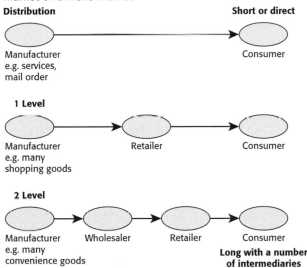

Channels of distribution

Examples of appropriate channels: two extreme cases

Baked beans are normally distributed via **long channels**. Wholesalers and retailers break down very large quantities of cans from the producer to take advantage of buying with economies of scale. The product is not complex and is easily transportable. This system of distribution allows baked bean manufacturers to target as many customers as possible (it is a mass market).

Industrial cranes for use in civil engineering are generally distributed via **very short** channels. The product is delivered by the producer to the industrial end user directly. The product is complex, difficult to move easily, and serves a very small niche market segment. Training, installation and supervision may be required before the end user can successfully operate the equipment. The product will be very expensive and may require continued customer support.

The role of agents in the distribution process: help or hindrance?

Wholesaling and retailing are the traditional way of distributing FMCGs (fast-moving consumer goods).

However, in some markets such as the real estate industry or the luxury car market, agents have been used to provide local knowledge or expertise to ensure a smooth exchange between buyer and seller. In the case of the real estate market, important legal procedures may require the need for an agent to conduct the transaction. Agents are paid a commission on completion of work undertaken.

However, in the role of human resource management, especially in the media and sporting industries, agents have been criticized for adding an intermediary function which may or may not ensure the smooth transition of an exchange between, for example, a soccer club (the buyer) and a potential player (the seller). Agents in these markets may delay the distribution process by, for example, bargaining for a higher price as their fee depends on the financial outcome. Interested students should look at the saga of footballer Carlos Tevez's transfer between West Ham and Manchester United in 2007.

In common with other distribution channels, the case for and against agents will depend on the nature of the good or service being traded.

- Agents can add an extra step in the distribution process and this will raise costs to the final end user.

But

- If a firm is looking to move into a new international market, it may be too expensive or risky to set up a distribution network in an untried region without local knowledge.

- An agent with local knowledge can act as a fast method to enable a firm to establish a market presence without spending large sums of money.

- There may be cost savings for primary data research as well.

> **DVD resource**
>
> The movie *Jerry Maguire* (1997) has some excellent material on the role of agents, mission statements and corporate social responsibility.

4.6 Place (2)

SUPPLY CHAIN MANAGEMENT AND LOGISTICS

Definition

Russell-Walling (2007) defines a supply chain as:

> *a chain that is made up of physical and information links between suppliers and the company on one side and the company and its customers on the other.*

- Activities in supply chain or logistics management include production planning, purchasing, materials handling and (within logistics) transport and storage (using warehouse and distribution centres).
- Vertical mergers (see page 26), both upstream and downstream, focus on the importance of managing the supply chain.

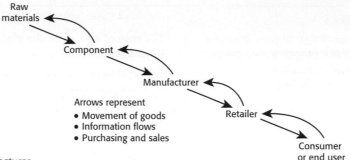

Arrows represent
- Movement of goods
- Information flows
- Purchasing and sales

The supply chain for a manufacturer

Globalization, outsourcing and the supply chain

Given our earlier comments surrounding the impact of globalization and the growth of outsourcing, supply chain management has taken on a whole new competitive focus and there is an urgency for large firms to trim costs and improve efficiency.

However, there can be problems.

- When a Finnish mobile phone producer manufactures a mobile phone in China to ship to a retailer in Australia, the supply chain is potentially stretched to breaking point. The more links in the chain over a greater distance, the more likely that mistakes will occur.

- As we saw in previous studies on the impact of ICT and globalization (page 48), some countries are not as well 'connected' as others. In some very cheap cost centres, a phone and a fax line is the most advanced ICT available. It may be hard to build a reliable logistical chain around these two.

However, Russell-Walling concludes that:

> *it is not surprising that many companies feel that, in order to draw every last cost saving, outsourcing in the new millennium has become the mantra for proponents of the global supply chain. A number of manufacturers have outsourced every link in the logistics process.*

As Kevin O'Connell from IBM remarked in 2005:

> *The supply chain is no longer a back-office activity. It has become **the** competitive weapon in the boardroom.*

4.7 Entry into international markets (1)

OPPORTUNITIES

In previous units we have discussed some of the reasons why considerable opportunities exist for an organization that intends to enter a foreign market.

- The growth and spread of globalization and the potential cost savings which can be made.

- The growing importance of offshoring (page 46) which has allowed firms to subcontract work into overseas countries. Offshoring can also provide an opportunity to gain knowledge of these markets at a relatively low cost, before committing to fully enter the market, thus offshoring helps to minimize the risk of entering.

- An improved economic tie through regional trading blocs has increased the attractiveness to firms entering these regions. By being inside a member country new firms may be able to avoid quota and tariff restrictions and take advantage of government incentives or relocation allowances.

- Increased information and the availability of training to understand local economies and cultural differences to minimize misunderstandings.

- The Ansoff and Porter growth models strongly advocate market development or differentiation to define a new competitive strategic position. Both could be achieved by operating in an overseas market.

- The improvement in ICT with opportunities for larger spans of control and to structure an organization according to geographical region.

THREATS

The threats to moving into an overseas market can be classified as weak or credible. Weak threats normally turn up in examination answers where students may have been asked to consider a number of threats to a firm moving into a new overseas market and have not thought through the discussion as part of their answer.

Credible threats need to be considered before a firm decides to take action, and can be considered alongside some of the external constraints which we identified in our earlier work on the decision-making process.

Weak threat 1

- **The firm will have to be aware of language and cultural barriers**

It is unlikely that a firm would not enter into a new market just because the management were not fluent in the local language. We have already noted the availability of support to help firms overcome some of the barriers to communication identified in unit 2.3.

Weak threat 2

- **The product may not be successful in this new market**

This could be true for any market and not just an overseas market. We must assume that the firm will conduct extensive primary and secondary research before they enter, in order to understand the competitive nature of the market, either by conducting a SWOT analysis or by analysing Porter's five forces. The Ansoff matrix does not assume that market development will be risk-free.

Weak threat 3

- **There will be competition from local producers**

Again we must assume that the firm will do its homework. They should be able to determine the needs and wants of existing customers and be able to determine whether a market gap exists and whether the market can grow significantly beyond its current size.

Credible threat 1

- **Legal issues**

A new firm entering into an overseas market must ensure that they comply with local rules and regulations regarding the conditions of work and employment (particularly if they wish to bring in expatriate managers on work visas) and any minimum wage legislation. They will need to consider local taxation rules such as corporation tax and indirect tax.

(continued)

4.7 Entry into international markets (2)

THREATS *(continued)*

Credible threat 2

- **Economic and political instability**

Given the prevailing deteriorating external environment, firms looking to penetrate overseas markets will need to be aware that some developed countries have launched 'buy local' campaigns in favour of locally produced goods rather than imported products. (This move has been discredited by some writers as being counter-productive as a 'buy local' campaign may jeopardize potential export markets due to retaliation.)

However, perhaps more significantly, economic recession can lead to political instability in some overseas markets as governments struggle to tackle the growing list of problems created by the 'credit crunch' and the global downturn. This can impact considerably on a firm's ability to be successful in a new international market. The tragedy of Zimbabwe will be known to many but there is also growing unease in the UK, Ireland and other parts of Europe where concern over rising unemployment is most acute.

Credible threat 3

- **Exchange rate volatility and capital controls**

Although very large firms can protect themselves from currency fluctuations by buying and selling forward in the financial market known as the 'futures' market, there still exists a danger for firms moving into new markets that financial gains could be lost when funds are repatriated from the overseas market back to the country of origin, if exchange rate volatility is present.

In more extreme cases, if the economic environment deteriorates as dramatically as it did in South East Asia during the financial crisis of 1997, some countries may impose capital controls on the movement of funds. This could present a firm with an insurmountable threat if they have already invested heavily in new international markets.

4.8 E-commerce (1)

INTRODUCTION

We shall begin our investigation into e-commerce by considering a quotation from one the world's most successful and wealthiest investors, Warren Buffet.

> I pay for only three things on the Internet: the Wall Street Journal, online Bridge and books from Amazon. They must be doing something right.

Amazon rightly takes its place as one of the great e-commerce success stories of recent times and we shall be looking at their business model to see how e-commerce (or the buying and selling of goods using the Internet) can benefit consumers.

First, the case study below is given as an example of how the development of an online presence can impact on the marketing mix of a firm.

It is modelled on the type of question that a student could expect in the new HL or SL Paper 2. The case will not be used in an IB examination and the company is fictitious.

ANALYSING THE EFFECT OF E-COMMERCE ON THE MARKETING MIX

The case of Rare Retro

Rare Retro is a specialist music store owned by 75-year-old former jazz guitarist, Lee Carlton, known by his customers as "Bluey". Rare Retro sells hard-to-find Blues, Jazz and World Music CDs. The store is in Toronto, Canada. Bluey and his 10 staff travel all over the country to purchase and listen to live music from unknown bands. They enjoy a friendly relationship with customers who are encouraged to browse, chat and discuss the latest CD releases over a coffee or to listen to live music. This loyalty to Rare Retro allows them to charge above market prices. Rare Retro rarely needs to use above-the-line promotion and relies on positive word-of-mouth recommendation.

However, recent ill health has forced Bluey to spend less time in the store. Control has passed to his son, Jaco, a change which has not been popular with the other staff. Jaco had been working as a
management consultant. He feels that Rare Retro needs to adapt to a changing market.

Jaco has researched B2C (business-to-consumer) relationships in other competing stores. He thinks that Rare Retro should have a website, an online ordering service and a customer loyalty scheme. Jaco has recommended that Rare Retro adopts an e-commerce focus.

Jaco also conducted a quota survey of customers and friends. His results revealed that many customers use the Internet to search for and purchase new songs. A trip to Rare Retro is now viewed more as a social visit and less as a purchasing experience.

From this brief case study, we can speculate on the type of marketing mixes which existed at Rare Retro before and after Jaco's decision.

Marketing mix before Jaco's decision	Marketing mix after Rare Retro decides to adopt a 'greater e-commerce focus'
Product: Niche market selling of Blues and Jazz CDs	Product: An opportunity to stock a wider range of CDs by linking to other websites?
Price: Higher than market. Rare Retro may be skimming to a certain degree	Price: Given the transparency of the Internet, Rare Retro will have to adopt going rate or market pricing?
Promotion: Minimal apart from some below-the-line	Promotion: Online to accompany the word of mouth? Rare Retro may need to create a Bebo, MySpace or Facebook presence (which is what a number of aspiring musicians do)
Place: Music distributed from one store only. Very short channel	Place: The store will remain but Rare Retro will need to consider supply chain management and overseas distribution channels. Channels are likely to get longer if the firm expands
People: Bluey's staff loyal and knowledgeable about the products they are selling. Emphasis on customer service	People: Some customers may look for online recommendations rather than travel to the store to discuss purchases. Will Rare Retro be able to support the current level of staffing?
Process: CDs sold in store over the counter	Process: Online security payment systems will need to be set up
Physical evidence: We can guess that the store encourages browsing and discussing music. A coffee lounge type of experience?	Physical evidence: A physical and a virtual store? Will Rare Retro have to create a presence on Second Life?

It is hoped that the above analysis will demonstrate that simply opting to develop a business online through e-commerce will have significant implications for the marketing mix.

4.8 E-commerce (2)

THE BENEFITS AND COSTS OF E-COMMERCE TO CONSUMERS

Example: Amazon

We saw in unit 1.5 how Amazon has responded successfully to changes in the external environment by launching its own music download service. Amazon in common with Google has been one of the e-commerce success stories of the last decade. Their survival and growth is testament to the success of their respective 'e-commerce models' which have prospered despite the shattering events of the dot.com boom and bust which occurred at the beginning of this new century.

Amazon has managed to maximize the benefits to consumers and minimized the threats of conducting business over the Internet so successfully that, during the 2008 Christmas period, online sales reached record levels. Such has been the threat of the e-commerce revolution and the deteriorating external environment that many 'high street' retailers have been put out of business.

The benefits for consumers, using Amazon as our model

- Significant cost savings to consumers by ordering online.
- Incredible range of choice for many products, not just books and CDs which established Amazon's core business.
- Direct customer feedback from previous customers allowing consumers to gauge product performance.
- In countries where Amazon operates, delivery can be the same day with substantial discounts for big orders.
- Amazon can customize web pages tailored to customer purchases or searches from previous transactions, allowing greater consumer targeting.
- Amazon and e-commerce in general have fostered a much greater degree of price transparency and consequently has made the marketplace much more competitive, to the benefit of all consumers.

The minimization of threats

The great drawbacks of the online model were:

- Concerns expressed by stakeholders about the transmitting of personal data such as address and credit card information over the Internet.
- Security issues and genuine concerns of consumers who felt uneasy about paying hundreds of dollars for a product that they could not physically touch or test before committing to purchase.

It would be fair to say that Amazon has managed to allay those fears, although we should note that the irritations of 'spamming' and 'phishing' have coincided with the proliferation of e-commerce organizations.

The trust and brand loyalty which Amazon has managed to create has had enormous impact through the online community. The number of me-too imitators has been considerable. Perhaps though it would be fair to say that Amazon has earned the marketing **attribute** of 'online retailing'.

THE GROWTH OF B2B (BUSINESS TO BUSINESS OVER THE INTERNET)

We have already noted the tremendous impact of the Internet and its important implications for businesses in terms of communication and the spread of globalization.

- **B2B** activity measured by the number of online transactions now outnumbers the number made via **B2C** (business to consumers transactions such as those conducted through Amazon).
- This growth can be explained by reference to the HL section on supply chain management (page 104), that linking the whole process of supplier-producer-consumer has become an integral part of defining a new strategic direction for many companies. The Internet has provided the ideal conduit to allow these linkages to develop with little regard for time zones or geographical isolation. Perhaps in terms of the growth of B2B, the world is now truly flat!

Before moving on to Topic 5, questions 4, 5 and 6, page 109, could be attempted.

Exam questions on Topic 4

1 Discuss the types of market research that the Walt Disney Company should carry out before deciding whether to build a theme park.   (November 2007)

2 **HL** Evaluate two methods available to the Fair Trade movement to select a sample for their market research.   (May 2003)

3 **HL** Examine the advantages and disadvantages of firms like the bank HSBC operating as a single brand around the world.   (May 2007)

4 Analyse how and when in the process of new product development, market research will assist Dyson (the innovative bag-less vacuum cleaner).   (May 2004)

5 Explain why the failure rate of new products is so high in the early stages of their life cycle.   (May 2004)

6 Analyse methods by which organizations can deepen their relationships with their domestic and overseas customers.   (May 2005)

5.1 Production methods (1)

NOTE FOR TEACHERS

We now begin a series of units on production or operations management. In the author's experience, if the study of human resource management and marketing are considered to be favourite topics of students in the Business and Management course, then the least popular subject areas are accounting and finance and, in last place, operations management. There are a number of possible explanations.

- Within the subject areas of human resources and marketing, students can view themselves as stakeholders (as part-time workers or full-time consumers!) and this increases engagement.
- Accounting and operations management may lack this stakeholder link and, as a result, immediate engagement is limited.
- Operations management may be perceived as conceptually difficult in some areas (network analysis, contribution and batch production) and in others (e.g. total quality management and break-even analysis) as rather obvious and thus there is a tendency to be a little complacent.

For business decision-making the importance of operations management cannot be overstated. Faced with maturing markets and an explosion of choice, firms are looking at efficiency, cost and profit centres, outsourcing, quality control and supply chain management as new cornerstones of strategic direction. The objective is to ensure cost reduction to boost potential profits to satisfy the growing demands of shareholders for increasing returns.

EXAMINER'S HINT

With the new structure of examinations for 2009 and the introduction of compulsory quantitative questions on both the HL and SL papers, it would be dangerous for students to ignore the accounting and operations parts of the course. On the contrary, these topics get to the very heart of business decision-making and can be challenging and engaging.

From the author's experience of moderating Internal Assessments at Higher level, projects based on accounting and operations management consistently satisfy the marking criteria more accurately than human resource and marketing assignments, and gain higher final marks.

DIFFERENT METHODS OF PRODUCTION CONTRASTED

The table below compares the features and applications of each method of production.

Production method	Description	Examples
Job	The production of a one-off project built to specific customer or industry specifications	The building of a ship or production of a film, or a house which is built specifically to customer requirements
Batch	Items are produced in consignments and undergo a part of the production process together. The whole consignment is then moved on to the next stage and another task is performed	Carefully planned groups of products with slight modifications allowed to customize batches. The best examples are bread-making and beer brewing. Batch production provides a good working model for network analysis
Flow	A continuous production process. Similar to batch but the consignment moves from one stage of the process to the next without stopping	The car industry provides the classic example for mass market car production. Note that luxury cars such as Ferraris are usually produced by the job method
Mass	Large-scale production based on flow production with production quantities in the millions	Large-scale food processing. FMCGs are usually mass produced

5.1 Production methods (2)

APPROPRIATENESS OF EACH PRODUCTION METHOD

From the above table we can draw some conclusions:

- Job production lends itself appropriately to niche markets as production runs are very small.

- Batch production allows a greater degree of flexibility of the consignment to perhaps cater and customize for larger production runs. Thus it can avoid the problems of standardization which is a feature of flow production. Batches can also be made to order for customers, allowing some economies of scale not available to job production

- For mass markets with predictable sales, flow and mass provide the most cost-effective methods of production. Significant economies of scale can be obtained.

- In order to achieve these economies of scale, investment in large-scale machinery is required. Financial, human resource management and technological issues can therefore be considerable in a flow environment.

Example: Job and batch production in a flow production world?

As a competitive weapon or marketing tactic, some producers now offer complete customization or some modification of a product even though it may be produced in a flow environment. This has been enthusiastically embraced by the fast-food and computing industries. For example:

- Burger King, McDonald's and Subway allow the consumer to customize their burger or sandwich (more salad or sauce or toasted?).

- Dell computers allow purchasers to upgrade RAM or add other features per customer requirement before delivery.

- Apple enable individual engraving to personalize the MP3 player when given as a gift.

Students are invited to think of their own examples as consumers and to analyse the human resource issues which may arise from adopting a customized approach to flow production.

Cell production

Cell production has been described as 'splitting a flow production line into self-contained units'. Each cell (or group of individuals) will produce a significant part of the finished product, giving the cell responsibility to complete a unit of work. Herzberg argued that this was a strong driver for firms to incorporate **job enrichment** programmes in their operations. The cell may also be responsible for setting the job descriptions, covering staff absence due to sickness, and offering advice to senior management on issues such as quality improvements and recruitment of workers. In some instances, the cell used in Japanese management systems may be allowed to decide on discipline and grievance procedures in cases of conflict.

Not surprisingly, cell production has been given high status in Athenian cultures and organizations where problem-solving and teamwork are viewed as a powerful motivational force.

5.2 Costs and revenues (1)

COSTS

The table below defines, explains and gives an example of each different type of cost.

Types of cost	Definition	Explanation	Example
Fixed	Costs which have to be paid but are not dependent on the level of output. They can also be referred to as overhead costs	These costs are incurred if the firm produces zero output	Rent and rates on the premises, insurance
Variable	Costs which are output dependent	As production increases, so do variable costs	Raw material costs, wages of production workers
Semi-variable	Costs which may have a fixed charge initially but after a certain level of usage may rise dependent on production levels	See definition	Electricity and telephone charges. Some Internet fees are semi-fixed dependent on the plan used

REVENUES

- We can define revenue as the amount of money generated from trading activities: selling goods or services to customers.
- In accounting terms, revenue may be counted as money earned even if physical cash or electronic transfer has not been received. The amount of debtors listed under current assets on a balance sheet can be counted as revenue.
- If a company earns revenue from activities other than trading (such as dividends from investments or shares owned), this is referred to as non-operating income.

CONTRIBUTION

Contribution is an important but sometimes elusive concept. We shall use the example of a hotel to try and demonstrate how contribution can be a valuable concept to keep a loss-making firm open.

- **Calculation**: Contribution per unit is calculated by subtracting variable cost from price.

Contribution per Unit = Price per Unit − Variable Cost per Unit

Total contribution accruing to a firm from all its products in the marketplace is calculated by:

Total Contribution = Total Revenue − Total Variable Costs

Explanation

For a firm to make profits:

- We have to assume that total revenue will be greater than total costs.
- Total costs are made up of fixed costs and variable costs.

- Fixed costs have to be paid even if the firm produces nothing. Let us assume that the firm either pays these on 1 January or it will not be permitted to trade.
- Now that the firm is trading, as long as total revenue is bigger than total variable costs, then the firm is said to be making a contribution towards fixed costs.
- On 31 December, if the firm has gathered enough contribution to pay fixed costs for the following year, it can remain in business and avoid shutting down. Any additional money left over after fixed costs have been paid would be considered profit.
- If the firm does not have enough contribution to pay fixed costs on 1 January of the following year, it will have to finance the fixed cost payment using another method, or it may have to consider shutting down.

(continued)

5.2 Costs and revenues (2)

CONTRIBUTION *(continued)*

Example of contribution in action: hotels trading in the offpeak season

- Hotels do not close down in offpeak seasons (monsoon seasons or periods outside national or school holidays) even though they may have to reduce their prices considerably to attract customers. (Remember that the hotel has to pay overhead costs even if it does not receive any bookings.)
- For hotel guests who do stay during the off-season, as long as the price per guest charged is greater than the variable cost of the guest staying (food served, cleaning of the room, etc.) then the hotel will be making a contribution to its fixed costs.
- The implication for hotels in terms of pricing is that they may be able to adopt contribution pricing during these periods of low demand in an attempt to increase bookings.

Implications of contribution

The implications of contribution for business decision-making should be clear.

- Even if a firm is finding it difficult to cover all its costs, it will still be beneficial to stay in operation and not shut down if it is making a contribution.
- Second, as we shall see in a multi-product firm, it may be sensible to retain a product in a portfolio even if it is loss-making because it may be making a contribution to fixed costs (overheads). (The product may also be kept in for defensive or strategic reasons, as we will see in the example of TK Pictures on the next page, which is an HL extension topic.)

5.2 Costs and revenues (3)

COST AND PROFIT CENTRES

We saw in a previous unit on organizational structure (page 41) that some businesses have now organized themselves in such a way to split divisions, departments, products or brands into self-contained autonomous units called **centres** where costs and revenues can be easily identified.

- **Cost centres:** Centres are allocated their own direct costs and can set their own budgets to control and monitor efficiency.

- **Profit centres:** Similar to the above, but profit centres (usually separate divisions or departments) are allocated costs and revenues for the purpose of calculating individual profit. Unilever took a decision recently to convert all its major brands into dedicated profit centres for this reason.

- We must also remember that the centre, whether cost or profit, will be expected to absorb some of the overhead cost of the whole organization.

- The creation of these cost and profit centres has been driven by the idea that empowering managers of these units may lead to motivation via increased delegation. The cost and profit centre must now be accountable for its own actions and this may lead to greater efficiency and productivity.

- The main problem with these centres is that when individual managers are responsible for individual centre performance then potentially the centre may set objectives that are different from the overall objectives of the organization.

We consider profit centres in action and analyse the role of contribution in determining the viability of each product for a multi-product firm, by means of sample HL Paper 2 question written especially for this guide.

TK Pictures is a movie company, which has been in the film industry for 40 years. TK currently aim to produce 20 movies with their output in a typical year being:

Division or department	Number of films produced, 2009
Action/drama	8
Family/musical	6
Comedy	4
Debut	2

Steven Lucas manages TK. As a young movie director he found it hard to get his movies made. TK offered him a chance in 1998 to develop his own project and Lucas became hugely successful. In 2003, as the newly appointed CEO, Lucas created the Debut division with a vision to encourage and support other young film-makers.

However, Lucas has been worried with recent falls in profitability and especially escalating direct costs,

specifically actors' salaries. He is also frustrated that the Debut department 7 years on has not 'discovered' a great new talent. Many of Debut's films are loss-making. Lucas feels that with greater accountability, turning the four departments into individual profit centres may be the way forward.

Debut's manager George Pitt has urged Lucas to reconsider this idea, arguing that although the Debut division has been struggling, it still provides a contribution and has an important role to play in discovering new talent. Lucas is not too sure and has been approached by an independent producer, Harvey Tarrantino, about a possible sale of Debut.

The case study highlights a number of classic dilemmas for a multi-division or multi-product firm.

- *Should the firm continue to support Debut even though it is loss-making?*

- *Should the firm keep Debut to block potential rivals from entering into this market? (Some have described this as a 'Watchdog', adapting the terminology of the BCG matrix.)*

- *Should the firm sell Debut and receive a one-off cash boost from the sale and then use this to financially support the other divisions?*

- *Could the creation of a cost or profit centre allow Debut the opportunity to manage itself and with this increased empowerment and responsibility allow it to be more successful?*

The role of contribution in the decision-making process

The above four dilemmas cannot be solved by solely looking at contribution.

However:

- If the management has confidence in the cost and profit centre idea, then if Debut can make a sustained contribution it may be worth retaining.

- If the film-makers in charge of Debut become more motivated due to their new 'freedom', contribution could easily turn into profit.

- By supporting the contribution argument, TK is able to try and achieve its vision and discover new talent. Stakeholders may be reassured that the company is retaining a commitment to its future path.

- Of course, by ignoring contribution and selling the division, new talent could be discovered by the new buyer. The gain from a sale of Debut would simply be a one-off to TK Pictures and longer-term profitability would be transferred to the buyer.

5.3 Break-even analysis (1)

BREAK-EVEN EXAMPLE

The article below is a rare glimpse into the finances associated with a major media or sporting event.

It neatly introduces the importance of using break-even analysis at the start of the decision-making process.

Auckland Regional Council paid $2.9m for David Beckham and lost $1.7m

The Auckland Regional Council spent $2.91 million on travel, accommodation and promotion for the ill-fated football match between David Beckham's LA Galaxy and the Oceania All Stars in December 2008, a report has shown.

It was also revealed yesterday that the ARC banked on David Beckham's 'world superstar' status drawing Auckland's Asian community to its football game that lost $1.7 million.

'Beckham is a phenomenon in Asia and with Asian people,' councillors were told in a pitch from staff for staging the LA Galaxy fiasco at the ARC-owned Mt Smart Stadium.

The proposal for LA Galaxy v an Oceania All Stars team match was pitched as a concept devised so that a wide range of people of differing ethnic descent would be attracted.

The Auckland Football Federation was to help by promoting the event to its 20,000 registered players and clubs.

'Therefore, it was not expected that there would be too many problems in attracting a healthy crowd for the event,' said the report.

The 'break-even' crowd needed was 25,000 and considering a similar event in Wellington had attracted 31,800 people in 2007, the report said it was unlikely that this crowd size would not be achieved.

The report suggested the ARC set ticket prices for a 30,000-seat capacity, with 29,000 paying ticket sales.

A profit of $484,350 was expected if 30,000 tickets were sold.

However, on the night a crowd of 16,587 turned out, but 'a portion of these were complimentary or were offered in a two-for-one deal, resulting in lower revenue'.

Mr. Winder's review of what went wrong is highlighted in the following details:

- *A loss of $1.79 million.*
- *Costs of $3,057,602 were $151,052 or 5.2% above the original budget.*
- *Revenue of $2,075,599 was 61% lower than expected.*
- *Expected revenue from ticket sales was $2,577,100 but was actually $782,000 – 70% less than hoped for.*

What went wrong? Mr. Winder said the ticket price was too high, the marketing ineffective and the Oceania team were not good enough to be considered a creditable opposition.

Source: adapted from *New Zealand Herald*

Comments

Having read the article, one is tempted to make a number of comments about the use of forecasts and the accuracy of cost and revenue calculation. However, space precludes a full review.

What we can say is that the Auckland Regional Council's use of break-even analysis was correct but they did not take into account a number of other factors which may have impacted on the decision to bring David Beckham and the Galaxy team all the way to Auckland to play an exhibition soccer match.

Break-even analysis is an important element in the decision-making model but there are a number of drawbacks, which the Beckham example highlights.

- Costs and revenues in reality are not linear and predictable, as assumed by the theoretical model.
- A break-even analysis should not be static, but different break-even points under different cost, price and revenue scenarios should also be undertaken. Some writers refer to this as 'What if' analysis.
- Promotions which are used to try and boost revenue should be costed carefully.
- Non-financial factors outside the control of the users of break-even analysis will need to be considered once the break-even quantity and margin of safety have been calculated. There is some evidence from the David Beckham example that the ARC underestimated these.

5.3 Break-even analysis (2)

Break-even analysis: theoretical review

We shall summarize the important elements.

Consider the diagram below:

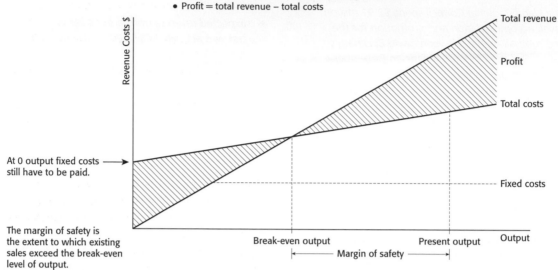

Break-even is the output at which revenue equals costs, i.e. no profit or loss is made.
- Total revenue = price × quantity
- Total costs = fixed costs + variable costs
  Fixed costs do not change with output, e.g. rent
  Variable costs vary directly with output, e.g. materials
- Profit = total revenue − total costs

At 0 output fixed costs still have to be paid.

The margin of safety is the extent to which existing sales exceed the break-even level of output.

Break-even analysis

Given that the diagram may be drawn inaccurately or the intersection point between total costs and total revenue may not be clear by eye, it is always useful to confirm the break-even point using the following formula:

$$\text{Break-even quantity calculated} = \frac{\text{fixed costs}}{\text{contribution}}$$

where contribution = price per unit − variable cost per unit

BREAK-EVEN QUANTITY WITH A PROFIT TARGET

HL

If the firm is looking to try and guarantee a minimum level of profit, perhaps to satisfy shareholders or ensure a sole trader's salary, fixed costs will need to be adjusted. The profit target effectively becomes an overhead and must be included. The break-even quantity will have to rise accordingly.

$$\text{Break-even quantity} = \frac{\text{fixed costs} + \text{profit target}}{\text{contribution}}$$

The margin of safety level of output

This is the amount by which the demand for a firm's product can fall before a firm incurs losses. Alternatively, it measures how close the firm is to the break-even level of output.

Current level of demand − break-even output

5.3 Break-even analysis (3)

EFFECTS OF CHANGES IN PRICE OR COST ON THE BREAK-EVEN QUANTITY, PROFIT AND MARGIN OF SAFETY

It was stated earlier that some students overlook the importance of break-even analysis in the decision-making process. When we consider changes in the price of a product charged or an increase in costs, then the impacts on the break-even quantity should be obvious. However, this is not always the case. Let us consider the following example.

Firm X has fixed costs = $3,000

Price of the product = $10

Variable costs = $7

Current level of demand = 1,500

The break-even quantity $= \dfrac{3,000}{3}$

$= 1,000$

Margin of safety $= 1,500 - 1,000 = 500$

Profit = total revenue − total costs

$= (1500 \times 10) - [3,000 + (1,500 \times 7)]$

$= 15,000 - 13,500$

$= 1,500$

If the firm cuts the price by 10%, the quick complacent answer is that the break-even quantity will need to rise by at least 10%.

The answer is actually 50%. Students should now work out the impact on profitability and the margin of safety.

From this straightforward example a number of issues arise.

- Is this 50% increase in demand achievable?
- Can we assume that demand will rise by this amount if the price remains at $10?
- Will a price cut affect the perception of quality of the product?
- What if competitors (if any) follow this price reduction?
- Can the additional demand required be produced quickly without significantly raising short-term variable costs, i.e. is there spare capacity in the organization? If not, fixed costs may need to increase if the firm needs to finance additional capacity.

The astute reader will have noticed that we have in the above questions identified a number of the limitations behind break-even analysis. To summarize:

- It is assumed that the firm can sell as much as it wishes at the same price. This is unrealistic. In order to sell higher quantities, the firm may have to reduce prices significantly.
- The law of demand which assumes a negative relationship between price and the quantity demanded does not result in a linear total revenue curve. It is dome-shaped.

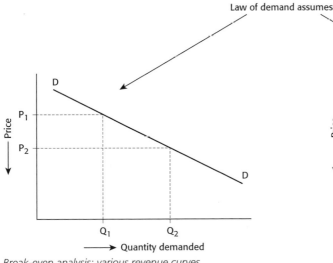

Break-even analysis: various revenue curves.

- On the cost side, the assumption that variable costs rise in a linear fashion can also be challenged. If large production runs are required then a firm's costs may fall due to economies of scale or rise due to diseconomies of scale.

- In keeping with other quantifiable decision-making techniques, external PEST factors are not considered.

You could now attempt question 1 on page 130.

5.4 Quality assurance (1)

INTRODUCTION

Although the Japanese have been rightly applauded for achieving outstanding levels of quality in the production of consumer goods, the original idea for adopting a total quality management philosophy which was at the forefront of a major change in thinking about approaches to quality came from an American statistician, W. Edwards Deming.

To summarize the paradigm shift away from traditional methods:

- Deming rejected mass inspection (the traditional method of quality control at the time) by one individual department.

- Quality was to be built into each stage of the production process, to be analysed carefully by use of statistical methods.

- Training was to be continuous and widespread to all workers to allow them to undertake quality inspections.

- Hierarchical barriers between departments and senior managers should be removed, with quality becoming everyone's responsibility.

- Deming called for a PDCA cycle of continuous improvement:

    1 Plan (find the right data, analyse the problem, plan the solution)

    2 Do

    3 Check

    4 Action (modify process as necessary)

Deming's ideas, incorporated with those of Kaoru Ishikawa (whose fishbone diagram we met in unit 1.6 HL page 23) began the total quality management movement, commonly shortened to TQM.

THE ROLE OF KAIZEN   HL

Kaizen is a Japanese word for the concept of continuous improvement which forms the basis of TQM and lean production (lean production is not stated explicitly in the course guide for 2009), and it incorporates a number of important elements.

- It should be the goal of the organization to introduce small incremental changes to operations to improve quality.

- Quality circles should be introduced for subordinates and management to work together to identify causes of poor quality, perhaps through use of a fishbone discussion. Hierarchical barriers should be removed to allow discussions to take place to solve problems and not to apportion blame.

- Workers should be encouraged to take ownership of their own work. This empowerment will lead to improved motivation and increased productivity, especially if the organization is structured in cells (see page 111).

- Kaizen can be extended to include continuous improvements in maintaining customer satisfaction as well. The objective is to produce products that have zero defects. ('Zero defects' is a term which is often misunderstood. Kaizen does not assume that mistakes will not happen; however, it is assumed from the start of the production process that there will be no failure rate.)

Approaches to quality improvement

Kaizen is not without its critics.

- In addition to continuous improvement, statistical control and data collection need to be rigorous. This will take time and use up scarce resources, especially if the intention is to achieve zero defects.

- Second, when successfully applied kaizen requires that managers and employees will be willing to change. As we saw in our work on force field analysis (page 32), establishing a new equilibrium can take time, given the existence of restraining forces.

- Quality circles will also involve changing the culture of the organization and the nature of the relationship between subordinates and managers. There may be some resistance from both sides, especially if the workforce is predominantly Theory X.

- Constant training is required and ongoing costs of disruption will need to be considered even if the training is both on the job and off. (In some quality circles, groups agree to work on solving problems during their lunch breaks. It is that important to them.)

5.4 Quality assurance (2)

BENCHMARKING

A second approach to quality management or quality assurance is through the process known as benchmarking. The idea behind this is that companies will try to benchmark or measure their operations, customer service, marketing or human resource management against what is considered to be the market leader in its industry and try to model their own behaviour on what could be considered to be industry best practice.

Examples of benchmarking

Examples can be found in the airline industry. Many airlines in Southeast Asia have tried to benchmark customer service on economy flights against that of the market leader, Singapore Airlines. Southwest Airlines in the United States has long been considered to be the benchmark provider which all no-frills or budget airlines should try to emulate.

ARGUMENTS AGAINST BENCHMARKING

Benchmarking has a number of critics. At a straightforward level, one argument put forward is that benchmarking represents a poor use of management time. Why spend time thinking about your competitors when you should be focusing on the strengths of your own company?

Next, there is a philosophical criticism that all benchmarking can do is make all companies look the same, leading to similar strategic positions and therefore a distinct lack of differentiation. Michael Porter would argue that this would be no source of competitive advantage for an individual firm.

Not surprisingly, on this point Jack Trout is unequivocal.

Benchmarking doesn't work because regardless of a product's quality, people perceive the first brand to enter their mind as superior. When you opt to benchmark a product and become a me-too, you are a second class citizen.

INTERNATIONAL SAFETY STANDARDS AND ISO CERTIFICATION

Finally, a third source of quality assurance would be to demonstrate a commitment to an internationally recognized standard of quality such as ISO 9001. For example, child car seat manufacturers are able to reassure customers that their product has satisfied a number of internationally agreed standards on safety.

Unfortunately, ISO certification highlights the fact that the company is following accepted manufacturing processes only, which could be considered to be leading the product to be viewed as a safe product. Certification in itself unfortunately does not guarantee the product's 'quality'.

Given this point, some commentators have argued that ISO recognition is simply a marketing tool designed to convince customers that the product has the quality stamp of approval from an independent body.

You could now tackle questions 2 and 3, page 130.

Quality assurance and control is an area of the course which many students take for granted and thus seem to have only a superficial understanding of what quality means.

Quality is now a given for many consumers, i.e. quality is expected in every purchase decision a consumer makes.

Students would probably agree that quality for a good or service is important and that companies perceived as offering poor quality would do everything in their power to rectify this situation.

However, this raises a number of questions:

- Which companies would actually admit to having a poor quality product or service?
- Given the tyranny of choice which started our marketing section, surely a product which is perceived as being 'poor quality' would be quickly upgraded or removed by competitive pressures from the market at the very least?

An interesting exercise for a teacher is to ask a group of students to write down a definition of quality, provide some examples and then compare answers throughout the class. There is likely to be wide variation in the perception of what constitutes quality.

5.5 Location

INTRODUCTION

This unit is one of our briefest as we have already discussed many of the factors affecting the location of a firm, without a direct reference to location theory, for example:

- The growth of multinational activity (unit 1.9)
- The impact of ICT on the ability of firms to communicate across many countries (unit 2.3)
- The increased possibilities of a firm structuring itself by geographic function (unit 2.1)
- The growing appetite for firms to engage in off-shoring parts of customer service and operations management (unit 2.2).

We have highlighted a number of factors which can influence a firm's decision to locate or relocate its operations. However, we shall also briefly summarize a number of other points which are commonly expanded upon in textbooks.

Location can also be influenced by:

- Accessibility to the market to limit transport costs which is especially important for firms where the production process involves weight gaining. This argument is strongly applied in 'heavy goods' industries (such as cars) and whiteware (fridges and washing machines).
- Access to government grants and allowances and tax considerations. Ireland has seen a surge in firms wishing to locate there due to favourable government incentives and tax environments.
- Availability of land will be an important factor for firms involved in large-scale production or perhaps looking to build a distribution network around large warehouse space. This is becoming very important in e-commerce firms such as Amazon or retailers such as Tesco and Wal-Mart that are looking to the Internet to provide extensive product ranges.
- The existence of reliable infrastructure such as energy generation and transport links. Traffic congestion and delays can significantly add to firms' costs.
- The ability to develop good reliable working relationships with suppliers. This is crucial if a firm wishes to employ just-in-time stock control methods and kaizen (unit 5.7).
- Availability and suitability of local labour to satisfy the firm's manpower requirements. This can be a powerful motivating factor, although increasingly with globalization, firms are able to offshore and outsource more and more of their labour input.

THE IMPACT OF GLOBALIZATION HL

The final point above illustrates the fact that some parts of traditional location theory are being challenged. For example, firms now do not have to locate in an area of high unemployment to find pools of labour. They can effectively transfer the responsibility to a geographic region offshore.

In the new global environment, the locations of key functions of a firm are not constrained by being necessarily in the same country as the head office.

We can summarize some of our previous arguments:

- For example, we have seen that with the growth of global branding, firms can now market their products successfully across the planet. Companies can now market regionally and allow a degree of decentralization, especially in marketing, to suit local tastes.
- The growth of offshoring has now enabled firms to concentrate their production in countries with lower labour costs.
- The growth of call centres and ICT, especially in Malaysia and the Philippines, has allowed firms to relocate their customer service programmes at greatly reduced costs.
- Finally, as we saw on page 63, the 'globalization' of modern finance and the growth of venture capital has seen firms being able to raise finance from all parts of the globe. This has been a vital source of funds transfer from the developed to the developing world.

5.6 Innovation HL (1)

THE IMPORTANCE OF RESEARCH AND DEVELOPMENT FOR BUSINESS **HL**

Research and development (R & D) is commonly defined as the ability to create and develop new products. This clearly has a number of benefits:

- Increased revenue and market share, especially if the new product forms the basis of a new Blue Ocean strategy
- Given the 'tyranny of choice', innovation can be – if the new product becomes 'first in the mind' – a very powerful differentiating factor.

Find out more

Interested students should read Steven Levy's excellent book about the creation and commercial realization of the Apple iPod, *The Perfect Thing*. It is striking that, before the iPod, the 'first in mind' product was the Sony Walkman and then the Discman. Sony's failure to fully appreciate the power of the music download from the Internet is viewed as a prime example of how it is possible to lose the 'first in mind' tag. The iPod is now synonymous with portable music.

Links with other topics

R & D, however, should not be restricted to the creation of new products.

- It is perfectly reasonable for a firm to investigate and develop non-tangible products such as new production methods, or customer service programmes, or innovative ways of advertising.
- R & D can also be applied to achieving new levels of quality assurance, hopefully leading to further opportunities for cost reduction and/or productivity gains.

- Finally, one of our conclusions from a previous unit (page 92) is that product life cycles are becoming shorter. R & D must have a commercial focus and not be locked away in a 'laboratory', because a firm's survival in some competitive markets may depend on its capacity to quickly bring an innovative product to market.

THE ROLE AND IMPORTANCE OF INTELLECTUAL PROPERTY RIGHTS **HL**

Research and development, invention and risk-taking by an entrepreneur will require some form of legal protection. This is referred to as the protection of intellectual property rights. Typically this will involve the use of patents, copyrights and trademarks.

To stress the importance of securing protection, let us first consider an example from the unit on PEST analysis (page 17) when we examined the Indian film industry and problems of film piracy. Illegal copying and downloading of movies from the Internet has become a major concern for film and media companies. The industry argues that illegal downloading denies artists and performers access to royalties, thus placing the very existence of the industry in jeopardy. Vietnam for example has very few local music artists who can support themselves financially, because of the widespread illegal burning of new albums onto blank CDs which are then sold in open markets.

Patents and copyright protection

Patents and copyright can both be used to protect intellectual property. In the case of patents (depending on in which country they are issued) a company may be awarded the exclusive right to produce a product for up to 20 years although the figure can vary.

It has been argued that patents protect the investment which many large companies undertake when researching and developing new products. In some cases these new products can have far-reaching consequences for a large number of stakeholders. The following example is a notable and popular defence for patents.

The creation of an anti-malaria vaccine would be an enormous step forward in improving the lives of millions of people in the sub-Saharan African belt where malaria is most prevalent. Large pharmaceutical firms would be willing to finance the enormous sums of capital required to find such an elusive vaccine if there was a guarantee that, if successful, they would have exclusive rights over production to allow them to recoup these substantial costs.

Source: adapted from IB examination (May 2009)

Trademarks

Once a successful innovative product has been established in the marketplace, a trademark or brand name can act as a powerful differentiating tool. Trademarks are thus fiercely protected by their owners and as we saw (page 73) can be an invaluable intangible asset.

5.6 Innovation HL (2)

INNOVATION

- **Definition:** Innovation in a business context refers to the successful commercialization of an invention. Successful commercialization means that it is brought to the market and achieves a significant level of sales. An invention which remains in the R & D stage only is not considered to be innovative.

Factors affecting opportunities for innovation and creativity

Innovation and creativity are very much intertwined. Innovative organizations need to be able to foster conditions that allow creativity and innovation to thrive.

- An organization needs to give space to those charged with being 'creative' and keep them away from unnecessary bureaucracy. Russell-Walling argues that, for innovation to thrive, management must not apply the same standards of budget, constraints or discipline as they do for other departments.

- A number of companies have developed innovative products and ideas through listening to customers and trying to respond or anticipate changing market trends. It is a not so well-known fact that many of the most popular items on the McDonald's menu were created not by the company but suggested by customers and/ or by franchisees.

- Innovation will take time. It is well-known in the history of the development of successful products that iconic brands such as Post-it Notes, Coca-Cola and Viagra were discovered by accident. These were happy (and very lucrative!) discoveries for the inventors concerned but they should not be considered typical. Successful innovation requires patience, continuous product testing and resources. Stakeholders must be wary of too much over-eager anticipation.

- Once innovation has been completed it will need to be communicated to the senior management for discussion to consider further action. The innovative idea will need to be presented in such a way as not to baffle or embarrass. It is argued that engineers and ICT specialists who may be at the forefront of the creative work may use excessive technical language and thus are not always the most appropriate people for this communication task.

Find out more

Even the creation of an innovative idea with a patent is still no guarantee of success. The personal computer was developed by a company called Micro Instrumentation Telemetry Systems (MITS). A young programmer called Bill Gates worked for them very briefly before leaving in 1975 to form Microsoft. We all know what happened to his company but what became of MITS? The interested reader is invited to find out.

5.7 Production planning (1)

INTRODUCTION

The term 'stock' refers to either unsold goods or components which are used in the production process. The same definition is used by the IB Business and Management course guide. In America, 'stock' is the name for a share owned in a company (e.g. IBM stock), while the term 'inventory' is used for unsold goods or components.

Stock control

The purpose of stock control is to be able to hold sufficient quantities of raw materials, work in progress and finished goods in order to enable production and sales to continue uninterrupted. A number of different ways have been suggested to try and achieve this. The two methods of stock control which we will consider are just-in-case (JIC) and just-in-time (JIT).

The costs of holding stock

These can be considerable and include:

- Costs of storage and if necessary warehousing.
- Insurance and security costs.
- Opportunity costs of tying up money which could have been used elsewhere in the business (see section on working capital, page 67).
- If the good being stored is perishable, firms may need to provide expensive refrigeration. If they do not, unsold stock may quickly become worthless.

JUST IN TIME (JIT) COMPARED WITH JUST IN CASE (JIC)

In JIT, firms try to minimize the costs of holding stock. Goods are made to order. The firm will hold stocks of components and materials subject to the prevailing level of demand, and only the absolute minimum is held.

JIT requires excellent communication and strong supplier relationships. In the car manufacturing industry, for example, component parts are delivered to the factory in real time (that is, just as they are about to enter the production process). Suppliers in JIT environments are consequently responsible for ensuring quality and zero defects.

In JIC systems, additional stock is held in order to provide a contingency against unexpected events such as a sudden increase in demand, or a breakdown in the production process or supply chain.

JIC is considered to be an expensive way of holding stock. However, it does reduce the risk of pauses or major stoppages in the production process which could be even more costly to the organization.

5.7 Production planning (2)

STOCK CONTROL METHODS

The figure below is a traditional stock control graph identifying lead times, buffer stocks and reorder levels.

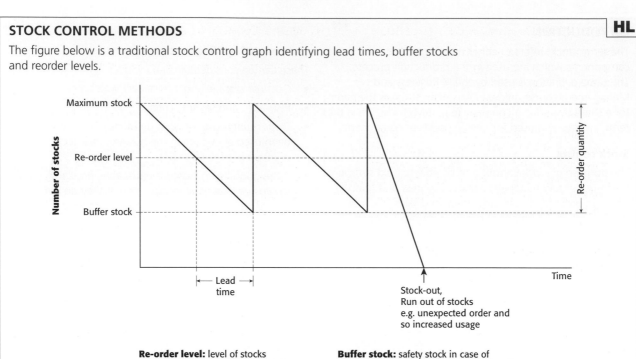

Re-order level: level of stocks at which new supplies are ordered

Re-order quantity: amount reordered

Buffer stock: safety stock in case of sudden increase in demand, or supply failure

Lead time: time taken from ordering supplies to supplies arriving

Traditional stock control graph.

Source: Gillespie (2001)

Appropriateness of stock control method

HL students should be able to explain different stock control methods and analyse the appropriateness of each method in a given situation. Students are recommended to reread earlier sections such as LIFO and FIFO stock valuation (page 74) and supply chain management (page 104).

- **How perishable is the product?**

In situations where the product might have a limited shelf life, JIC may be an inappropriate form of stock control. Firms will have to keep stock levels and buffer stocks to a minimum to avoid throwing away out-of-date products.

- **Can supply chain management relationships be guaranteed?**

JIT demands that there is a very strong and reliable relationship between supplier and final manufacturer. Until recently, Nissan's production plant in Sunderland, UK, demanded that suppliers of components sign contracts guaranteeing that components for its assembly line would be on-call (ready to deliver) 24 hours a day, seven days a week.

- **Is there available and suitable warehouse space?**

Although JIC is expensive, some online retailers such as Amazon and Wal-Mart have built their business infrastructure around huge warehouses stocked full of products to satisfy incoming online orders from customers. JIC is appropriate for Amazon given their enormous influence in the e-commerce environment. Small business start-ups may not be able to use JIC stock control and may have to service customer requirements by the use of JIT, usually at higher prices to the final end user.

- **What about economies of scale?**

By using JIC, Amazon is able to take advantage of bulk-buying economies of scale which firms using JIT will not obtain.

Students could now attempt question 4 on page 130.

5.7 Production planning (3)

OUTSOURCING AND SUBCONTRACTING HL

These two terms will be used here to mean the same thing.

- Outsourcing is the process by which firms will subcontract to (or use) independent suppliers rather than undertake the activities themselves.

- Outsourcing allows firms to concentrate on their core activities and benefit from the experience and knowledge of specialists. Examples of commonly subcontracted activities include catering, call centre and other customer service activities, security, office cleaning, market research and, in some industries, design.

Benefits of outsourcing for an individual organization

Outsourcing has been most commonly proposed by senior managers looking to remain competitive in an increasingly connected and transparent external environment. Our previous case studies from Telecom (page 45) and Fisher & Paykel (page 15) highlight these potential cost savings. Outsourcing differs from offshoring in that it can be achieved without the need to subcontract overseas. However, given the growing transparency around global labour costs, the two terms have become synonymous with each other in the media that report such events.

ICT functions remain the most outsourced function, with India being the main beneficiary. The growth in number of Indian university graduates has been noted by multinational firms in particular and has allowed firms to outsource administrative and call centre functions with no noticeable drop in the quality of service provided.

However there are possible costs, for example:

- Outsourcing may transfer quality responsibility to the outsourced company. This is a process which will need monitoring and senior managers may have to visit these centres regularly to enforce the host company's expected standards of performance.

- Concerns have been raised about the security of information, with host country firms having to share intellectual property with the outsourced company.

- Russell-Walling has argued that the cost savings from outsourcing are not as dramatic once 'cultural alignment activities have been completed'. Despite training and cultural awareness activities, there will be transitional costs in subcontracting a service.

- There may also be public relations issues to the firm outsourcing operations in the host country, as we have seen already in our work on Telecom and Fisher & Paykel. Given the deteriorating economic environment, firms may be regarded as unethical if they transfer work to other providers overseas while the rate of unemployment increases in the host country.

MAKE-OR-BUY DECISIONS HL

When considering make-or-buy decisions, management chooses whether to buy in components or make them in-house themselves.

We have already discussed several factors behind the decision for firms to outsource production. However, we can also consider some figures.

For example, if a certain component will cost firm X either $12 to produce in its own factory or $10 by outsourcing to company Y, the firm will have to consider the following issues:

- Is the $2 saving significant, given quality control concerns about another firm producing the component?

- The $2 per component saving could be used as a contribution to overhead costs for company X.

- Will company Y be able to guarantee delivery and sufficient batch size?

- What are company X's core activities and should it be producing this component?

- Given time, larger batches and economies of scale, will company Y be able to charge a price lower than $10 in the future?

Students could now tackle questions 5 and 6, page 130.

5.8 Project management HL (1)

ACTIVITY

An engaging way to understand the processes behind network or critical path analysis without the need for technical terms is to undertake the following task in conjunction with your college or school's Food Technology department (or it could be carried out at home).

Students are invited to bake a simple jam cake. A recipe with instructions could be downloaded from the Internet or obtained from the Food Technology department.

Consider the following tasks required in order to make a basic cake.

Activity	Task	Estimated time taken to perform task = duration in minutes
Turn on the oven	A	1
Find the cooking utensils and ingredients from cupboard	B	4
Mix cake ingredients in bowl	C	5
Put finished cake mix into baking tins	D	3
Bake cake mixture	E	20
Wash up utensils already used and clean work surfaces	F	10
Put utensils and unused ingredients back into cupboard (must be carried out before cooling and eating!)	G	7
Remove cake from oven and leave to cool	H	10
Prepare jam filling	I	2
Add filling and serve	J	5

- From the process of baking a cake, students understand that some activities need to be done in a certain order, e.g. B, C, D, E.

- Next, the estimated duration of all the stages to complete the cake totals 67 minutes. However, some activities in baking a cake can be carried out at the same time. For example, the washing up and cleaning of work surfaces can be carried out at the same time as the cake is baking in the oven. These are called parallel activities.

- If some activities are delayed, such as putting the cake mix in the oven to bake, then delays in the overall project time will occur. The cake will not be ready to eat at the expected time. Activities which, if delayed, lengthen the whole project duration are called critical activities.

- Having finished washing up and cleaning, there may be some free time to prepare the filling or to ensure that other future critical activities are not delayed. This 'free time' is called float time.

5.8 Project management HL (2)

CONSTRUCTING A NETWORK FROM THE BEGINNING

A network diagram consists of a series of nodes and arrows to represent stages in a project. Arrows represent activities and often have a letter next to them to identify them; the length of time the activity takes (its duration) is put underneath the arrow. Circles or nodes represent the start or end of an activity.

A node has three sections.

- The left-hand side shows a node number to make it easier to follow the sequence of tasks.

- The top right segment of the node reveals the earliest start time (EST) which is the earliest time the next task can begin.

- The bottom right segment of the node shows the latest finish time (LFT) which is the latest time the previous task can finish without delaying the next.

Starting a network diagram

- **Step 1:** Given our duration and activity order from the table (page 126) for baking a cake, we can construct a diagram, labelling the nodes and adding duration times but leaving the rest blank.

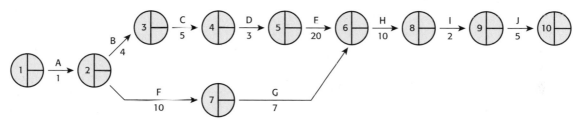

Planning the network

- **Step 2:** The next step is to calculate the EST for each activity.

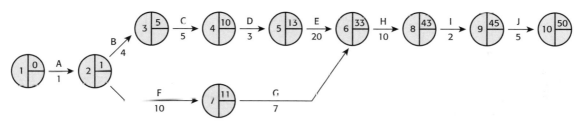

Adding ESTs to the network

This is a straightforward exercise except for node 6 where two arrows converge. The baking of the cake and the clean-up operation need to be completed before the cake is 'cooled' for final preparation (otherwise students may be tempted not to wash up!).

At node 5, the EST of the baking is 13 minutes.

At node 6, the EST of putting away the utensils is 15 minutes.

Activity H, the cooling, can only begin after the cake has been baked, so the EST at node 6 must be 13 + 20 minutes = 33 minutes. As a general rule when calculating EST, if two arrows arrive at a node, the longest time taken is added to the previous EST.

- **Step 3:** With the ESTs added, we are now ready to calculate the LFTs. We start calculating the LFTs from right to left in a process which is known as roll-back. (We saw this process before when calculating expected monetary values in the decision tree, page 35.)

Given that activity J is the last activity, the latest finish time is the same as the EST of the next activity, which does not exist. This equals 50 minutes.

LFTs are then calculated by subtracting the durations from the last LFT.

(continued)

5.8 Project management HL (3)

CONSTRUCTING A NETWORK (continued)

LFTs calculated

Critical path is A, B, C, D, E, H, I, J.

Points to note

From the network diagram and calculations, the estimated time of completion is 50 minutes. Without using a network diagram and simply adding up all the minutes of the tasks in sequence, we thought the cake would have been ready in 67 minutes; there has been a significant time saving of 17 minutes.

If the EST and LFT in a node are the same, then these activities are deemed to be critical. The latest finishing time of the previous activity is the same as the start of the next. Any delay will result in additional time being taken and, as a result, this will delay start times of following activities. If the network diagram was referring to a complex building project, these delays could lead to significant increases in costs and penalties for the construction firm.

In the above situation, activities where the EST and LFT in the same node are equal are called critical, and lie on the critical path.

On another branch of the diagram, it is clear that for node 7, the EST and LFT are significantly different, giving the project manager an opportunity to examine some float time.

5.8 Project management HL (4)

TOTAL FLOAT AND FREE FLOAT **HL**

Total float

Total float is the longest an activity can be delayed from its own EST without delaying the project.

It is calculated by using the LFT (of that activity) − duration − EST (of that activity)

For activity F, the total float is 26 − 10 − 1 = 15 minutes

For activity G, the total float is 33 − 7 − 11 = 15 minutes

However, total float is not specific to an activity but to an uninterrupted path, and this has implications for how we can use this free time.

We cannot delay both F and G by 15 minutes as this will add time to our baking. To avoid this 'knock-on' effect we calculate the free float.

Free float

The free float is defined as the amount of delay possible on an activity without affecting the earliest start time of following activities.

It is calculated by using the EST (next activity) − duration − EST (of that activity).

For activity F, the free float is 11 − 10 − 1 = 0 minutes

For activity G, the free float is 33 − 7 − 11 = 15 minutes

We conclude that activity F cannot be delayed without affecting the free time available to activity G. This information will be needed by project managers when considering how to use float time effectively by shifting workers or resources to ensure that critical activities are completed on time.

Before we discuss the value of critical path analysis (CPA) for project management, students are encouraged to attempt question 7, page 130.

EVALUATING THE VALUE OF A NETWORK IN THE MANAGEMENT OF PROJECTS **HL**

We can identify a number of important benefits to managers from using a network diagram. For example:

- Managers can experiment and can consider 'what if?' without having to commit to spending vast amounts of time and money on projects that are later abandoned.

- Potential delays in activities can be identified and pre-empted by use of subcontractors if required, or the re-allocation of resources from activities where there is float time to those activities where there is none.

- CPA computer programs now exist which avoid the need to draft networks by hand and changes can easily be incorporated before the final diagram is decided. Thus the schedule and final diagram can also be updated easily if external factors (such as the weather, for building projects) change without warning.

Issues to bear in mind, however, include:

- Depending on the number of activities, some large-scale projects may not lend themselves well to a simple diagram and can become too complex. Additional managers may be required for supervision of additional tasks, which will raise costs.

- The durations for each activity may need to be objectively assessed by an industry expert to see if they are realistic and achievable, given the labour and capital constraints of the firm.

Judgment

We have seen throughout this study guide that the need for clear planning is imperative. Students are encouraged to read about the opening of Terminal 5 at London's Heathrow Airport which was announced with much fanfare by the owners, BAA, as the model way to plan, construct and complete a complex infrastructure project. Unfortunately events did not turn out as they expected.

Examination questions on Topic 5

1 Paolo's Pasta

Paolo sells his pasta for a price of $7 per kilogram

Full capacity is 12,000 kg pasta per year

Current output is 10,000 kg per year

Paolo's expenses:

Lease costs	$200 per week
Mortgage payment	$500 per month
Paolo's salary	$300 per week
Raw materials	$1.25 per kilogram (kg) of pasta produced
Wages	$1.60 per kilogram (kg) of pasta produced
Electricity/Gas/Water	$0.15 per kilogram (kg) of pasta produced

Construct a break-even graph showing the break-even level of output, the margin of safety and the amount of profit at current output level. (Show any relevant workings.)   (May 2007, adapted)

2 HL Evaluate the methods for achieving a Total Quality Culture in large organizations like Jaguar.   (May 2005)

3 HL You are given the following information concerning Coffee-Cool's stock control system which is presented in the following graph. Coffee-Cool roast and distribute coffee beans to café's and retailers.

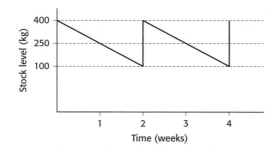

Identify the following for Coffee-Cool

  i lead time

 ii buffer stock

iii reorder quantity   (May 2006)

4 Evaluate the marketing, human resource and finance implications for Bubbleflow if it introduces mass and cell production.   (May 2006)

5 Explain the advantages and disadvantages for Jaguar of using just-in-time (JIT) production rather than the more traditional just-in-case systems.

6 HL Network analysis

Construct the diagram for the following project, clearly showing ESTs, LFTs and the critical path, and calculating the respective total and free floats.

Activity	Duration	Details of the sequence
A	2	The first task
B	6	Must follow A
C	8	Must follow A
D	10	Must follow B
E	16	Must follow C
F	6	Must follow E
G	8	Must follow only after D and F are completed

(**Source:** adapted from Gillespie 2001)

6.1 The pre-issued case study (1)

Introduced in 2002, the pre-issued case study as an assessment tool was a significant step forward for Business and Management. It has allowed students to prepare material before the examination and importantly allowed ESOL students a great opportunity to save time in the final examination and focus on displaying their knowledge of Business and Management.

PREPARING FOR THE PRE-ISSUED CASE STUDY

Since 2002, it is assumed that IB Diploma centres will have developed their own way to help students prepare for the final pre-issued case. The analysis below is offered as a guide to help students navigate through the material and should not be considered exhaustive.

Students could focus on the following:

- Identify the current position of the firm – a great starting point is to draw up a SWOT analysis from the information given in the case.

- Sketch out the main characters in the case study. Who are they? What are their roles? If there are leaders, what are their qualities or styles?

- Identify and define the key business terms in the case study. Make sure you have exact definitions and explanations which have direct relevance to the case study. This is known in examiner 'jargon' as context. (Your answers to questions must be in context: they must refer to the business in the case study and not just any other possible organization.)

- Identify a mission or vision if one is not given. What are the organization's main objective(s)?

- Which market is the organization currently operating in? Is it a niche or a mass market? Who are the key competitors?

- Linked to this point, try to determine who the key internal and external stakeholders are.

- What about the external environment? A good idea might be to undertake a PEST or STEEPLE analysis from the stimulus material.

- Do any areas of concern within the organization immediately present themselves? You may wish to consider motivation, communication, leadership and management issues.

- What is the organization's current financial position? Are there any immediate liquidity and profitability concerns?

PREPARING FOR THE PRE-ISSUED CASE STUDY **HL**

In addition, we can identify some HL extension areas:

- What is the prevailing corporate culture in the organization? Is it appropriate given the current financial position, leadership style adopted and external environment?

- To what extent does change need to take place? What are the key driving or restraining forces for change? HL students could draw up a force field analysis for the firm.

- From the information given, is the company too centralized or decentralized? How important is the informal organization?

- Try to ascertain the degree and nature of any conflict suggested within the case study.

NOTE FOR TEACHERS

The above analysis may seem intimidating but, if it has been carried out effectively, a student will feel empowered going into the examination room knowing that they have covered every significant dimension of the case. They may also feel that they have pre-empted some of the potential questions and may have ready some pre-prepared answers.

However, we must sound a note of caution. The new pre-issued case study has been written for two examination sessions – May and November. The number of possible questions arising would fill many pages. Students should not try to prepare for them all and then learn pre-prepared answers.

Furthermore, HL students in the final examination will be given additional new information to help them answer the compulsory strategy question in section C (see below).

6.1 The pre-issued case study (2)

PAPER 1 SECTION C: THE STRATEGY QUESTION FOR HL ONLY

Before studying this section, students are advised to read pages 40–43 of the IB *Business and Management Guide* as this contains information and advice on tackling this compulsory question for Higher level students.

Here is an important extract:

This topic does not add any new content to the diploma programme business and management course but gathers and synthesizes business ideas, concepts and techniques from the topics in the HL course. The use of these ideas, concepts and techniques will allow informed decisions to be made about the future direction of an organization. This will be assessed through a question in section C of paper 1 requiring a strategic response.

Source: IB *Business and Management Guide*, p.40

It is expected that students will have seen the specimen question for this paper available on the online curriculum centre. This study guide was written before the first May examination, and hence it does not contain any questions from 2009.

Strategy: definition

Russell-Walling cites the work of Johnson and Scholes, defining strategy as:

The direction and scope of an organization over the long term which achieves advantages through its configuration of resources within a challenging environment to meet the needs of the market and to fulfil stakeholder expectations.

Russell-Walling (2007, page 48)

Michael Porter puts it succinctly.

Strategy has to do with what makes you unique.

Relevance to the HL Section C question

In the final section of Paper 1 HL, the student will have to be able to discuss possible strategic options for the organization featured in the case study.

You will be given additional *new* material which will guide you (in addition to the material which you have pre-seen) in analysing the strategic choices which may need to be made by the organization in question.

This new information could include but is not limited to:

- Additional financial information which has come to light since the original case was issued, which will be given to the student with a fresh copy of the case study material
- New updated economic data or forecasts in the form of graphs and tables
- New information on other changing external factors

- New market research data from surveys or interviews
- Quotes or excerpts from newspaper articles or other secondary sources which may be of direct or indirect relevance to the strategic decision under consideration.

Strategic tools and methods to guide strategic options

Throughout the guide, reference has been made to strategic decision-making tools and methods which could help in this process of formulating a new direction.

They could include use of:

- The Ansoff and BCG matrices
- Changing the marketing mix as *part* of a new strategy
- Possible joint ventures or strategic alliances with other firms
- Franchising
- Porter's generic strategies given the competitive nature (Five Forces) of the industry in which the firm operates
- The creation of a Blue Ocean strategy (not on the syllabus but a useful new strategic way of thinking)
- Moving into new international markets as suggested from Ansoff
- Downsizing, retrenchment and restructuring the organization to reduce management costs as part of a new competitive strategic direction
- Offshoring and outsourcing parts of the production process to accompany the above choice.

Evaluating a new strategic direction: a recent example

- Throughout the syllabus but especially in the Marketing parts of the course, the Business and Management course asks students to demonstrate higher-order learning skills such as discussion and evaluation. To achieve this, HL students are often asked to try and evaluate a strategy or a change in the strategic direction of a company.
- For part C of the new HL Paper 1, students will be asked a *compulsory* question on this. Strategy questions could also form part of a HL Paper 2 question.
- Students will need to practise their technique in this area. The marks offered for these types of questions are invariably higher than for questions asking for a definition or explanation of a business term.
- Let us take a real example from 2007 of a strategic change and then try to evaluate whether it has been successful. It concerns the launch of a very popular product as part of a new strategic direction.

6.1 The pre-issued case study (3)

APPLE LAUNCHES IPOD TOUCH

Today, Apple has launched a new MP3 player, the iPod Touch, a music player with a touch-sensitive screen that can browse the Internet wirelessly. It has also introduced a range of products to replace its successful iPod Nano range and has cut the price of its more recent product the iPhone by $200.

Apple is trying to consolidate its position as the market leader when the company is facing renewed attacks from its rivals including Microsoft which has cut the price of its own music wireless device, the Zune.

Apple had also announced that it had struck a deal with Starbucks to form a joint venture to allow customers to buy music from Apple's wireless iTunes Store, whilst they are at one of the chain's coffee shops.

Apple's share price fell on the news by 3.5 per cent. There was concern over how successful the launch would be given the problems many American cities have in sustaining reliable networks and a recent survey conducted by the German government about the associated health risks from using mobile devices with wi-fi connectivity. There have also been further concerns about the possibility of a US economic recession.

Source: adapted from Reuters, 7 September 2007

Outline of the strategic change

- Apple is attempting to launch a new product to compete with its rivals in a rapidly changing technological market
- Increasing its range of products to widen its product portfolio
- Cutting the price of one of its new innovative products, the iPhone
- Joining with a well-established chain to allow greater distribution of its services such as ITunes via wireless networks.

Identifying external factors from a PESTLE analysis

- Problems with unreliable wireless networks (Technological)
- Health concerns over the use of these networks (Ethical?)
- Threat of economic recession and reaction from major competitor, Microsoft (Economic)

Evaluation of the strategy

As this case study was written in 2007, hindsight is clearly valuable here and we can note that the launch of the iPod Touch has been a major success and consolidated Apple's position as the market leader in MP3 devices and legal downloadable music.

However, how would we have evaluated this strategy before we knew that it had been a success?

We can do this by asking a number of questions:

- How will this new product change the product portfolio of Apple?
- What will be the impact on revenue with the introduction of new models and the price reduction of the iPhone?
- How will stakeholders other than shareholders react?
- With the new product range, will Apple's marketing mix have to be altered? Will new distribution channels have to be opened and a new promotional mix created?
- Is there a danger that with the release of the new MP3 player Apple may begin to cannibalize its own market share?
- Will the corporate cultures of the two organizations be compatible to allow the joint venture flourish?
- How significant will the external factors be? Does Apple need to consider its social responsibilities given the health concerns highlighted in the material? How deep will the US recession be?
- What time frame will we require before we can judge objectively whether this strategy has been a success?

The important point to note is that we are trying to evaluate the strategy and providing sound analysis to justify its introduction. Students do not need to ask all of the above, but it is a good habit to get into to ask challenging questions of the material. Finally:

Strategy is about asking questions: what, why, when, how and who?

Source: IB *Business and Management Guide*, p.40

6.2 Extended Essay: alternative insights (1)

NOTES FOR TEACHERS

The IB *Bulletin* for 2007, which publishes statistics on the number of students entering particular subjects, reveals that group 3 subjects (including Business and Management and others) are the most popular subject areas in which Diploma candidates submit extended essays.

From the author's experience, Business and Management extended essays are popular for a number of reasons:

- An Extended Essay in Business and Management allows students to pursue and develop knowledge of and insight into a topic such as human resource management or marketing which has engaged them.

- Anecdotal evidence from a number of students who have applied to tertiary institutions in the United States, Australia, New Zealand and Europe suggests that university admissions tutors regard the preparation of an Extended Essay in business as a valuable higher-order learning skill which will allow students to flourish on a degree or equivalent course.

- Finally, if the student is a stakeholder in an organization such as a family-run business, the Extended Essay can provide an opportunity to objectively examine a current or future issue with the possibility of suggesting feasible solutions. (This is also true for the Business and Management Internal Assessment, which we will come to later.)

The distinction between the Extended Essay and Internal Assessment

New assessment (or marking) criteria for the Extended Essay that came into operation in 2009 make a much clearer distinction than previously between the Extended Essay and the Higher level Internal Assessment for Business and Management.

- With its 'positioning' firmly established, the Extended Essay has taken a major step forward to be regarded as an opportunity to practise and develop tertiary academic research skills because of the importance of collecting predominantly secondary data sources.

- The Internal Assessment for Higher level requires much greater use of primary data (with some secondary of course!).

Extended Essay: avoiding the common problems

Students fail to narrow the research focus

One of the most common problems which consistently resonates from the annual examiner reports on Extended Essay performance in Business and Management is that, given the 4000 word limit, students try to cover too broad an area of a particular topic.

Below is an Extended Essay title which would fit this description.

- An evaluation into company X's new marketing strategy designed to launch a new product into a new international marketplace.

This type of essay, focusing on evaluating a new marketing strategy, appears quite often. It is the author's view that the submission of a marketing-strategy based Extended Essay needs to be handled carefully. Close scrutiny of the research topic needs to be carried out before the student begins.

A more appropriate focused research question would be:

- Should company X release product Y into country Z?

or

- Given the changing economic environment, to what extent should company X attempt to change its marketing mix for product Y?

These questions may not be perfect and both require fine-tuning and negotiation between the student and supervisor, but each is more realistic within the word limit to complete, and significantly narrower than our first example.

Here are some potential examples for students and supervisors to discuss:

1 Should company Z remove product X from its current portfolio?

2 Will company Y be able to survive the significant downturn in economic activity in its host country?

3 Will the release of product Z save company Y from insolvency?

4 What are the implications of company X moving from a niche market to a mass market?

- **Justification**

All of the above titles or research questions have been written to convey how narrow a good Extended Essay research question should be. They leave little room for doubt as to the scope of the investigation and perhaps may provide a clue into the possible theoretical framework which may be employed.

- In example 1, *product portfolio analysis* and *contribution* may be important theoretical concepts.

- In example 2 the *external environment* is clearly going to be an important theoretical framework on which to build an argument around whether company Y will survive.

- For example 3, *cash flow*, *liquidity* and *marketing* may be important theoretical topics to guide this essay.

- Students are invited to discuss the merits (and demerits!) of example 4.

6.2 Extended Essay: alternative insights (2)

Students try to 'reinvent the wheel'

There has been a temptation for some students to try and undertake an Extended Essay which might try to challenge current paradigms.

Examples for discussion include:

- Is all marketing unethical?
- Given the growth of e-commerce, is the 7P marketing mix model now redundant?
- Is there a more accurate way for a firm to calculate probabilities on a decision tree, to make the expected monetary values more valuable for decision-making?

These attempts are very laudable but, without wishing to dampen student enthusiasm, this type of Extended Essay topic is too vast for effective treatment within the word limit. These topics may lend themselves more appropriately to a class TOK discussion, especially the first marketing question on marketing and ethics.

Students focus on the subject-specific criteria and neglect the general criteria

The Extended Essay is marked according to a set of prescribed criteria and students need to be issued with the criteria early in the process of selecting possible topics for investigation.

However, a crucial part of the relationship between the supervisor and the student in determining success is – on submission of the penultimate draft – to make sure that they carefully check that they have satisfied the general criteria as well as the subject-specific criteria.

For example:

- Is the research question clearly stated in the introduction?
- Are the arguments presented reasoned and balanced? (that is, do they attempt to show both sides?)
- Has sufficient analysis has been carried out including the use of numerical data?
- Have sources have been referenced according to the IB guidelines?
- Has the abstract been included and does it conform to the expectations of the marking criteria?

In common with the word limit, these aspects of the Extended Essay are within the control of the student.

In the race to finish, attention to detail can sometimes be overlooked and important marks lost. This is frustrating for the student, the supervisor and the final assessor!

6.3 Internal Assessment (1)

INTERNAL ASSESSMENT: HIGHER LEVEL

From the author's experience as a senior examiner and moderator, the Higher level Internal Assessment (also referred to as the Business Report) provides many students with a challenging but very rewarding experience.

Over the last six years the author has moderated a number of superb, professional-looking business reports which would have been of significant practical value to senior management of an organization as a forward-looking document to aid decision-making.

However, despite clear guidelines in the IB *Business and Management Guide*, the availability of online advice and guidance in senior examiner reports which are published after each examination sesssion in May and November, a significant number of students are not producing business reports which satisfy the assessment criteria.

One consistent area of weakness in this latter group is that an increasing number of projects do not include financial information or costs of any kind.

This point is important for two reasons:

- Without cost information incorporated into the analysis, the scope for discussion and evaluation is limited and therefore the number of marks available is limited too.

- Secondly, the report must have *practical value* to management. Without a single cost or sales forecast included, changes to a marketing mix, for example, could not seriously be considered by senior management.

Suggestions for improvement

- **Access to data and confidentiality issues**

A number of candidates continue to ignore the following advice from the IB online support materials.

> *Students must ensure that the organizations selected for the project are willing and able to provide the necessary data. It is not uncommon for organizations to fail to provide this. This will seriously undermine the quality of the final written report. If students have not gathered sufficient material, they may have to give up the project and start another.*

Each year, HL students have claimed in their research proposals and conclusions that a potential difficulty or limitation of the report has been either the presence of confidentiality issues or simply that the owner of the business was unwilling or unable to submit the relevant primary data.

These projects are unlikely to score highly. The student and their supervisor need to decide early on in the investigation whether data collection is going to be a significant issue, and find a different project if necessary.

- **Primary data collection: interviews and questionnaires**

It is unlikely that any business would undertake a significant strategic or tactical change based either on the opinions of 20 or even 50 customers from a single questionnaire (even if it was 100% accurately

and completely filled in) or from one interview conducted with the senior management team or CEO.

However, a number of projects submitted in recent examination sessions have placed their entire justification for a particular course of action on the responses of perhaps 25 individuals or fewer, to one questionnaire.

Before a student begins a project they must ask themselves this important question again:

- Will I be able to collect significant primary data to allow me to make reasoned judgments on the suitability of a particular course of action?

- **Length**

In 2009 the word limit of 2000 words will be explicitly applied as part of the marking criteria. Before 2009 this was not the case and students have been able to extend their analysis and evaluation beyond this limit without loss of marks.

Students are advised to check carefully the marking criteria at the end of the assignment writing process to ensure that they are within the required word limit. It would be frustrating for students to lose marks unnecessarily on aspects of the assignment that are under their control.

- **The suitability of family businesses**

There are a number of compelling arguments why a student may wish to undertake for their Business Report an investigation of a family firm. They include but are not limited to:

- quick and readily available access to data

- prior knowledge of the workings of the organization.

However, as a basis for Internal Assessment projects the choice of a family business can suffer from one vital flaw.

The decision in the Business Report needs to be one that has not yet been previously considered or undertaken, i.e. the project needs to be forward looking and not reflect backwards on something which has already happened.

It is the objective of the Business Report to try and ascertain through good analysis and evaluation that a business should either accept or reject a particular future course of action. A number of recent reports submitted which featured a family company gave the impression that the student was already aware of the final decision and was in a sense working backwards from the conclusion to the introduction to justify this. This type of project is effectively a descriptive essay and will score lower than expected marks.

If two students have two separate family businesses which they wish to use as models for their Business Report, it may be useful to ask each student to swap families for the duration of the project, for the sake of objectivity.

6.3 Internal Assessment (2)

INTERNAL ASSESSMENT: HIGHER LEVEL *(continued)*

Examples of appropriate research questions

- Should company X purchase a new combined fax, printer and scanner?
- Should company X lease or purchase laptop computers for its senior managers?
- Should company X advertise its products on the outside of buses?

All of the above titles are appropriate. They share a common factor that they are narrow in focus and are proposing tactical changes to an organization's operations which lend themselves to effective treatment within the word limit. Another important justification is that these research questions will require the student to include numerical data in their project.

- In the first example question, company X will have to look at the purchase cost and the depreciation on a new fax machine and future costs savings.
- In the second, the student will have to directly compare leasing costs and purchase costs of laptop computers and consider depreciation.
- Finally, the last example will require the firm to consider (and cost) the other alternative methods of promotion to see whether advertising on buses is cost-effective and would achieve sufficient audience reach.

INTERNAL ASSESSMENT: STANDARD LEVEL

From May 2009 the Internal Assessment for the Business and Management course for Standard level students takes the form of a written commentary.

The intention for the new Standard level assessment is that students will use mostly secondary data sources (some primary data is of course allowed) to analyse and discuss a real issue or problem facing an organization. The title must be phrased as a question.

Three to five supporting documents must be given as evidence and students must highlight sections of the articles that have been used as research material in their commentary. A range of different points of view is encouraged.

The articles must be as recent as possible and published not more than 2 years earlier than the submission of the commentary. For example, for students submitting written commentaries for the examination in November 2009, the articles presented must be dated no earlier than November 2007.

NOTE FOR TEACHERS

This study guide was published in late 2009, a few months after the first Standard level commentaries were received by the IB from the May session. Therefore it would be disingenuous to comment further on the structure and format of the commentary at this early stage. If the student follows the advice above and, in the case of the Higher level assessment, keeps the focus narrow, then the author is confident that a student's efforts, if they adhere strictly to the marking criteria, will be well rewarded

References

Chan, Kim W. and Mauborgne, Renée (2005) *Blue Ocean Strategy*. Harvard Business School.

Dearden, Chris and Foster, Mike (1994) *Organisational Decision Making*. Longman.

Economist (2004) *Business Miscellany*. The Economist/Profile Books. New edition due to be published 2009.

Friedman, Thomas L. (2005) *The World is Flat*. Allen Lane.

Gabriel, Vincent (1998) *Management of Business for GCE A level and LCC 1,* 2nd edn. Oxford University Press.

Gillespie, Andrew (2001) *Oxford Revision Guide*. Oxford University Press.

Handy, Charles B. (1976) *Understanding Organisations*. Penguin.

Handy, Charles B. (1995) *Gods of Management*. Arrow.

Hashemi, Sahar and Hashemi, Bobby (2007) *Anyone Can Do It*. Capstone.

Herzberg, Frederick (2003) *One More Time: How do you motivate employees*? Harvard Business Review.

Lines, David, Marcouse, Ian and Martin, Barry (2004) *The Complete A–Z Business Studies Handbook*. Hodder & Stoughton.

Powell, John (1991) *Quantitative Decision-Making*. Longman.

Russell-Walling, Edward (2007) *50 Management ideas you ought to know*. Quercus Publishing.

Trout, Jack (2001) *Big Brands, Big Trouble*. John Wiley.

Trout, Jack with Rivkin, Steve (2008) *Differentiate or Die*. John Wiley.

NOTES FOR TEACHERS

The suggested answers in the following pages should not be treated as model or perfect answers. In keeping with the objectives of this guide and the IB learner profile, suggested answers are given for selected questions only, with in some cases, hints and tips on how to answer.

Reflections on student performance from the author's experiences as a marker of Higher level scripts over the last 6 years are also included . New teachers to the IB Business and Management course may find these comments particularly useful.

The temptation to provide 'model answers' is resisted, in part because of the author's and the IBO's intention that this guide is perceived as a learning guide and not positioned as a revision crammer. It is also to fulfil the author's commitment to an old proverb, which has underpinned much of his teaching practice in this subject.

> *Give a man a fish and he can eat for a day,*
> *Teach a man to fish and he can eat for a lifetime.*

Particular attention will be given to command words in the question. Failure to follow command words such as 'examine', 'analyse' and 'evaluate' is one of the most critical reasons why many candidates fail to achieve high marks in final examinations despite the fact that their knowledge of theoretical concepts may be sound.

In many cases, not the whole question but part only is covered, in order to allow greater focus on technique rather than knowledge. More detailed answers are given to numerate questions from units 3 and 5, in order to allow students to gain confidence in tackling these types of questions, since – for both HL and SL – a compulsory quantitative question in the examination cannot be avoided.

The material covered in these questions is suitable for both HL and SL students, unless designated HL.

Topic 1 Business Organization and Management (1)

1 (a)

On page 13 in unit 1.3 of the guide we saw that a firm could implement an environmental audit to respond to growing concerns of climate change and threats to sustainability.

Possible practices to minimize the 'carbon footprint' of the BMW Group include but are not limited to:

- Recycling of materials such as tyres and steel used in construction
- Investing funds in designing more environmentally friendly cars that use less unleaded petrol
- The installation of environmentally friendly technology which is used in the production process of cars to limit noise pollution and to minimize harmful emissions.

To become a more attractive employer the firm could:

- Offer flexible working patterns given the significant changes in the demographic landscape for the developed world as identified in unit 2.1 (page 36)
- Encourage greater employee involvement in the decision-making process and increase training opportunities to encourage 'personal growth' as argued by the job enrichment school
- Extend profit-sharing schemes or employee share ownership schemes, if currently offered, or introduce if not.

(b)

- It would be fair to say that many companies consider the adoption of greater corporate social responsibility (CSR) towards its stakeholder groups as a vital part of their mission and vision and not only for commercial success.
- A strong commitment to CSR could be used to motivate workers or to satisfy government guidelines or to pre-empt pressure group action.

However, a key point to remember is that commercial success is the criterion being used to justify a CSR approach in the question and very good students will define in their answer what commercial success could imply.

Commercial success could be defined in terms of:

- Increased revenue leading to increased market share
- Increased profitability
- Improved goodwill leading to benefits or cost savings throughout the supply chain (HL only).

Given that we have defined our terms of reference, it will be now up to the student to prepare analysis based on the information given in the unit about the benefits and drawbacks of adopting a CSR approach with reference to a car manufacturer, rather than Nike or McDonalds which were given as examples in unit 1.3. (It is likely that environmental concerns and the costs of compliance are likely to feature strongly in the CSR analysis.)

For evaluation questions at HL and SL, it is imperative to note that this question is not asking just for a list of the advantages of adopting such an approach (something that many students would be able to do) but is asking for a balanced justification – the negatives of adopting such an approach will need to be considered, and to reach the top of the marking band a substantiated judgment reached.

Without resorting to too much examiner jargon, the command word – evaluate – implies that a final answer, based on the analysis which has preceded it, will need to be given. This analysis will also need to show both sides of the argument and be related to BMW and not just any company.

2

The important command words in this question are 'analyse the potential effects on stakeholder groups'.

Students will need to speculate on the potential positive and negative effects of a large global conglomerate investing in China. Specific knowledge of the Disney Company and China is not required in the answer, although information from the stimulus given in the question could be quoted to highlight a potential stakeholder concern. However, this quotation alone would not be considered as good analysis; additional depth and detail and explanation would be required.

For positive effects, we could identify:

- Increased capital and new technology transfers to the host country (China).
- Improved infrastructure, employment opportunities and thus an increase in the standard of living for local Chinese residents.

- Greater choice for consumers in the industry in which the Disney Company operates.

However, negative impacts could be felt by some stakeholder groups:

- Increased competition for local businesses and potential redundancies for some workers.
- Possible government financial incentives given to the Disney Company to encourage them to locate in China may increase local and national tensions if the same assistance is not offered to other Chinese firms (particularly pertinent given the bailout packages being awarded to some but not all firms in many countries).

Given time constraints, students would be expected to come up with perhaps one more negative stakeholder impact. However, a simple list of concerns should be avoided. Analysis requires that there will need to be some development of each point.

Topic 1 Business Organization and Management (2)

3

As we have seen from our investigation into the stakeholder model in unit 1.5 and the impact of offshoring, the number of potential effects is considerable.

We could look at the impact on:

- Suppliers
- Employees
- Shareholders
- Competitors
- Government
- Local community
- Consumers

The command word 'assess' generally tries to put a value on the magnitude of the effect. Not all stakeholders will be affected in the same manner and good answers will try to look at both positive and negative impacts.

Consumers and shareholders may, for example, be positive about the move if the cost of the finished product is reduced, in the case of the former, and thus higher revenue and profitability is achieved in the case of the latter.

The local community, the affected workers domestically and the government may all be fearful of the move. As we have seen, given the rise of unemployment recently (and in our NZ Telecom case study) in a number of developed countries, such a move could be deeply unpopular.

Competitors may be indifferent about the move but may be forced to consider a new strategic option, if the move leads to much lower costs and increased market share to the company undertaking the offshoring.

4

Again as we saw with our Fisher & Paykel example, firms can find it very difficult to reconcile all stakeholder demands and avoid conflict. Given the enormous influence of oil companies in our daily and business lives, the growing concerns about sustainability, and the ability of pressure groups to exert influence via improved ICT, companies such as BP have to tread a very careful line between all of these concerns. Students are invited to analyse these concerns in more detail.

5

This is a demanding question and many students failed to reach the top marking band, not because they did not know what the external environment was, on the contrary, many students went into great detail and highlighted a number of external factors which constitutes STFEPLE analysis.

The two issues where students let themselves down was a failure to relate their answers to both the size and the number of mergers and takeovers and to answer the command word which was 'to what extent'.

'To what extent' questions are evaluation-type questions but they require students to 'measure' the impact of a factor or variable on a continuum or sliding scale where at one end the factor or variable has no impact (0%) to the other end where the variable completely determines the objectives or motives of a firm behind a merger or takeover (100%).

In this question, in order to 'measure the impact' of the external environment, students were required to provide detailed analysis highlighting both drivers and restrainers (HL extension term) of merger activity or reasons why the external environment had a role to play in determining merger activity and instances where perhaps it did not.

Some information was provided by the stimulus material in the case study but students had to look beyond the external environment to argue why internal influences such as the motives or objectives of senior management might also be important. Many students did not look inwardly enough, if at all. A final conclusion stating the overall impact demanded by the question was also absent in many responses.

NOTE FOR TEACHERS

In May 2008, when this question was set, the external environment did have a role to play in determining the size and number of mergers, but one is tempted to speculate how different student answers would have been if the same question had been set in May 2009.

6 **HL**

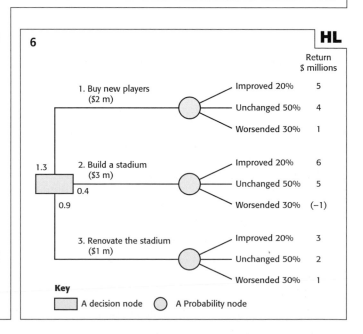

Topic 1 Business Organization and Management (3)

9   **HL**

Although a Lewin force field diagram is not required, it might be helpful to sketch out an idea of the competing forces. The command word is 'analyse' so a list of drivers and restrainers would not be appropriate. The appropriate command word for a list of points would be 'identify'.

Driving forces which could be analysed include but are not limited to:

Sales

- Increased global market share with flow-on effects for profitability and shareholder value

Manufacturing

- Allows larger production runs to take advantage of economies of scale
- Cheaper sources of raw materials and labour

Operations

- Improvement in global communications technology has allowed firms to decentralize and offshore with additional cost savings

Restrainers could include:

Sales

- Increased competition in overseas markets may reduce profit margins and prices.
- Investment in the marketing effort will be required to create new distribution channels and other elements of the mix such as promotion.

(continued)

Topic 1 Business Organization and Management (4)

9 *(continued)*

Manufacturing and operations

- Outsourcing will raise quality control concerns and additional money will be needed to finance training to maintain and ensure quality standards
- Decentralizing operations may lead to cost savings but, if unsuccessful, production costs may rise and goodwill may be lost in the supply chain.

To achieve full marks on this question, students need to cover all three areas of the question, but sensible time allocation is required to ensure that the student does not overwrite and therefore use up valuable time, which could be spent on other parts of the examination paper.

EXAMINER'S HINTS

11

At first glance this discussion question on globalization seemed straightforward and many answers did contain relevant analysis on the issues surrounding globalization.

However, a closer look at the question reveals that the 'context' of the question is asking for students to focus on leadership and motivation only.

- Students therefore had to consider and discuss the leadership responses when a company decides to move into a global marketplace and the impact on motivation of perhaps senior managers affected or workers who may have to adapt to a new working environment.
- Outstanding answers included reference to traditional existing leadership and motivation theories, and discussed whether they would be appropriate in a global context.
- In contrast to the command word 'evaluation', discussion questions do not explicitly require the student to provide a final judgment. (It would be very hard to provide a judgment in the above question.)
- However, it would not hurt a student's response to include a comment, perhaps in the last sentence, summarizing the overall mood or tone of the discussion.

10

Suggested answers to these two questions have been combined, given the similarity of the topic and context, although it is accepted that the command words are different.

As we saw with our analysis in unit 1.9, the spread of globalization has been enhanced by the commercial development of the Internet and the significant growth in communication technologies such as e-mail, video conferencing and VOIP (e.g. Skype).

Students are encouraged to review unit 1.9 and the role which ICT has played in rapidly changing technological markets.

Evaluation questions on globalization, in the examiner's experience, tend to attract the descriptive, unsubstantiated, one-sided argument, predominantly that the spread of globalization is solely down to a number of generic factors based on communication such as the ability of senior managers to e-mail, video conference and speak foreign languages.

As we have seen from the work by Paul Krugman especially, the answer is not so clear-cut. It is unlikely that globalization would not have happened without the help of the World Wide Web, but the arguments run deeper and are more varied than just greater use of ICT.

Explaining how technological change has affected the way global businesses operate also requires an up-to-date understanding of technological change. A number of students in this examination session did not really appreciate this.

According to the IB mark scheme, technological change may be linked to human resources (automation), marketing (e-commerce), organizational structure (retrenchment and downsizing or outsourcing and offshoring) or design (the use of CAD in the new product development stage) and communication (on-line collaboration through social networking or wikispaces or remote working through the use of bluetooth or wi-fi).

Of course, given Moore's law, some of these points may already be out of date!

Topic 2 Human Resources (1)

EXAMINER'S HINTS

1

What was perceived as a straightforward explanation question proved to be difficult:

- Many students did not understand the term 'work pattern or practice'.

- The creation of part-time work and increased female participation was mentioned but the explanations soon ran dry. Many talked of 'training' as a working pattern, which is not technically correct.

- A number of students also felt that it was essential that employers needed to adapt to every demographic or social change. The question is slightly ambiguous as it asks how management *may* adapt work patterns. Good answers included comments about how some employers in industries such as the public sector may find it difficult to adapt work practices.

EXAMINER'S HINTS

2 HL

Regularly each year in the senior examiner's report on Business and Management there are comments that students do not answer 'analysis or evaluation' questions in enough detail and depth. The reverse is true for 'explanation' type questions: many students write too much.

The question was worth 6 marks. Assuming that 80 marks was available for the whole paper sat over 2 hours and 30 minutes, a student should take about $150 \times \frac{3}{40} = 11.25$ minutes to explain two advantages and one disadvantage, or one point every 4 minutes.

Good explanations are brief; they define clearly terms or concepts and wherever possible provide a concise example to illustrate a point being made.

Possible advantages of moving to a matrix structure:

- Experts can be brought together from different departments increasing the knowledge pool available to find a solution to the task

- Increased motivational possibilities created by job enrichment

- Greater co-operation between departments with longer-term benefits for the informal organization.

Possible disadvantages:

- Costly to implement in terms of time, resourcing and disruption to departments with key workers removed in order to take part in the matrix project.

- A new leader will need to be appointed to run the project team. There could be loyalty issues and tensions if an appointed 'temporary' leader is not valued by the whole team.

- Potential cultural clashes between workers from different departments.

EXAMINER'S HINTS

3 HL

Motivation continues to be a very popular area of the course, given the large number of students who chose to answer this question.

Financial rewards and payment systems, tied into theories such as Taylor's 'Economic Man' approach, are well understood, and it is always good practice to include a theoretical model in an answer wherever possible, if time allows.

However, issues identified earlier such as a lack of balanced discussion and appropriate context continued, undermining the final marks available for this type of question.

- Many answers were too one-sided and did not include analysis as to why financial rewards *may not* enable firms to recruit and retain skilled workers.

- Some students listed endless theories as to why workers are motivated by financial rewards, in a sense repeating information gleaned from their textbook.

- This second point is crucial as the context of recruiting and retaining skilled workers was often ignored.

- One could have argued that skilled workers may value opportunity, respect and self-actualization as much as their financial reward, given the job enrichment opportunities proposed by writers such as Herzberg as a mechanism to recruit and retain workers in an organization.

- It is likely that, as skilled workers, they may have already met a number of the lower-order needs as specified by the Maslow Hierarchy of Needs.

Answers including balanced discussion with specific reference to skilled workers were rare.

A good tip for students is to take a highlighter pen after the 5-minute reading time has finished and mark out the key command words or contexts of a particular question to remind them that they must try to answer the question presented to them on the exam paper, rather than one that they had expected and prepared for.

Topic 2 Human Resources (2)

4

This was a relatively 'open' and straightforward question. The key to explanation questions of this kind where a number of alternative solutions are feasible is to clearly identify the terms in the question and your perception of an open and informal relationship, and then use appropriate business theory to back up your points.

Suggested answer

(Examiner's reflection is in italics)

A flat management structure is defined as one where there are wide spans of control requiring few layers of hierarchy. We tend to find flat management structures in smaller firms (defined here as an organization with fewer than 10 employees) where communication is easier than in larger organizations with many departments or layers.

Given the nature of smaller chains of command in a small firm, more open and informal relationships may be possible and even encouraged between line managers and subordinates. Decision-making may be flexible and more inclusive than in larger organizations, leading to high levels of empowerment and thus motivation. Greater use of delegation may also lead to increased motivation.

Open and informal should not be viewed as a form of laissez-faire management. Some formal decisions will still need to be made and responsibilities clearly articulated to line workers, otherwise even in small firms, confusion will arise and mistakes could be made.

- *The answer is brief and contains a good deal of terminology which has been applied appropriately although no specific context is mentioned. The last part of the answer perhaps introduces material which is not necessary. The assumption being made that 'open and informal' implies a laissez-faire management style is not always the case.*

5

(Examiner's reflection is in italics)

A piece rate system is a way of rewarding labour by paying workers for each unit produced. In the example of Fish Packaging, it would be appropriate that workers are paid for each kilogram of fish 'landed' or caught.

- *Even though a definition has not been asked for, it is always good practice to define key terms, especially in an explanation question.*

- *Second, it is even better to define the term 'in context' and apply to the company in question. As one can see above it is possible to do both in three lines and not use up unnecessary minutes in the final examination.*

Disadvantages and advantages will depend on whose point of view we are considering. For the workers a key advantage is that the weekly or monthly wage will be directly influenced by the amount they produce. The harder somebody works and catches more fish, then the higher the wage. This type of advantage would suit employees who are influenced by FW Taylor's Economic Man approach.

Two disadvantages for the worker could be that, in the fishing industry, it would be assumed that external factors such as weather are crucial. Wages being directly linked to output will be lower if the boat cannot sail as the case suggests. If this is prolonged, workers may have to move to other occupations. This would then lead to labour shortages for Fish Packaging when the external factors turn in their favour.

For Fish Packaging Limited, increased productivity is possible if wages are tied to production. However, the firm will need to monitor the use of a piece rate system especially if workers are driven to work harder but neglect quality control in a race to satisfy higher production targets. Second, making the firm's output level a function of the workers' motivation instead of customer demand does run the risk that waste may occur and losses may be incurred if Fish Packaging can only sell additional fish at deeply discounted prices.

- *The second part of this answer overcooks the explanation a little. The question does not specifically ask for advantages or disadvantages from the point of view of the firm or worker. However, the intention was to raise points which had not been covered in the text and to show that if the question does not explicitly state which stakeholder group is being affected, then appropriate answers in context will still be rewarded.*

Topic 2 Human Resources (3)

6

Again there is no definitive answer here, given that there are a number of competing theories of motivation.

Here is a brief tutor answer with one comment in italics.

Clearly, with JIT being employed at Jaguar there would need to be a significant change in the degree of delegation and empowerment in the organization, especially with respect to quality control in the car manufacturing process.

Maslow's hierarchy of needs would clearly be relevant, especially the higher-order need of esteem. Leadership approaches leaning towards Theory Y would also be appropriate.

- *Again the focus and context of the question needs to be considered at the beginning. It is a good habit to develop.*

Pride and commitment could be driven by a host of factors and clearly ongoing training, appraisal and feedback would be important factors to bear in mind to introduce JIT successfully. Herzberg was unequivocal in his support for the 'personal growth' of the worker as long as the work which he or she was given was 'meaningful'. Here lies the essence of the 'motivators' in his contribution to the motivational debate.

There are four aspects to this question.

- Appropriate motivational theory
- Jaguar – a car manufacturer
- Introduction of JIT
- Increasing pride and commitment.

Each will need to be considered in the analysis, but only briefly, as the above example illustrates.

7 **HL**

A little context is required here to explain this merger to help us understand the two corporate cultures.

Kmart in wanting to compete with Wal-Mart's dominance of the retail market merged with Sears in an $11bn deal in 2004, creating the third largest retail chain in America.

Kmart's traditional customer base has been the older consumer shopping at out-of-town stores, with Sears focusing more on local shopping malls targeting younger and more 'adventurous' customers.

We can speculate that Kmart may be more traditional in its structure along the lines of Apollo, with Sears being more Athenian in nature. The question asks how we can bring these two opposing cultures together under the management of one merged company, which was going to be predominantly run by Kmart senior managers.

Potential problems in this question could be examined by use of a stakeholder model:

- Employees from the merged companies may have different beliefs and values regarding customer service, quality control and training.

- The new management team will have to decide how the predominantly Apollo bureaucratic-style culture of Kmart can be adapted to fit a more problem-solving and teamwork culture of Sears to minimize the inevitable problems with 'cultural alignment'. (How will we get along?)

- Customers loyal to both Kmart and Sears may require guarantees through promotion and public relations exercises that the new enlarged group will retain elements of both companies. This will be a difficult balancing act.

- Given the merger, there may be a period of fear and suspicion from Sears workers who may feel that their job may be under threat.

- Any other stakeholder conflict on culture could be identified.

Topic 2 Human Resources (4)

8

The stimulus provided with this question made reference to the growing practice of offshoring customer service operations from the UK to India.

Unit 2.2 covers in some detail the benefits and costs of offshoring, but we have not provided analysis when a trade union emerges in an organization where one had previously not existed.

The command word 'examine' is considered to be equivalent to the command word 'analyse' and hence a balanced examination showing both positive and negative consequences should be given.

No overall judgment is required.

Positive effects of introducing a union to a call centre:

- Workers may be given more achievable targets in answering customer enquiries. Working hours could be agreed and, given the nature of call centre work which can be monotonous, may lead to improvements in working conditions.

- Pay could be linked to agreed measures of productivity between the union and management, again providing a boost to motivation.

Negative effects could include:

- Some firms may choose to avoid India as an offshoring destination if the practice of union representation becomes widespread. This could represent a vital source of employment opportunities lost.

- Clear lines of bargaining, negotiation and responsibility will need to be drawn up by the management and the union and this will take time and resources.

- As this is the beginning of the union's existence, initial tension and misunderstanding could result if the above is not clearly articulated and communicated to the members of the union.

Topic 3 Accounts and Finance (1)

2 (a)

	July	August	September	October	November	December
Inflow						
Sales	4000	4000	4000	4000	4000	4000
Outflow						
Costs of buying and holding stock	700	700	700	700	400	400
Costs of Ordering stock	100	100	100	100	200	200
Promotion	200	200	200	200	200	200
Electricity	400	-	-	-	-	-
Drawings	2400	2400	2400	2400	2400	2400
Finance charge	100	100	100	100	100	100
Repayment of loan	-	-	2500	-	-	-
Total outflow	(3900)	(3500)	(6000)	(3500)	(3300)	(3300)
Net cash flow	100	500	(2000)	500	700	700
Opening balance	400	500	1000	(1000)	(500)	200
Closing balance	500	1000	(1000)	(500)	200	900

(b)

In September and October the company will be short of cash due to the first repayment of the loan. This liquidity deterioration, however, will be eased by December and thus should not be viewed as significant. If the owners can for a short time reduce their own generous drawings from the business, then this would improve the liquidity situation considerably. Overall, Coffee-Cool's liquidity position is good and is expected to improve.

Coffee-Cool is selling coffee beans and the cash flow forecast is written for a perishable product. Some of the outflows of cash are assumed to be constant. Given potential changes in external factors, the firm may wish to redraw and update the forecast in a few months, if new cost information becomes available.

Topic 3 Accounts and Finance (2)

3 (a) **HL**

The first three months of the solution is given in each case, and the final answer.
The layout in LIFO/FIFO questions is crucial in obtaining the correct answer.

FIFO

Date	Purchases	Issues/Sales	Balance	Value
July Opening stock			8 @ 6200	49,600
July	20 @ 6300	8 @ 6200 17 @ 6150	3 @ 6300	18,900
August	35 @ 6150	3 @ 6300 29 @ 6150	6 @ 6150	36,900
September	28 @ 6400	6 @ 6150 24 @ 6400	4 @ 6400	25,600
October				
November				
December				
Closing stock in December under FIFO			6 @ 6500	**39,000**

LIFO

Date	Purchases	Issues/Sales	Balance	Value
July Opening stock			8 @ 6200	49,600
July	20 @ 6300	20 @ 6300 5 @ 6200	3 @ 6200	18,600
August	35 @ 6150	32 @ 6150	3 @ 6200 3 @ 6150	18,600 18,450
September	28 @ 6400	28 @ 6400 2 @ 6150	3 @ 6200 1 @ 6150	18,600 6,150
October				
November				
December				
Closing stock in December under LIFO			3 @ 6200 1 @ 6150 2 @ 6300	18,600 6,150 12,600 **37,350**

etc.

(b)

	FIFO	LIFO
Sales 211 hot tubs @ $8500	1,793,500	1,793,500
Opening stock	49,600	49,600
Add purchases	1,319,850	1,319,850
	1,369,450	1,369,450
Less closing stock	39,000	37,350
Cost of goods sold	1,330,450	1,332,100
Gross profit	**463,050**	**461,400**

Topic 3 Accounts and Finance (3)

4

For the first part of the question, students are advised to re-read the section on intangible assets in unit 3.5, page 73.

The second part of the question is looking specifically at a large oil company (which presumably has significant physical assets which may act as insurmountable barriers to entry for new firms looking to take market share away from Shell).

Intangible assets for Shell could include:

- Goodwill or customer loyalty through improved customer service, given Shell's financial strength

- Brand value through product recognition and image. (The Shell logo is distinctive and has not changed significantly. This may create trust in the mind of the consumer.)

- Patents and other forms of intellectual property on new forms of petrol designed to be environmentally sustainable or economical for car owners given concerns in mid 2008, for example, about the diminishing size of the world's potential supply of oil.

5

This question covers elements of unit 3.1, sources of finance, and unit 5.6 on innovation.

Possible discussion points:

In a previous question, we looked at evaluating the potential sources of finance available to a small engineering firm – Gemel – and how they could finance stock of finished goods for resale, delivery vans, or land and buildings.

For this question the context is innovative products. Given that they may not have been brought to the marketplace in large quantities or be fully positioned in the minds of consumers, the developers of innovative products face a number of different challenges in trying to raise finance.

'Traditional' bank loans and other sources of finance may be problematic as they may be derived from risk-averse institutions or lenders who may be unwilling to finance untried products. This could be frustrating even though the makers of the Segway will we assume have certainly provided a detailed business plan on how they intend to successfully use the funds to ensure that the risk of failure is minimized.

For innovative products perhaps some different sources of finance may be required. Venture capitalists that may sense that the Segway represents a significant leap forward in personal mobility without impacting too much on the environment may be tempted to fund the launch of large production runs of the scooter in the hope that the scooter is exploiting a market gap.

If social responsibility issues are involved, the Segway developers could apply for funding from philanthropic investors or institutions such as the Grameen Bank or the Acumen Fund. The growth of e-finance has been considerable, especially in socially responsible projects. A financial partnership with a non-governmental organization may also be possible given this point.

There is no definitive answer here and original thinking would be well rewarded in context as long as the discussion is balanced. To achieve a mark in the top marking band, students are reminded that they should apply some overall form of judgment to the analysis.

6

In May 2005, this question was referring to the founder of Subway, Tom de Luca, who at 17 opened his first sandwich outlet.

One could argue that an empathetic approach could be useful here. Imagine going into a bank yourself and asking for $5 million to fund your idea for a new start-up. What do you think the reaction from the bank manager would be, even with a detailed Internal Assessment project under your arm?

Here is a selection of responses from the markscheme of that year.

- Younger people may suffer from a lack of a previous 'track record' and banks may be reluctant to lend large sums of start-up capital to someone with limited retail or business experience.

- Younger entrepreneurs may lack the knowledge to prepare detailed cash flow forecasts and other financial documents or may be unable to finance and undertake substantial market research to convince the potential lender that their business plan is viable.

- Younger people may also lack the required collateral required by the lender or institution to guarantee a start-up loan.

Topic 4 Marketing (1)

1

The context of the case study needs to be given. The Disney Company were looking to build a new theme park in China to extend the Disney brand in the leading emerging economy. A theme park already exists in Hong Kong and the company were looking to take advantage of the growing affluence of the young Chinese professional worker and increasing desire of the Disney Company to be considered as a global entertainment organization.

- Many students were able to write down a number of market research methods from both primary and secondary sources.

- Textbook treatments (implying generic methods and not specific to the issue facing the Disney Company) and thus long lists were common.

- The issue of discussion was rarely tackled and many students felt that if the Disney Company effectively 'did their homework and researched the market' then success was inevitable.

Some areas where discussion could have occurred:

- Secondary data collection would be low cost and easy to obtain but how relevant would it be to a new theme park in China?

- Could Disney easily compare costs of the Disney theme park in Hong Kong and the one to be built in China?

- Would this secondary data from Hong Kong be already out of date?

- How relevant would primary data be to the company if it were to ask Chinese people about their understanding of a company which may not yet have a significant influence in this growing economy?

- Would questionnaires/interviews be effective, given the above?

- Should Disney consider the potential cultural and linguistic problems?

- Should Disney employ a specialist organization to carry out their market research to increase objectivity?

- However, this will increase costs significantly and will take considerable time to report back to Disney before a final decision can be made.

2   **HL**

The Fair Trade movement has been a key stakeholder in the drive to promote a 'fairer deal' for producers or growers of commodities such as coffee beans.

The intention is to give producers, who are predominantly in the developing world, a much larger share of the value added – similar to but not exactly the same as profit – which the processed coffee gives to the final retailer.

The current share of this value added to the growers is very low as a percentage of the final purchase price. It is argued that the retailer enjoys a significantly higher share of the value added and this has been considered to be unethical.

- A company which is essentially trying to promote itself as ethical and socially responsible under the Fair Trade Agreement will need to conduct its market research carefully, given that many consumers many be unaware of the values of the movement and may feel embarrassed when questioned if they show a certain degree of 'ethical ignorance'.

- For this reason, a random sample of a chosen population may be inappropriate. A quota survey may also prove to be ineffective if the group selected is unaware of the mission and vision of the Fair Trade movement.

- To increase accuracy of the data collected the firm may have to pre-select its market research respondents and perhaps could either choose a cluster group or a stratified sample with tightly defined criteria such as monthly spending on ethically traded goods and services.

- These groups may be small and unrepresentative of a general population but the issues being discussed here are unlikely to appeal to the mass market.

- Finally, a few well-chosen 'ambassadors' may be selected to go out in to the marketplace with the specific task of 'spreading the message' of the Fair Trade movement through 'snowballing'. This would not be as costly as the other two previous methods. However, the Fair Trade movement will need to ensure that a consistent message is being given by the ambassador. Word-of-mouth recommendations could also be difficult to objectively measure for research purposes.

Topic 4 Marketing (2)

3 HL

- This question was very popular in this examination session and students could name a number of marketing advantages as to why global branding could be successful.

- However, they were mostly focused around one central point; namely, marketing economies of scale. The same point was often just 'dressed up' using different language.

- For disadvantages, once students had mentioned the problems of a global brand trying to reflect local tastes, cultures and variations, the examination again began to run dry with inevitable duplication.

- If a student examines just one point for an argument and one against, it is unlikely that they will be able to reach the top marking band and score 5 or 6 marks.

- Instead of focusing on the marketing advantages or disadvantages, students could have considered the *accounting advantages* (brand value boosting goodwill or other intangible assets) or *operational* or *organizational disadvantages* (how much will it cost to maintain and monitor a global brand to ensure that it is consistently relevant in all markets? Is it possible to be centralized in a global marketplace?).

- The question asked was quite open in that it did not specify marketing advantages or disadvantages.

- The advice given here is that sometimes a topic such as branding may cut across different sections of the syllabus.

- If the marketing ideas have been exhausted or are repeated, a student may wish to see if the topic can be applied in other areas of the course.

- This type of approach will make the examination much more thorough and of course will command higher marks.

4

James Dyson's creation has won a number of design awards especially in Japan. The question was attempting to examine how and when market research will assist a company that is trying to bring a new innovative product to the market.

Some possible ideas could include:

- Primary data collection through focus groups, surveys or consumer panels to indicate reaction to early prototypes or design plans. This could allow the company to gauge initial feedback before major production runs are launched.

- This primary research could also be used to gauge initial consumer reaction when the new product is compared to existing competitors. Of course, given that the product is new, the effectiveness of secondary information based on existing rival products may be a concern.

- Clearly, based on this feedback from the first round of consultations, Dyson may begin to consider the impact on the creation of the new product's marketing mix especially price and promotion.

- After the design phase is completed, Dyson will perhaps release small samples of the vacuum cleaner to test markets to gauge reaction to the finished product. It will be too late at this stage for wholesale changes to the product, but this new information may be used to further shape price methods or strategies and also to help decide on appropriate distribution channels.

5

The question here does not explicitly refer to innovative products. Line extensions could also be considered. Whichever context is chosen it is always a good idea to state how you intend to interpret the question.

Possible explanations:

- A lack of customer recognition and loyalty given the fact that the product has yet to be launched. Positioning new products against existing ones is hard to do immediately. It may take time for the perception of the product to be established.

- Market research methodology may have been flawed due to inappropriate method or sample used. There may have been a lack of funds to finance an objective review of the product by an independent market research agency.

- Based on poor research, inappropriate channels of distribution or an incorrect pricing method were chosen.

- The 'tyranny of choice' and the presence of strong established brands may limit the possibilities of growth for new products to build a market following.

- Since the launch of the product, external factors, especially the economy, may have impacted on consumer confidence and consumers may have been unwilling to purchase new, unknown brands.

- A lack of finance to support a new product during the introduction phase of the life cycle when promotion is crucial.

Topic 4 Marketing (3)

EXAMINER'S COMMENTS

6

This question proved to be very popular with students and there were many good answers concerning the role of loyalty programmes (an example being air miles), Internet-based advertising and online membership schemes. The first part of the question was clearly well understood.

Whilst it is true to suggest that some of these schemes may deepen relationships with domestic customers, it may not be so true for overseas customers who may not share the same degree of loyalty and whose only experience with the company may be through a casual search on the Internet or through a third-party intermediary such as an agent or retailer.

A number of candidates missed this aspect and assumed that the answers to both domestic and overseas customers would be the same, thus limiting their final mark. It is not good practice to merely repeat information.

Possible ideas to strengthen overseas customer relationships include:

- Adaptations of products and the marketing effort to suit the overseas 'local markets' tastes more closely. (McDonald's have been very good at this.)

- Linked to this point is an attempt to adapt to local cultural norms which could strengthen the link between the overseas firm and its customers.

- Form a joint venture or strategic alliance with an incumbent local firm to increase brand awareness and spread the mission or vision of the company. The use of locally based agents could enhance this process.

- Community projects could be introduced or the development of an overseas corporate social responsibility programme (linked to the environment or greater use of social marketing?) to develop goodwill or create a new ethical positioning in the minds of the overseas customers.

Topic 5 Operations Management (1)

1

Contribution

Variable costs	$1.25 + $1.60 + $0.15 = $3.00 per kg of pasta
Selling price	$7 per kg of pasta
Contribution	$7 − $3 = $4 per kg of pasta

Break-even level of output

Fixed costs	($500 × 52) + ($500 × 12 = $6000) = $32,000
Contribution	$4 per kg of pasta
Break-even quantity	$\frac{$32,000}{4}$ = 8000 kg of pasta per year

Margin of safety

Current output level − break-even level

10,000 kg − 8,000 kg = 2,000 kg

Profit at current capacity

margin of safety × contribution: 2000 kg × $4 = $8000

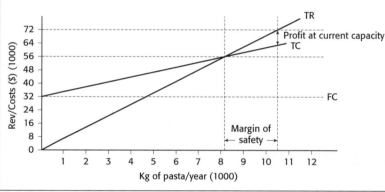

2

HL

As we have already stated the case for TQM, kaizen and quality circles in the analysis in section 5.7, we shall concern ourselves here more about the difficulties of introducing a total quality culture in order to fulfil the requirements of the command word, evaluate.

A number of writers have dismissed TQM as a new management fad or tool. Jack Trout is particularly scathing:

I was startled to find out that 81 per cent of the 5,600 executives I surveyed said that management tools (including TQM) promised more than they delivered. That is a polite way of saying that "we wasted a great deal of money".   (Trout 2001, page 151)

Moreover, there are substantial costs of training the workers to be able to take the required responsibility which TQM demands. These costs are ongoing as the firm recruits and inducts more labour into the workforce.

Potentially, TQM increases the degree of bureaucracy and record keeping in ensuring that objectives are being met and that the new working environment is being maintained. Jaguar's line managers in particular could be put under significant pressure to ensure that TQM is being followed and will have to record significant amounts of data to be able to justify that a total quality culture is having the desired effect.

Judgment:

Introducing any new management philosophy is not without risks. It can be simpler in small organizations with a flatter hierarchy and smaller spans of control. In large organizations such as Jaguar, small incremental improvements in quality may have to be accepted as changing a workforce with many thousands of workers to a total quality culture will take considerable time and capital.

Topic 5 Operations Management (2)

3 **HL**

(i) lead time = 1 week; (ii) buffer stock = 100 kg; (iii) reorder quantity = 300 kg.

4

This question is linked with the LIFO/FIFO question which was set in May 2006 and appears in the answers section for Topic 3. It is a demanding question so a more detailed suggested answer is given than normal.

Bubbleflow manufactures hot tubs for use in the garden and produces them in batches to supply to Jetstream Hot Tubs, the company at the centre of the case study.

To change from batch to flow production, Bubbleflow will need to consider the impacts on the three areas in the question. We will discuss these briefly in turn.

Marketing implications:

- The move to mass production will standardize the hot tubs to an extent although it would be hoped that, with cell production, quality of the finished tubs will improve.

- These two elements will clearly have an impact on the product part of the marketing mix. There will also be the need to change current pricing methods, given that the tubs will be produced in much larger quantities, aimed at perhaps new market segments.

- A move to mass production implies mass marketing and thus the promotional mix will need to be changed to ensure a higher audience reach. New distribution channels will also need to be researched. Further market research will need to be undertaken.

- Marketing costs will rise. Marketing economies of scale will be limited until sales of the new hot tubs enter the growth phase of the product life cycle.

Human resource implications:

- Mass production will require greater automation; redundancies will be inevitable although, if the firm expands, then some of these workers may be redeployed.

- Training, in preparation for the new technology via automation, the displaced line workers and the arrival of cell production will need to be undertaken. Management styles will have to be adapted to take into account the new working culture of cell production.

- The introduction of cells will demand greater empowerment and teamwork. The effect on motivation in the short run will be uncertain. Bubbleflow may have to undertake some contingency planning if the transition to cells is not as seamless as expected.

Finance implications:

The transfer to mass production will have a significant impact on the financial resources of the firm in terms of the investment in new technology and the upskilling of workers. Greater attention to payback and discounted cash flows will be needed to judge the viability of such an investment. A PEST analysis will also be needed to check on the state of the external environment.

Judgment:

The move to mass markets is not without risk, as this brief survey of three affected areas highlights. Planning for the change will be very important despite the significant potential cost savings which could by achieved through higher productivity and greater teamwork. However, the change in culture and working practices will need to be managed carefully otherwise the long-term future of the organization could be put in jeopardy.

Topic 5 Operations Management (3)

5

Students are advised to look back at unit 5.7 concerning stock control methods to check their understanding of the generic differences between JIT and JIC. They will not be repeated here.

Questions such as this can sometimes lead the student to list every single point they have revised. Descriptive lists of advantages or disadvantages with no detail or depth and no context are unlikely to score above the lowest possible mark band.

Bullet point answers in the final IB examination are generally to be avoided. However, if the bullet point is detailed and does try to explain the advantage being presented, it is acceptable to offer this style of answer.

In the context of Jaguar we can note the following advantages:

- JIT as part of kaizen demands an approach where TQM is at the centre of the philosophy of operation. Quality becomes the responsibility of a number of stakeholders and thus Jaguar should benefit from a reduction in waste, and improved finished product quality, to name only two of the benefits from a study of kaizen.
- As JIT demands minimal level of stocks (it is estimated that the Nissan car plant in Sunderland had managed to keep stocks to only one day's worth of production),

working capital is not tied up unnecessarily. Some opportunity costs of holding too much working capital can be avoided.
- Linked to this point is the reduction in storage costs, including power, electricity and security, which are not needed as warehouse space to house stocks of components and semi-finished vehicles is not required.

Disadvantages:

- JIT requires a complete change in culture and a thorough review of the supply chain (HL only.) With both of these needing to be undertaken the adjustment and transitional costs can be significant.
- Economies of scale of ordering bulk quantities of components in the assembly process of vehicles are not experienced.
- Some aspects of quality assurance for the final vehicle coming off the production line are taken out of the hands of Jaguar. There are potential short-term difficulties as suppliers come to terms with the new working culture. (Nissan had their suppliers on call for components 24 hours a day when they were running production during the night.)

---

6 HL

From the diagram, we can see that the critical path will be ACEFG. The total duration of the project is 40 hours.

Float time:

Any float time will be on the part of the diagram where the ESTs and LFTs are not equal.

- At Node 3, the EST of activity D is 8 and with a duration of 10.
- However G cannot begin until D and F are finished. G cannot begin until 32 hours have passed.
- Hence we have float time for D = 32 − 10 − 8 = 14 and this is also the free float. (Node 3 is the only node in the diagram where the ESTs and LFTs are not equal.)
- Activity D can be delayed for up to 14 days without delaying the whole project time of 40 days.
- Alternatively, the workers employed to complete activity D could be redeployed for up to 14 hours on critical tasks such as C, E and F to ensure that G is started by day 32, and therefore not delay the project overall.